MW00824934

WHY BORDERS MATTER

Western society has become estranged from the borders and social boundaries that have for centuries given meaning to human experience. This book argues that the controversy surrounding mass migration and physical borders runs in parallel and is closely connected to the debates surrounding the symbolic boundaries people need to guide them on the issues of everyday life.

Numerous commentators claim that borders have become irrelevant in the age of mass migration and globalisation. Some go so far as to argue for 'No Borders'. And it is not merely the boundaries that divide nations that are under attack! The traditional boundaries that separate adults from children, or men from women, or humans from animals, or citizens and non-citizens, or the private from the public sphere are often condemned as arbitrary, unnatural, and even unjust. Paradoxically, the attempt to alter or abolish conventional boundaries coexists with the imperative of constructing new ones. No-Border campaigners call for safe spaces. Opponents of cultural appropriation demand the policing of language and advocates of identity politics are busy building boundaries to keep out would-be encroachers on their identity.

Furedi argues that the key driver of the confusion surrounding borders and boundaries is the difficulty that society has in endowing experience with meaning. The most striking symptom of this trend is the cultural devaluation of the act of judgement, which has led to a loss of clarity about the moral boundaries in everyday life. The *infantilisation of adults* that runs in tandem with the *adultification of children* offers a striking example of the consequence of non-judgementalism.

Written in a clear and direct style, this book will appeal to students and scholars in cultural sociology, sociology of knowledge, philosophy, political theory, and cultural studies.

Frank Furedi is Emeritus Professor of Sociology at the University of Kent, Canterbury. Author of more than 20 books, Furedi's studies have been devoted to an exploration of the cultural developments in Western societies. His research has been oriented towards the way that fear and uncertainty is managed by contemporary culture. Dr Furedi's studies on the problem of fear has run in parallel with his exploration of the problem of cultural authority and cultural conflict.

WHY BORDERS MATTER

Why Humanity Must Relearn
the Art of Drawing Boundaries

Frank Furedi

Routledge
Taylor & Francis Group

LONDON AND NEW YORK

First published 2021
by Routledge
2 Park Square, Milton Park, Abingdon, Oxon OX14 4RN

and by Routledge
52 Vanderbilt Avenue, New York, NY 10017

Routledge is an imprint of the Taylor & Francis Group, an informa business

© 2021 Frank Furedi

British Library Cataloguing-in-Publication Data
A catalogue record for this book is available from the British Library

Library of Congress Cataloging-in-Publication Data
A catalog record for this book has been requested

ISBN: 978-0-367-41681-2 (hbk)
ISBN: 978-0-367-41682-9 (pbk)
ISBN: 978-0-367-81568-4 (ebk)

Typeset in Bembo
by Apex CoVantage, LLC

CONTENTS

PREFACE

The idea for writing this book first emerged during the early months of 2016. I was asked to give the keynote lecture on the topic of borders to open the Philosophy Festival in Leuven, Belgium on 16 March 2016. Coincidentally I was requested to present the keynote on the same subject to the Dutch National Day of Philosophy at the University of Tilburg on 16 April 2016. This was a time when the issue of mass migration to Europe dominated the headlines and the subject of borders was widely debated throughout Europe. As a former Hungarian refugee, who was forced to leave his country of birth and cross a border into another country, I enthusiastically embraced an opportunity to seriously reflect on the issues at stake.

Two years later, my interest in borders was also unexpectedly provoked by a research project that I undertook to investigate the history of identity and the crisis that is often associated with it. After studying historical and philosophical reflection on this subject, I became convinced that the problems associated with what is known as an identity crisis, interweaved with the issue of borders. I came to the conclusion that conflicting attitudes towards physical borders between nations were often echoed in debates about the meaning of symbolic boundaries between adults and children, man and woman, humans and animals, the private and the public sphere. It seemed to me that Western society had become estranged from hitherto conventional borders and boundaries. I drew the conclusion that the problem of identity was a sublimated expression of society's alienation from the making of moral judgement and the drawing of lines. Explaining why borders provide the signposts that assist humanity to gain meaning is what motivated me to write this book.

I am grateful to the intellectual companions and friends who put up with my questions and arguments regarding borders. In April 2019, I was able to test out some of my ideas at the Academy of Ideas Symposium on Culture Wars. The

Twenty-First Century Foundation in Budapest encouraged me to develop my ideas on the cultural meaning of borders. My friend and colleague, Dr Jennie Bristow, read the draft manuscript and provided much needed criticism. I gained important insights from the feedback offered by my colleagues, Dr. Simon Cottee and Dr Michael Fitzpatrick.

A Leverhulme Emeritus Fellowship provided support for this project, which gave me the opportunity to discuss border-related issues in Washington DC, New York, Berlin, and Paris.

As ever I am grateful to my wife for her constant lectures about the importance of moral judgement and choice.

Frank Furedi
November 2019

1

INTRODUCTION

The paradox of borders

Borders have become one of the most divisive issues of our time. Donald Trump's campaign slogan 'Build the Wall' on the United States–Mexico border may have won him the support of millions of voters, but it also provoked the wrath of some of the dominant influencers of American culture. In the media, borders have a bad press and are often portrayed as sites of inhuman practices directed at helpless refugees. The prevailing narrative presents borders as oppressive, discriminatory, exploitative, and characteristically, violent. It is frequently suggested that borders nurture racism and xenophobia. In some instances, these narratives imply that the main purpose that borders serve is to promote and reinforce extreme nationalism.

The prevailing anti-border narrative looks down on people who take borders seriously and regard borders as essential for their security. According to this narrative, people's support for border security and national sovereignty is not only misguided but also a source of conflict. Animosity towards borders is not merely confined to the physical boundaries separating nations. Western culture frequently displays unease towards its symbolic boundaries such as the one separating adulthood from childhood or the one that divides the public from the private sphere. In recent times, even the boundary that distinguishes between male and female is condemned by activists, who insist that it oppresses transgender people. Conventional symbolic boundaries, like physical borders, are often dismissed as archaic and oppressive by influential members of the cultural establishment. In theory – if not in practice – the ideal of open borders enjoys cultural ascendancy and traditional moral and symbolic boundaries are often rejected for being outdated or arbitrary or discriminatory.

The aim of this book is to explain why the call to erase borders is held up by so many as a cultural ideal. It also seeks to draw attention to the close link between the rejection of physical borders and society's alienation from the symbolic boundaries that give meaning to human life. The chapters that follow discuss how such symbolic boundaries – between health and illness, men and women, children and adults, the private and public spheres – have become the target of so much criticism. The rejection of borders between nations and communities runs in parallel with the *unbounding of cultural norms* in all dimensions of social life. Even the boundary between humans and animals is called into question on the grounds that it has been drawn 'rather starkly'.[1]

The book also discusses what it calls *the paradox of borders*. Paradoxically the hatred directed at Trump's Wall and the disdain towards physical and symbolic boundaries coexists with a constant demand for new boundaries. Opponents of building walls and border security are often drawn towards constructing and policing other forms of boundaries. Recent decades have seen a proliferation of gated communities on both sides of the Atlantic. Though hostile towards the call for national security, many are devoted to constructing institutional boundaries to protect their own sense of individual psychological and physical security. As one commentator explains, despite the 'recent pejorative association with wall-ing' there is a 'striking popular desire for walling today'[2]! Opponents of Trump's call to 'keep America safe' have no problem about demanding 'safe spaces' to quarantine themselves from unwanted comments and criticism.

Many who idealise open borders take a starkly opposite attitude towards the policing of *cultural* ones. Culture has become a fiercely contested resource, to the point that accusations of cultural appropriation feature in the news as the 21st century's moral equivalent of religious sacrilege. In the Anglo-American sphere, individuals and businesses who dare cross cultural boundaries are fre-quently condemned; here they do not have the right to free movement.

A Keep Out sign reminds the would-be transgressor that in the cultural domain, borders and symbolic boundaries matter more than ever before. Actors who presume to play a role of a person who possesses an identity different from them are denounced for daring to cross the boundary of identity. It has 'never been ethically or politically justifiable for cisgender people to play trans roles' argues an advocate of the policing of cultural boundaries.[3]

Opposing views about borders are integral to the conflicts over cultural val-ues. Arguments about borders tend to mirror conflicting attitudes towards the status accorded to national identity, citizenship, multiculturalism, family life, and traditional conventions. References to 'illegal aliens' or 'migrants' as opposed to 'undocumented immigrants' or 'refugees' tend to be underpinned by competing values, attitudes and identities. A recently published study of the history of walls noted that in the contemporary era, 'by some cruel irony, the mere concept of walls now divides people more thoroughly than any structure of brick or stone'. David Frye, the study's author, stated that for 'every person who sees a wall as an act of oppression, there is always another urging the construction of newer, higher, and longer barriers'. Frye remarked, that 'the two sides hardly speak to each other'.[4]

That people are divided by the 'concept of the wall', rather than the physical structure of brick or stone, is an astute observation. What is principally at stake is the political, symbolic, and cultural significance of a border, not its physical characteristics. To a significant extent, opposing attitudes toward the 'concept of the wall' mesh with the conflicts over values in the so-called 'Culture Wars'.[5] In these conflicts, a mobile and globalist class of professionals and managers adopt a very different attitude to borders than sections of society who are bounded to their community's territory. Pointing to the tension between 'globalists' and 'territorialists', one recent study of borders explains that:

> in many aspects of life, territorial allegiances have become a class-specific property; they have in effect bifurcated. Those who tend to occupy the supervisory positions in politics and the economy – in the non-profit or the electronically based economy, the research centers, financial firms, but in many units, too, of the manufacturing, agriculture, and mining sectors – claim to transcend territory. They aspire to make it archaic, depriving it both of real power over their particular activities and of symbolic power, as well.[6]

In contrast, for billions of ordinary folk, 'territory remains an important principle of structuring existence in the world. The protection they derive from borders is fragile, but they are dependent on them, and their sense of national or ethnic identity remains higher'.[7]

As the following chapters explain, arguments for open borders are founded upon the idealisation of openness and unboundedness in all spheres of life. Such sentiments are reinforced by the conviction that drawing boundaries necessarily implies limiting human behaviour and experience. Borders and symbolic boundaries are portrayed as not merely instruments of control but also as markers of fear and danger. This point was clearly voiced by the Italian playwright Dario Fo, when he argued that it is 'extremely dangerous to talk about limits or borders', and that 'it is vital instead, that we remain completely open'. Though it is far from clear what the call to remain 'completely open' signifies, it resonates with the current *zeitgeist*.

The borderless spirit

Just Google the words 'without borders': what you'll find is not just Médecins Sans Frontières (Doctors Without Borders) but a bewildering array of organisations that aspire to achieve the highly acclaimed status of being 'without borders'. Engineers, musicians, chemists, veterinarians, executives, librarians, builders, plumbers, lawyers, astronomers, creatives, journalists, rabbis, herbalists, women, sex workers, acupuncturists, clowns . . . these are just some of the occupational groups now flaunting their virtue of being 'without borders'. During the course of the debate around Brexit, even animals were recruited into the open borders movement. 'Cats without Borders' were joined by 'Border Terriers Against Borders'.[8]

Some display their enthusiasm for being 'without borders' as an expression of their risk-taking spirit, a bold and pioneering desire to explore the unknown. And it would indeed be inspiring if attempts to go beyond borders were actually imbued with a pioneering temper and the impulse of breaking new ground. Unfortunately, that is rarely how matters stand. Though there are many contradictory impulses fuelling the contemporary cultural reaction against borders, its dominant driver is not the aspiration to discover but to leave behind duties and responsibilities that are experienced purely as onerous burdens. As Western culture struggles to uphold the conventional boundaries that provide guidance to the conduct of life, there is little risk attached to the act of breaking them.

The drawing of lines and the defence of borders contradicts one of the most unquestioned, though rarely discussed, values of contemporary society – *openness*. Western culture is wedded to the idea of openness as a virtue, in and of itself. The cultural authority of openness even trumps the integrity of intimate life. That is why the historic distinction between the public and the private spheres of life often unravels in recent times when confronted with the claim that the 'personal is political'. Openness undermines discretion to the point that it encourages a voyeuristic disregard for intimacy. The industrialisation of pornography illustrates that the age-old boundary between what one should or should not see has lost much of its cultural significance.

In his classic exploration of *The Civilizing Process*, the sociologist Norbert Elias remarked that with the 'advance of civilization the lives of human beings are increasingly split between an intimate and a public sphere, between private and public behaviour'. Yet today, the prevailing *zeitgeist* has become uncomfortable with maintaining the border between the intimate and the public domain. Popular culture encourages the open display of intimate thoughts and those who take their private lives too seriously are often assumed to have something to hide. This is the age of the therapeutically inspired 'confessional' and the reluctance to 'share' is often ridiculed as symptomatic of a dysfunctional personality. According to one psychologist, a 'psychological preoccupation' with borders is a 'sign of regression'.[9]

The cultural influence of a borderless sensibility has acquired its most systematic and explicit form in the domain of geopolitics. National borders are frequently denounced as artificial, exclusionary, unjust or anti-human. Robert Schuman, one of the founders of the European unification movement, regarded 'borders as the scars of history'. Secure borders are condemned on the ground that they draw on racist and xenophobic sentiments. Claude Juncker, the former President of the European Commission, contends that 'Borders are the worst invention ever made by politicians'.[10] Rutger Bregman, author of *Utopia for Realists*, argues that borders are the biggest source of inequality in the world.[11] Pope Francis claims that 'peace has no borders, and he added that 'if one seeks the good of peoples and the world, it is foolish to close spaces, to fight against each other'[12]

In popular culture, hostility to borders and boundaries enjoys significant moral authority. The country singer Willie Nelson echoed this sentiment, when he sang, 'I don't believe in closing the border. We have a statue that says: Y'all come in'.[13] The lyrics of John Lennon's *Imagine* speaks to this borderless sensibility:

> Imagine there's no countries
> It isn't hard to do
> Nothing to kill or die for
> And no religion, too

It is very rare to encounter a movie, television programme, or a musical hit that celebrates national sovereignty or secure borders. Antagonism towards physical and symbolic boundaries is even more prevalent in high and academic culture. On university campuses, even cognitive boundaries and lines of demarcation have come under fire by opponents of so-called 'binary thinking'. Binary thinking – that is, making sense of the world in contrasting categories – is often caricatured as narrow-minded, intellectually lazy, and an inflexible way of interpreting experience. Binary thought is also attacked on the grounds that the drawing of lines and distinctions is both discriminatory and unjust.

The meaning of borders

The dividing up of space into distinct territories, and their demarcation through symbolic markers, has been an integral feature of human development. Such efforts probably date from the time when the first Sumerian cities were fortified with walls.[14] In fact, Frye claims that there is a 'nearly universal correlation between civilization and walls',[15] and that the 'creators of the first civilizations descended from generations of wall builders'.[16] Walls and boundaries were constructed because it was believed that they provided the inhabitants of urban civilisations with security and peace. They marked out a space where commercial and intellectual life could flourish. The existence of walled and fenced burial sites in numerous nomadic communities indicates that the human impulse to draw lines is not confined to fixed settlements or urban settings.[17]

Precisely because the demarcation of physical spaces was a human accomplishment, it possessed an important meaning for people. Border markers and spatial boundaries were often endowed with unique spiritual significance. Virtually every society possesses boundaries that demarcate and protect sacred sites. This setting aside of spiritual and religious symbols, such as a holy site, divided the secular from the sacred and also bestowed a moral significance onto spatial divisions.

The marking out of space and the tendency to draw lines constitutes humanity's need for signposts and guidance. Advocates of 'openness' or 'borderlessness', who possess a negative orientation towards boundaries, sometimes claim that the drawing of lines is merely a Western preoccupation and linear consciousness is alien to many non-Western societies. As Tim Gold in his study of the history of lines points out:

> Anthropologists have a habit of insisting that there is something essentially linear about the way people in modern Western societies comprehend the passage of history, generations and time. So convinced are they of this, that any attempt to find linearity in the lives of non-Western people is liable to be dismissed as mildly ethnocentric at best, and at worst as amounting to collusion in the project of colonial occupation whereby the West has ruled its lines over the rest of the world[18]

Yet the drawing of lines can assume a variety of forms in different cultures, and colonialism was not 'the imposition of linearity upon a non-linear world, but the imposition of one kind of line on another'.[19] As Gold observes, 'it is surely the case that, ever since people have been speaking and gesturing, they have also been making and following lines'.[20]

That borders and the drawing of lines are regarded by many as an unnatural and potentially pernicious accomplishment says far more about their own cultural attitudes than about the human condition. In 1909, the German sociologist Georg Simmel gave us an eloquent reminder of the human desire to draw borders: Only to humanity, in contrast to nature, has the right to connect and separate been granted, and in the distinctive manner that one of these activities is always the presupposition of the other.[21'] Simmel drew the conclusion that people situated and conducted their lives in accordance with the meaning forged within distinct boundaries. 'Man's position in the world is defined by the fact that in every dimension of his being and his behaviour he stands at every moment *between two boundaries*', he argued, claiming that 'this condition constitutes the formal structure of existence' as human beings orient themselves to find direction in 'the infinite space of our worlds'.[22] As the sociologist Keith Tester explains, Simmel is 'in no doubt that without boundaries, life in the world (that is existence) would be barren' and 'it would be largely incomprehensible'.[23]

The significance that Simmel attached to the role of boundaries was based on the recognition that these markers help to endow human experience with meaning. Tester echoes this point when he writes that 'the emergence and consolidation of bounded forms were identified as the only way in which life could be given direction, meaning and location'.[24] Physical borders and different forms of territorial demarcations create a space within which individuals develop a sense of belonging and community, as well as cultivate their identity. The Norwegian anthropologist Fredrik Barth developed the concept of an 'ethnic boundary' to refer to the cognitive or mental boundaries that guide people to situate their community in relation to others. From this standpoint, boundaries play a crucial role in the constitution of the self, for they provide the framework within which identity can be cultivated.[25]

Borders are not just physical and geographical realities; they also have a powerful symbolic significance through which communities gain insights into themselves and the meaning of their existence. As the cultural sociologist Robert Wuthnow noted, 'order has somehow to do with *boundaries*'. Why? Because 'order consists mainly of being able to make distinctions – of having symbolic demarcations – so that we know the place of things and how they relate to one another'.[26] People's very sense of social reality is often forged, and internalised, through their engagement with symbolic boundaries. These boundaries – between the 'self' and 'other' – influence people's sense of 'us' and 'them'. Today, as in the past, our attitudes towards physical and spatial borders are influenced by our attitudes towards symbolic borders. When symbolic borders lose their meaning, a cultural crisis ensues. Without the guidance provided by symbolic boundaries, young people find it difficult to make the transition to adulthood. The most striking expression of this development is what the psychologist Erik Erikson characterised as an 'identity crisis'.

Symbolic boundaries have proved to be essential for the development of human thought and have sensitised individuals to understand where they stand in relation to others.[27] Symbolic boundaries provide people with guidance about their relation to others and influence the way reality is perceived. Symbolic boundaries afford communities with guidelines about how to differentiate and make spatial, temporal, and cognitive distinctions. They help in creating a mental map that outlines the boundaries within and between groups.

Historically, symbolic boundaries have played an important role in providing communities with the cultural resources necessary for the making of moral distinctions between right and wrong, good and evil or between the realms of the sacred and the profane. They also stake out a limit. Moral boundaries remind members of the community of the distinction between acceptable and non-acceptable forms of behaviour. Though these boundaries are sometimes experienced as constituting a limitation on the activities of individuals, communities rely on them to maintain moral order.

Moral boundaries are omnipresent to the point that most people are not conscious of their influence on their behaviour. Teaching children to 'know their boundaries' plays an important role in their socialisation. When boundaries are breached, people are told that 'they have crossed the line'. The phrase 'crossing the line' is a colloquial way of signalling that someone has violated the prevailing moral code. Someone who has crossed the line has migrated from the territory of acceptable behaviour to one that is unacceptable. Line related metaphors are often used to convey moral sensibilities about limits. 'The 'blurring of lines' draws attention to the absence of moral clarity. The phrase a 'fine line' highlights the difficulty of making a clear distinction in some instances between right and wrong. Public figures refer to the term the 'Red line' to signify their point of no return; the point beyond which they are not prepared to negotiate. They sometimes use the phrase, the 'line in the sand' to indicate the limit beyond which they will not go.

The following chapters will argue that a lack of clarity about moral boundaries has estranged individuals and wider society from the activity of drawing lines. The confusions that surround the question of 'where to hold the line' intermesh with the controversies surrounding physical borders and the status of national sovereignty. They not only fail to take borders seriously but they also unbound cultural norms.

The demand for security

The rejection of borders on grounds such as that it is discriminatory, artificial or arbitrary overlooks their role in providing communities with meaning and a sense of belonging. It also ignores the significance that borders play in providing a secure space within which all the important features of public life and culture – legal and moral obligations, norms of solidarity and citizenships and the social practices and rituals of everyday life – are cultivated. The bounding of space and the differentiation of places are essential elements for the conduct of human activity and the construction of political and social institutions.

From the standpoint of the ideology of openness, borders constitute divisive obstacles to human development. However as one historian of borders notes, 'borders are more than just barriers; for some they guarantee community and belonging' and they 'organize the spatial structure of our collective life'.[28] It is not merely political and ethnic allegiances which are territorial. The ties that bind people together and which serve as the foundation for public life occur within a space of common belonging. Such ties also serve to distinguish people from others and may lead to acts of exclusion and discrimination but without their existence any form of solidarity would possess a fragile and abstract character.

Advocates of open borders deterritorialise people's identity and seek to denationalise the status of citizenship. In this way, they deprive citizenship of moral content and undermine the capacity of human beings to think of themselves and act as a people. The political philosopher Hannah Arendt has forcefully argued that 'a citizen by definition' is a member of a 'particular community'. She explains that a citizen's 'duties must be defined and limited by not only those of his fellow, but also by the boundaries of a territory', and concludes:

> Philosophy may conceive of the earth as the homeland of mankind and one unwritten law, eternal and valid for all. Politics deals with men, nationals of many countries and heirs to many pasts: its laws are the positively established fences which hedge in protect, and limit the space in which freedom is not a concept, but a living, political reality.[29]

Political institutions and customs can only gain meaning if they are territorially bounded. 'A people ought to fight for the laws of the city as if they were its walls', stated the Ancient Greek philosopher Heraclitus. Indeed, for the Greeks, laws, like walls, served to protect the *polis*. That is why the Greeks and later Arendt used the metaphor of the city walls to outline the demarcation of the public realm.

Arendt advanced an imaginative theory according to which the emergence of boundaries was expressed through *nomos*, the laws of the Greek city-states. She suggested that *nomos* conveys the idea of demarcation and appropriation. Through the stabilising of boundaries, *nomos* provided the precondition for a durable public and political realm. Arendt argued that a political community can only thrive if it is territorially limited: 'legislation creates first of all a space in which it is valid, and this space is the world in which we can move in freedom'.[30] Political freedom and its exercise are inconceivable without the spatial institutionalisation of public life.

Arendt was by no means the only philosopher to emphasise the significance of territorial demarcation for the flourishing of political life. John Locke, one of the founders of liberal philosophy along with Jean Jacques Rousseau and Immanuel Kant, conceptualised the demarcation of space as the foundation of political sovereignty and as the precondition for the maintenance of political order.

Given the close connection between the clear demarcation of borders and national sovereignty, it is not surprising that the latter has also become a target of the borderless worldview. National sovereignty is often belittled as an outdated prejudice that has become irrelevant in a globalised world. It is also criticised for dividing people and for setting one nation against another. Criticism of national sovereignty sometimes goes hand in hand with the belittling of the status of a citizen. Proponents of boundarylessness condemn national citizenship as far too exclusivist and criticise it for failing to give equal moral status and concern to people who inhabit a different part of the world.

Arguments against national sovereignty and of the status of citizenship have as their premise the supposed superiority of universal and humanitarian values. However, universalism becomes a caricature of itself when it is transformed into a metaphysical force that stands above prevailing national institutions through which human beings make sense of the world. The attempt to deterritorialise sovereignty and citizenship rights reduces people to their most abstract individual qualities. In consequence, citizens are deprived of the cultural values through which they give their lives meaning. Humanity does not live above or beyond the boundaries and institutions it created through great struggle and effort. That is why Arendt argued that: The establishment of one sovereign world state, far from being the prerequisite for world citizenship, would be the end of all citizenship. It would not be the climax of world politics, but quite literally its end.[31] Whatever its advocates' motives, the project of deterritorialising citizenship and weakening national sovereignty constitutes a direct challenge to democracy and public life. Whatever one thinks of nation states, there can be no democratic public life outside their confines. It is only as citizens interacting with one another, within a geographically bounded entity, that democratic decision-making can work and achieve remarkable results.

In his essay *Perpetual Peace* (1795), Immanuel Kant, the founder of modern cosmopolitan philosophy, developed the idea of 'cosmopolitan right', which required that strangers who entered the territory of a foreign state should not be treated with hostility. He called this requirement the 'natural right of hospitality'.[32] However, Kant's concept of the right to hospitality did not imply the right to settle, and it certainly did not call into question the legitimacy of territorial borders. He objected to the advocacy of a borderless world and argued that a world state would lead to global tyranny. Rather, Kant supported a federal union of free and independent polities, which he believed 'to be preferred to an amalgamation of the separate nations under a single power which has overruled the rest and created a universal monarchy'. He took the view that laws that transcend the nation state lacked the moral depth necessary for the exercise of authority, warning that: 'laws progressively lose their impact as the government increases its range, and a soulless despotism, after crushing the germs of goodness, will finally lapse into anarchy'.[33] His vision of cosmopolitanism is very different to the outlook of anti-border cosmopolitans today

Identification with people born into a common world is the main way that solidarity between people can acquire a dynamic political character. People exercising their citizenship rights have interests that are specific to their circumstances and which provide the foundation of their solidarity. If they were to be dispossessed of those interests, their capacity to act as responsible citizens would be diminished. Paradoxically, the best protection for refugees and migrants is that which is provided by nation states, where citizens feel confident about their role and where, as a result, they are able to extend their solidarity to those beyond their national borders.

Not just merely limits

Critics of borders often adopt a contemptuous and patronising posture towards people who believe that physical boundaries can assure their security. People who demand the building of walls are depicted as the manipulated victims of the politics of fear. The political theorist Wendy Brown caricatures the current demand for borders as being akin to a religious quest for divinely sanctioned certainty. Accordingly, the 'clamor for walls' is dismissed as the outcome of psychic and religious fantasies that misguide people to allow their illusions to overcome the sense of reality.[34]

Yet borders and walls constitute a tangible reality for the lives of human beings. They pose limits and sometimes serve as obstacles to people wishing to embark on a journey beyond them. But borders and boundaries are much more than barriers to exploration and the free movement of people. As Simmel explained in his essay, the 'Bridge and Door', a border both separates and connects people and helps establish the terms on which people relate to one another. He wrote that 'things must first be separated from one another in order to be together'. This imperative to connect and separate transcends the realm of physical boundaries. He wrote that 'in the immediate as well as the symbolic sense, in the physical as well as the intellectual sense, we are at any moment those who separate the connection or connect the separate'. A boundary sets limits, but its existence is also necessary for creating the precondition 'for a social or a cultural activity which might seek to go beyond the boundary'.[35]

The German philosopher Martin Heidegger wrote that a 'boundary is not that at which something stops but, as the Greeks recognized, the boundary is that from which something begins its presencing'.[36] Both physically and metaphorically, boundaries constitute the starting point for human activity. Throughout most of history, physical borders and symbolic boundaries have coexisted with the aspiration for adventure and experimentation. Boundaries serve as a terminus, a final point in space and time but also as a point for beginning something new.

Paradoxically the cultural devaluation of borders has unleashed a wave of anxiety, leading to an explosion of demand for new boundaries. Characteristically the demand for new boundaries possesses not so much a communal but a personal or privatised form. Boundaries are necessary for the conduct of human relationships and for the constitution of an individual's identity. That is why, in a further paradoxical development, there is a veritable self-help industry that offers guidance and support to those who apparently need to learn how to set their boundaries.

Self-help books with titles such as *Where to Draw the Line: How to Set Healthy Boundaries Everyday* or *Boundaries: Where You and I Begin* speak to a culture where people feel that they have lost the skill of drawing lines. Such anxieties are also exacerbated by the awareness that the signposts provided by the conventional borders of the past can no longer be taken for granted. One important focus of borderless anxiety is the securing of *personal space*. 'Most people value their personal space and feel discomfort, anger, anxiety . . . when their personal space is being encroached', explains an expert offering guidance on how to deal with this threat.[37] A heightened sense of preoccupation with protecting the self suggests that the defence of space and territory has acquired a hyper-personal form.

However one views borders, it is important to acknowledge that humanity has always been in the business of drawing lines. Symbolic borders embody values that give people a sense of moral equilibrium and help them lead their lives. The human imagination often inspires us to soar above borders in order to experience the unknown. But even such flights of fancy have, as their precondition, a sense of limits and of boundaries that must be overcome. The very act of rebelling against the boundaries set by society presupposes that those boundaries exist in the first place. Every limit constitutes a restraint on human activity – physical borders limit freedom of movement, and symbolic boundaries limit options for human behaviour. Yet, these limits also serve as an invitation for their transcendence. We need borders both for the realisation of existential security as well as for providing a starting point for acts of transcendence.

The rejection of borders is celebrated by some commentators – particularly those of a postmodernist disposition – as a manifestation of a positive impulse of transgression. From their standpoint, transgression conveys a sense of daring and even of courage. However, when transgression becomes an end in itself, the act becomes emptied of meaning. What I characterise as *transgression without an object*, highlights the purposeless character of the reaction against borders in the 21st century.

Western society's estrangement from borders is not an enlightened step forward – rather it expresses a self-destructive sensibility of estrangement from the conventional sign posts that guide everyday life. Consequently, it finds it difficult to hold the line that separates the positive from the negative dimensions of human experience. Having embraced the evasive tactic of non-judgementalism, society must relearn the value of making distinctions. In this context, it is essential to reject the idea that borders between nations are simply artificial props, unworthy inventions designed merely to keep people out. Borders are essential for the maintenance of national sovereignty, which is so far the only foundation that humanity has discovered for the institutionalisation of democratic accountability. Without borders, a citizen becomes a subject – subject to a power that cannot be realistically held to account.

Historically, conflicting attitudes towards borders were driven by two contradictory, but very human, passions. The human aspiration for freedom of mobility clashed with people's existential need for a sense of security. Neither of these sentiments can be ignored, which means that society has some very difficult choices to make. The answer to this current crisis lies in the reconciliation of the aspiration for freedom of movement with the existential need for spatial and symbolic security.

Notes

1 Russell (2010) p. 17.
2 Brown (2017) p. 38.
3 Meredith Talusan (2018) 'Why Scarlett Johansson – or any CIS actor – should never play trans roles', *them*, 4 July, https://www.them.us/story/why-scarlett-johansson-or-any-cis-actor-should-never-play-trans-roles.
4 Frye (2018) p. 7.
5 For a discussion of the Culture Wars, see Furedi (2018a).
6 Maier (2016) p. 290.
7 Maier (2016) p. 290.
8 See James Walsh (2016) 'Border terriers against borders', *The Guardian*, 22 June, https://www.theguardian.com/lifeandstyle/2016/jun/22/border-terriers-against-borders-your-pets-on-the-eu-rufferendum.
9 See Molly Castelloe (2016) 'Border Psychology', *Psychology Today*, 27 July, https://www.psychologytoday.com/gb/blog/the-me-in-we/201607/border-psychology.
10 Cited in Savage, M. (2006) 'Borders are worst invention ever, declares Juncker', *The Times*, 23 August.
11 See Joe Dunt (2017) 'Rutger Bregman: why open borders would make the world richer', *Business Insider*, 11 March, https://www.businessinsider.com/rutger-bregman-worldwide-inequality-borders-economist-author-journalist-2017-3?r=US&IR=T.
12 See Chiara Biagioni (2019) 'Peace has no borders. Always without exception', *SIR, Agenzia d'informazione*, 16 September, https://www.agensir.it/europa/2019/09/16/pope-francis-peace-has-no-borders-always-without-exception/.

13 Rebecca Bengal (2018) 'Interview: Willie Nelson: "I don't believe in closing the border. We have a statue that says: Y'all come in"', *The Guardian*, 28 September, https://www.theguardian.com/music/2018/sep/28/willie-nelson-i-dont-believe-in-closing-the-border-we-have-a-statue-that-says-yall-come-in.

14 See Szary (2015) p. 13.

15 See Frye (2018) p. 6.

16 Frye (2018) p. 8.

17 Diener and Hagen (2012) pp. 27–28.

18 Ingold (2016) p. 2.

19 Ingold (2016) p. 2.

20 Ingold (2016) p. 3.

21 Simmel (1994).

22 Simmel (1918) p. 353.

23 Tester (1993) p. 7.

24 Tester (1993) p. 19.

25 See Barth (1969).

26 Wuthnow (1989) p. 69.

27 According to a study of this phenomenon, 'symbolic boundaries are conceptual distinctions made by social actors to categorize objects, people, practices and even time and space. See Lamont and Molnár (2002) p. 168.

28 Maier (2016) p. ix.

29 Arendt (1970) pp. 81–82.

30 See Lindahl (2003) pp. 881–901.

31 Arendt (1970) p. 81.

32 For a discussion of this point see Miller (2016) p. 14.

33 Kant (1991) p. 113.

34 Brown (2017) pp. 144–145.

35 Tester (1993) p. 7.

36 Heidegger (1997) p. 100.

37 See 'Invading Personal Space, Boundary, Privacy – Workplace, Social, Home – Get Out Of My Face: How Close Is Too Close', BIZSHIFTS-TRENDS, 24 November 2013, https://bizshifts-trends.com/invading-personal-space-boundary-privacy-workplace-social-home-get-face-close-close/.

2

JUDGEMENT AND THE MORAL RELEVANCE OF BORDERS

Prevailing contemporary cultural attitudes are drawn far more towards the sensibility of boundarylessness than towards respect for the internal and external lines of demarcation that frame the meaning of people's lives. Most accounts of the influence of boundarylessness perceive it as a direct outcome of the powerful forces unleashed by globalisation. They attribute it to a changing world, in which the forces of globalisation render borders porous and turn symbolic boundaries into outdated relics. They claim that in this fluid global setting, traditional loyalties and identities lose their salience. Typically, they point to the disruption of traditional hierarchies, the influence of media consumption, and the proliferation of newly invented lifestyles. One sociologist explains that 'a series of changes involving migration, transnational capital, communication technologies, and cultural exportation . . . have been destabilizing identity in the West and throughout the world'.[1]

As against objectivist accounts that assign a central role to the influence of structural shifts in the patterns of social life, this chapter argues that the main driver of the turn away from the practice of drawing lines is the diminishing cultural status accorded to the act of moral judgement. Borders and boundaries are founded on and legitimised through the distinctions arrived at through an act of judgement. In this way, moral norms become bounded. The unbounding of cultural norms – their detachment from boundaries and space – has as its corollary the belittling of judgement. The unbounding of cultural norms – of normativity – challenges the capacity of a community to gain meaning from its experience.

The moral relevance of borders

Superficially, the siting of borders and boundaries can appear merely as an arbitrary act. Border critics never tire of emphasising that the act of drawing a line is an outcome of human convention. They often portray borders as a negative imposition on people's lives. They condemn borders on the ground that they are divisive and are designed to exclude and discriminate against those who live on the wrong side of the divide.

Of course, the construction of new boundaries can divide communities and be experienced as irrational and unfair. Because of events outside their control, communities discover that new borders separate them from their families, friends, and members of their social group. The symbolic boundaries that permeate everyday life can also appear irrational and unfair. Rules and conventions about the age of consent, marriage, and adulthood are queried by many people and for understandable reasons. In England and Wales, the age of criminal responsibility is 10 years old; in Sweden and Denmark, no one can be subjected to a criminal sanction if they are under 15. Such variations in the age of responsibility encourage many to regard socially constructed and culturally specific boundaries as arbitrary impositions that lack moral significance.

Some advocates of open borders claim that the artificial lines that separate one group of people from another are morally insignificant. Others adopt a more pragmatic approach, claiming that although borders might have had some moral meaning in the past, globalisation renders such qualities irrelevant. For example, the political scientist David Held contends that:

> any assumption that sovereignty is an indivisible, illimitable, exclusive and perpetual form of public power – entrenched within an individual state – is now defunct . . . the boundaries between states, nations and societies can no longer claim the deep legal and moral significance they once held.[2]

Along with most cosmopolitanism-oriented commentators, Held questions the legitimacy of the borders of the nation state. The sociologist Ulrich Beck goes a step further, calling for a 'cosmopolitan revolution' to overcome the 'lie of the national age', by which he means the divisions and boundaries that allow the citizens of one nation to enjoy rights that are denied to others.[3]

Open border activists and advocates of a cosmopolitan world order take the view that borders are not only unnatural but also immoral. They contend that regardless of their origin and nationality, all human beings are morally equal and should therefore enjoy the same rights and obligations as any other member of the human community. In their appeal to what they term 'global justice', they suggest that different forms of local patriotism are a vice, and that members of a political community do not owe a special duty of care to one another. Yet in the very act of denouncing borders as immoral they recognise that the lines that separate one nation from another are, in some sense, morally relevant.

Despite the claim that borders and boundaries are artificial, almost everyone – at least implicitly – acknowledges their necessity. Though there might be differences of opinion about where the line should be drawn between those capable of consent and those who are not, most people acknowledge the need for making such a distinction. It is unlikely that any human being passes through life without possessing a consciousness of boundaries. Without an awareness of the limits that shape people's actions, the human imagination is deprived of the capacity to meaningfully process life's events. A consciousness of boundaries provides an arena within which people possess a sense of duty and moral obligation, which influences everyday interactions.[4] Even a fervent advocate of cosmopolitanism, such as Beck, recognises the necessity for the drawing of lines: having questioned the status of national borders, he argues that new borders can be chosen, which will 'have to be redrawn and legitimated anew'.[5]

Particular boundaries and borders may indeed be unjust, but the drawing of lines that distinguish one community from another has been an integral feature of human history and development. These important universal impulses that emerged over the centuries were not founded on an abstract global experience but emerged from the cultural life of local communities who had to figure out how to deal both with their neighbours and with the strangers that they encountered from time to time. The important qualities of empathy and solidarity presuppose the capacity to forge attachment within a particular community. Centuries before the idealisation of human friendship, people had to develop an appreciation of close human attachments through the relationships they forged within their communities. In the very act of forging such attachments, people make a distinction between those they considered to be 'one of us' and those whom they viewed as outsiders.

It is inconceivable that the qualities of empathy, solidarity, and a humanistic outlook towards the world could have emerged without the existence of territorial borders. Bonds of attachment were guided by distinct cultural influences, developed in different settings and underwritten by place-specified rights and duties. A sense of place allowed people to feel that they belonged not just to a physical location but to a meaningful moral community. The political scientist Paulina Ochoa Espejo observes that 'borders are morally relevant' because 'there are genuine moral differences between people living on either side of a territorial border, and their territorial presence justifies differences in their rights and obligations'.[6] Though Western border critics tend to be indifferent to the moral significance of space, they often make an exception to the sensibilities of non-Western communities. Many of them call for the protection of their sacred sites from the intrusion of Western tourists. They thoroughly approve of the recent decision of the Australian Government to ban visitors from climbing the *Uluru* Rock, on the ground that it is a sacred site in Aboriginal folklore.

Borders and boundaries provide both psychological and social closure, symbolically separating individuals and cultures. As the sociologist Rogers Brubaker remarks, borders demarcate lines of inclusion and exclusion and serve to define a political community in terms of 'who we are' and 'who we are not'.[7] However, the impulse to differentiate, particularise or individualise is in the first instance about understanding yourself and your identity: it is not about discriminating or excluding those who are different so much as recognising that there *is* difference. In the course of differentiating ourselves from others we gain an insight into our own separate identity: 'I am me because I am not you'. We think of ourselves as being similar to some people because of *x*, and different to others because of *y*.

Most of the time, the drawing of lines is not an arbitrary act but requires a degree of certainty that the distinctions are right and legitimate. Throughout human history, acts of judgement were made through appealing to an external moral authority. As Delsol contends, 'thoughtful moral judgement establishes a relationship between a situation and certain points of reference' Delsol (2003a).[8] Individuals justified their judgements by referring to a recognised moral source, whose authority was recognised by their community. As one account of the changing status of moral authority explained: "Traditionally man points beyond the limitation of his own judgements of value to some ultimate source that he expects will authenticate and give validity to the conviction that these decisions are universally 'right'".[9] The Old Testament is full of references to borders and boundaries. The old Hebrews would understand *Micah* 7:11 that instructs that this is

> A day for the building of your walls!
> In that day the boundary shall be far extended.

Those who uphold the Christian tradition could appeal to the authority of the New Testament for endorsing the moral status of boundaries, pointing to the passage where St. Paul tells the men of Athens at the Areopagus that God 'made from one blood every nation of men to dwell on all the surface of the earth, having determined appointed seasons, and the boundaries of their dwellings'.[10]

At the present time, the status of moral authority is relatively weak and constantly held in question. In public life, arguments and statements that are communicated through self-consciously moral language tend to be regarded as outdated and irrelevant and treated with scorn. This trend is particularly evident in communications within academic circles and among cultural elites. Policymakers and politicians find it difficult to justify their work and outlook in the vocabulary of morality and promote policies on the grounds that they are 'evidence-based' rather than because they are right or good. Even religious voices feel compelled to hide behind the rhetoric of 'Research shows . . .' in order to overcome the resistance to moral discourse.

The unravelling of moral authority has important implications for the way that borders are perceived and discussed. It tends to deprive territory and place of moral content, meaning that those who wish to defend national borders often find it difficult to base their arguments on a normative foundation and find it difficult to counter their opponents' arguments. The weakening of normativity also has important implications for wider boundary-related issues. Societies feel uneasy about drawing lines and upholding symbolic boundaries when they cannot assuredly draw on culturally sanctioned norms. In such circumstances, it becomes difficult to make moral judgements.

The unravelling of judgement

There is an intimate relationship between the drawing of distinctions and the construction of moral codes. Symbolic boundaries and distinctions help to distinguish between desirable and undesirable actions and maintain the 'authority of particular moral commitments'.[11] That is why the reluctance to take boundaries seriously may diminish people's ability to endow their actions with meaning. 'Any erosion or blurring of each boundary, therefore, constitutes an area in which one might look to identify potential crises in moral authority', wrote Wuthnow.[12] From this perspective, society's estrangement from the drawing of distinctions can be interpreted as a loss of judgement. In Western societies, the main response to the problem of judgement has been to evade the problem by calling into question its very value and desirability.

Anglo-American societies have accommodated to the blurring of symbolic boundaries through turning their reluctance to draw lines into a positive virtue. In higher education, ambivalence, hybridity, fluidity, and transgression are favourably contrasted to boundedness. The acclamation of the virtue of boundarylessness rests upon a consensus that judgement has negative connotations. This sentiment, conveyed through the lauding of 'non-judgementalism', has a commanding influence on regard for the symbolic boundaries that frame everyday life. In contemporary culture, judgemental behaviour is defined in entirely negative terms.

It is worth noting that historically, the term 'judgement' was endowed with positive connotations. The *Oxford English Dictionary* (*OED*) defines judgement as 'the ability to make considered decisions or to arrive at reasonable conclusions or opinions on the basis of the available information; the critical faculty; discernment, discrimination'. It also points out that qualities such as 'discretion, good sense, wisdom' are also conveyed by this word.[13] Today, although there are some circumstances in which judgement is still regarded as connoting discernment and critical thought, in its everyday usage, many of the term's positive qualities have been lost.

The diminishing cultural status of judgement is illustrated by the word's rhetorical mutation when expanded into the term 'judgementalism'. The *OED* defines judgementalism as a form of 'overly critical or moralistic behaviour' and suggests that the term was virtually unknown until the 1950s, when it was used in conjunction with the term 'moralism'.[14] My investigation into the genealogy of the term indicates that it first began to be used in social work and gained wider currency in the 1950s and especially in the 1960s. According to the *Google Ngram Viewer* database, the usage of this word took off in the 1970s, when it entered into everyday speech.[15] Since the 1970s, judgementalism has acquired an increasingly negative connotation as an act of narrow-minded prejudice: as in the complaint, put forward in one newspaper article, about 'censorious judgementalism from the moralising wing, which treats half of our countrymen as enemies'.[16]

The obverse of the negative portrayal of judgementalism is the legitimation of *non-judgementalism*, which currently enjoys a formidable cultural authority in Anglo-American societies. As far back as 1948, the liberal literary critic, Lionel Trilling, wrote of a 'characteristically' American impulse not to judge people too harshly, noting the assumption that the consequences of judgement 'will turn out to be "undemocratic"'.[17] In the present context, where there is a widespread reluctance to draw moral boundaries, a non-judgemental orientation towards life has become the defining feature of the prevailing cultural sensibility.

The transformation of non-judgementalism into a core value was documented by Alan Wolfe's 1998 study of what middle-class Americans think about political, cultural, and social issues. They 'are reluctant to pass judgement on how other people act and think', writes Wolfe, before suggesting that 'Thou shalt not judge' has become the Eleventh Commandment of middle-class Americans.[18] Wolfe's finding that judgement had become associated with bad manners is also echoed by the political philosopher Jean Bethke Elshtain, who commented that 'judging has been in bad odor for quite some time in American culture'. She claimed that judgement 'is equated with being punitive, or with insensitivity, or with various "phobias"', and that therefore it is better 'to be something called "open minded", a trait thought to be characteristic of sensitive and supportive persons'.[19]

Popular culture associates non-judgementalism with a refusal to pigeonhole people and a reluctance to accept boundaries. In her song 'Born This Way', Lady Gaga praises a 'race which bears no prejudice, no judgement but boundless freedom'.[20] According to this outlook, the idealised state of 'no judgement' is not just freedom, but a freedom that possesses 'boundless' qualities; the acclamation of the 'open-minded' and of the value of openness. As we note later in this chapter, the framing of openness as a foundational value, like its companion virtue of non-judgementalism, contributes to and reinforces the cultural distancing of people from boundaries.

Although non-judgementalism is represented as an enlightened and liberal attitude towards the world, it is nothing of the sort. The authority of non-judgementalism legitimates the attitude of evading judgement about different, often competing, values and cultural practices. It is true that off-the-peg judgements arrived at through stereotyping are merely manifestations of conformism and prejudice. But the valuation of non-judgementalism *itself* possesses no inherent positive ethical qualities. It is symptomatic of indifference at best, and moral cowardice at worst, reflecting a reluctance to struggle with the meaning of moral boundaries. The reluctance to criticise and confront others' beliefs and opinions closes the door to the elaboration of a mutually agreed public consensus. Paradoxically, the practice of non-judgementalism reinforces the psychic distance between people and fortifies the boundaries that separate them.

Anglo-American society has become so alienated from making value judgements that it has developed an entire vocabulary of euphemisms to avoid being unambiguous, clear, and blunt in its statements. The term 'inappropriate' is paradigmatic in this respect, obfuscating the distinction between what is morally right and wrong and censoring while refusing to condemn outright. The trend towards the adoption of a non-judgemental rhetoric is particularly visible in schooling and education, where a veritable Orwellian vocabulary has emerged to provide teachers and others with a language that spares them from the responsibility of making a judgement. In some universities, exam boards are instructed to offer the verdict of 'not passed' instead of 'failed'. Opaque terms such as 'inappropriate', 'uncomfortable', 'unwelcome', or 'problematic' hint that not all is well without clarifying the nature of the transgression. The word 'inappropriate' does not clarify why something is not appropriate and avoids the drawing of a line that clearly distinguishes between what is right and what is wrong about a word or act. Yet while being explicitly ambiguous and opaque, claims about 'inappropriate behaviour', 'inappropriate pressure', 'inappropriate content' or 'inappropriate touching' shun engaging explicitly with a coherent system of right and wrong, whilst also acting to condemn. Thus, the commanding rhetoric of non-judgementalism does not merely obscure but also constrains free and spontaneous verbal communication.

Hannah Arendt characterised the reluctance to judge as an expression of a disinclination towards public association. She wrote of the 'blind obstinancy that becomes manifest in the lack of imagination and failure to judge'. From a humanist perspective, judgement is not simply an acceptable response to other people's beliefs and behaviour, but a public duty, which establishes the basis for dialogue between an individual and others. Drawing on Kant's *Critique of Judgement*, Arendt writes of an 'enlarged way of thinking, which as judgement knows how to transcend its own individual limitations'. The current endowment of the act of judgement with overwhelmingly negative qualities is premised on the view that this act discriminates, excludes, and in some cases harms those who are judged. Instead of perceiving the act of judgement as a deed through which people can establish connections and develop a shared understanding of one another's outlook, its critics depict it one-sidedly as a source of conflict. But contrary to the claim that judgement closes down discussion, 'the power of judgement rests on a potential agreement with others', states Arendt. Judging plays a central role in disclosing to individuals the nature of their public world: 'judging is one, if not the most, important activity in which this sharing-the-world-with-others comes to pass'.[21]

Non-judgementalism discourages society from discussing issues that implicitly raise questions about right and wrong. The French philosopher Marcel Merlau-Ponty wrote that 'a truth always means that someone is judging'.[22] The quest for truth is undermined when a society is reluctant to encourage judgement. The positive potential of an act of judgement depends on the degree to which it is based on experience, reflection, and impartiality. Not all judgements are of equal worth and, as Arendt remarks, the quality of a judgement 'depends upon the degree of its impartiality'. But partial and hasty evaluations are not an argument against judging, only for adopting a more responsible attitude towards it.

The philosopher Mary Midgley points out that judging makes it possible for us to 'find our way through a whole forest of possibilities'.[23] Freedom itself is based on the human potential for action; without the exercise of judgement, freedom itself becomes denuded of moral content. The implications of the sacralisation of non-judgementalism was grasped by the sociologist Zygmunt Bauman, when he warned about the trend towards what he called 'adiaphorization': the exemption of a considerable part of human action from moral judgement and, indeed, moral significance.[24]

One of the few occasions when adiaphorization, or moral indifference, turns into its opposite is when it is confronted with those who take moral boundaries seriously. Those who persist in making distinctions and drawing lines are condemned for their failure to embrace the openness of non-judgementalism, and those deemed 'judgemental' are unambiguously judged to be not worthy of respect. This response indicates that even the most zealous advocate of non-judgementalism cannot entirely abandon judgement. Appearances to the contrary, the ethos of non-judgementalism is almost always implicated in covert and not so covert judgement. However, it is rarely able to acknowledge its own role and tends to associate the act of judgement with individuals and groups on the other side of the cultural divide.

The transformation of moral indifference into a core value

Originally, the emergence of support for what would become codified as the value non-judgementalism was motivated by the worthy motive of avoiding prejudiced or discriminatory behaviour. Around the turn of the 20th century, critics of the prevailing order called into question the manner in which judgements evaluated differences between classes of people, men and women, cultures and races. Judgements concerning the superiority and inferiority of different groups and races were rightly contested on the ground that they legitimised and perpetuated different forms of oppression and exploitation. Critics questioned what they perceived as unfair and demeaning distinctions. Going a step further, they also argued against the legitimacy of making judgements from a common point of reference: for example, applying the standards of Western societies to judge societies in Africa or Asia.

The intellectual underpinning for the emergence of non-judgementalism as a powerful social ideal was initially provided by cultural anthropology. Some of the discipline's founders, led by Franz Boas, criticised the rigid distinctions that Western scientists and commentators drew between different cultures and races. Boas developed a concept of culture that 'entailed a rejection of belief in any single, external standard of evaluation that could be used to rank a society as a whole'.[25] As one study of this development explains, Boas's idea of culture 'made possible a form of identity, "cultural identity", that was less susceptible to evaluative judgement than were other forms of identity – such as national or racial identity'.[26] Back in the 1950s, the cultural anthropologist Melville Herskovits explained that 'cultural relativism developed' because of the 'difficulty of finding valid cross-cultural norms'. He stated that the need for a 'cultural relativistic point of view has become apparent because of the realization that there is no way to play this game of making judgements across cultures except with loaded dice'.[27]

During the interwar years, cultural anthropology played an important role in transforming the manner with which group differences were discussed and evaluated, gaining influence for a view that regarded 'many differences among social groups in less judgemental term, i.e. more as merely "differences" and less as signs of inferiority or superiority'.[28] The main objective of this project was to isolate cultural and social differences from evaluative judgements. As Marie Moran explains, the new 'conceptions of culture were deliberately non-evaluative (in intent at least), and thus less susceptible to judgements of superiority and inferiority'.[29]

From the standpoint of cultural anthropology, differences in custom and behaviour could not be judged as superior or inferior to one another. Herskovits underlined this point when he stated that American anthropologists had 'given a clear and unequivocal answer' that 'objective indices of cultural inferiority and superiority cannot be established'.[30] Cultural differences were presented as simply different habits and customs that should not be the object of invidious comparisons. According to the anthropologist Ruth Benedict, even the 'very concepts of the true and the false' were bound up with a specific cultural tradition and could therefore not be used to make judgements about other people's way of life.[31] With the passing of time, an act of judgement regarding the values of another culture was increasingly regarded as illegitimate, an expression of intolerant behaviour.

There was and remains one striking exception to the animosity that cultural relativists display towards judgement. Frequently, when it comes to their own society, cultural relativists lose their inhibitions about the making of negative judgements. On occasions, Benedict appeared to regard American culture as inferior to those of other communities. Her description of suburban Middletown is infused with a sense of patronising contempt. According to Benedict, Americans in Middletown feared to act 'different from their neighbours'. She depicted this community as one suffocating in its conformity, and Benedict concluded that the 'fear of being different is the dominating motivation recorded in Middletown'.[32]

In the post-Second World War era, the reluctance to make judgements about cultural differences mutated from a morally neutral stance to the acclamation of difference as a positive value in its own right. During the 1950s and 1960s, anthropology's concept of culture, which was deliberately non-evaluative, succeeded in acquiring a hegemonic influence over deliberations on the subject.[33] According to one account, '"cultural diversity" became increasingly construed over the course of the twentieth century as something to be valued: and even as exotic, "Cosmopolitan" and sophisticated'.[34] With the cultural turn of the 1960s, a non-evaluative orientation towards different identities and forms of behaviour gained traction. In most instances, personal attitudes and behaviour ceased to be subject to moral judgement. Yet while there are many positive aspects to this development, a price has been paid.

Back in the late 1940s, Trilling associated the rising trend of non-judgementalism with the generosity of spirit of American liberalism. But he was nevertheless troubled, noting that 'we cannot help observing' that non-judgementalism is 'often associated with an almost intentional intellectual weakness'. To illustrate his point, he wrote of 'an almost conscious aversion from making intellectual distinctions' on the spurious ground that an 'intellectual distinction must inevitably lead to a social discrimination or exclusion'.[35]

Cultural relativism was not the only driver of the practice of non-judgementalism. The term was first adopted by therapeutic professionals, social workers, and educators, who believed that the establishment of a space that was free from judgement would help their clients to open up and discuss their problems. In its early form, non-judgementalism was justified on instrumental grounds as a medium for gaining the trust of patients and clients. My investigation of the origins of the term 'non-judgemental' suggests that it made its appearance in the 1920s, when advice books directed at parents counselled them to refrain from imposing their judgement on their children. 'As loving parents, we try to stay in touch with our wayward children, keeping lines of communication open, being non-judgemental', counselled one commentator in 1925.[36] In 1934, one supporter of the National Council of Parent Education supported non-judgementalism on the ground that it created an environment where 'emotional conflicts may be worked out and a better balance of emotional stresses achieved'.[37]

During the 1930s, therapeutic professionals and sections of the helping professions began to refer to non-judgementalism as a positive character trait. For example, the Family Services of America, in their 1935 *Newsletter*, noted that for social workers, desirable 'personal qualities would include, among others, sensitivity, freedom from prejudice, non-judgemental and non-managing attitudes, a genuine feeling for people, maturity, capacity for self-development'.[38] During the decades to follow, non-judgemental attitudes became associated with an open, anti-authoritarian, and flexible personality.

The non-judgemental personality emerged as a cultural ideal in the second half of the 20th century, since which point schoolchildren have been educated to adopt it as a desirable character trait. By the 1960s, the creative public act of judgement was increasingly rejected as an undesirable and negative form of moralistic behaviour and portrayed as an expression of narrow-minded prejudice. Indeed, the distinction between prejudice – a judgement based on preconceived notions – and judgement gradually became blurred. Those who insisted on upholding moral boundaries and making judgements of value were often castigated for their archaic and inherently unpleasant behaviour.

The tendency to condemn the act of moral judgement was reinforced by the claim that this form of behaviour is harmful to those subjected to it. Initially, the claim that judgement caused psychological harm focused on children and individuals suffering from mental health problems. Since the 1980s, the pathologisation of judgement has acquired a powerful dynamic. The main driver of this trend is the growing influence of the view that people, especially children, lack the resilience to deal with judgement: a belief widely advocated by parenting experts and early years educators. Schoolteachers are trained to avoid explicit criticism of their pupils and to practice techniques that validate members of the classroom. The sentiment that 'criticism is violence' has gained significant influence on university campuses and among society's cultural elites.[39] Judgement is sometimes depicted as a form of psychic violence, especially if applied to children: the sociologist Richard Sennett echoes this sentiment when he writes of the 'devastating implications of rendering judgement on someone's future'.[40]

By the 1980s, therefore, the meaning of the word 'non-judgemental' had significantly expanded from its original use. At the turn of the 20th century, critics of judgement directed their fire at the use of a common standard of values for judging different groups and cultures, with the aim of undermining the attitude of superiority of Western culture towards other societies. In the decades to follow, the criticism of judgement was applied to a widening range of circumstances, and the avoidance of judgement transformed into a positive virtue to be inculcated in children and young people.

In his discussion of liberal resistance to the imposition of value judgements, Stephen Holmes claims that this turn 'helped deflate moral imperialisms' and was 'not meant to destroy morality itself'.[41] Unfortunately, the tendency to delegitimate the authority of judgement has gone way beyond deflating 'moral imperialisms'. It has encouraged institutions and wider society to adopt the attitude of moral neutrality. This, in turn, has fostered a cultural climate hospitable to the flourishing of moral indifference.

An important study of the widespread prevalence of moral indifference among young people illustrates the depth of this problem. The majority of young Americans interviewed by the authors of *Lost in Transition: The Dark Side of Emerging Adulthood* (2011) took the view that since morality is a matter of individual choice, it was inappropriate to judge others; those who insisted on doing so were perceived as legitimate targets of condemnation. One young adult claimed to view people who sought to impose their moral beliefs on others as 'sick'.[42] The predominant sentiment that prevailed among these young interviewees was that judging was associated with 'condemning, castigating, disparaging, or executing'.[43] Another survey, of 18–24 year-old Americans in 2012, indicated that most associated prejudices such as being anti-gay, or acts of hypocrisy, with being judgemental.[44]

Aversion to judgement also conveys a sense of moral indifference, not only towards other people, but also towards the authority of the boundaries that govern daily life. The cultural validation of non-judgementalism has a profound influence on how society and individuals alike make sense of the boundaries and borders that cross their lives. An act of judgement can be interpreted as a form of boundary work that assists people to understand where to draw a line. When the capacity for judgement is discouraged and discredited, the practice of boundary work loses much of its meaning and creative dimension. Discouraged from exercising their capacity for judgement, individuals have become psychically distanced from the art of drawing lines.

The blurring of the boundary between health and illness

The ascendancy of non-judgementalism as a dominant value has been paralleled by the growing influence of a trend that can be best captured by the term 'permissive therapeutics'. During the interwar era, non-judgementalism became integral to the practice of health professionals, particularly in the sphere of mental health. Practitioners of permissive therapeutics insisted that patients who were insulated from the pressure of judgement were far more likely to open up and communicate their problems. But the growing influence of psychology in modern society ensured that permissive therapeutics has expanded from the clinical setting into other spheres that demanded the management of human relations, such as the realms of parenting and education.

The widening influence of permissive therapeutics also interacted with and reinforced the non-judgemental attitudes of anthropologists towards their evaluation of different cultural values. Writing in 1950, the American anthropologist Clyde Kluckhohn drew a direct comparison between the practices and attitudes of psychiatrists and members of his discipline. He noted that the 'amnesty which the anthropologist gives to the exuberant variety of cultural patterns must be that which the psychiatrist gives to incestuous dreams'.[45] Unlike many others in his discipline, Kluckhohn was not entirely happy with the virtue that his profession made of its refusal to judge. He suggested that not all truths were culturally relative, and that the discoveries of science 'transcend cultural variations'.

Back when Kluckhohn and others debated the amnesty that ought to be extended to 'exuberant' cultural attitudes within psychology, the practice of permissive therapeutics tended to be confined within a legitimate clinical setting. As the sociologist Talcott Parsons explained, therapists seek to influence the internal life of their patients through empathising with their predicament, and to achieve this they establish a relationship of 'permissiveness'.[46] Through a relation of permissiveness – what today would be called being non-judgemental – therapists are able to gain a privileged access to people's subjectivity.

Through a diagnosis, therapists are able to assign the status of being sick to a patient. Parsons developed the concept of the 'sick role' to explain how an amnesty from judgement serves the objectives of therapeutic intervention. The sick role exempts individuals from having to behave in accordance with prevailing social and moral expectations, since 'being ill cannot ordinarily be conceived to be the fault of the sick person' and 'illness can justify certain exemptions from normal expectations of performance'.[47] In return for gaining these exemptions, sick individuals are expected to define their condition as undesirable and aberrant and to do everything possible to get well. Parsons regarded the sick role as a temporary one, during which the therapist could establish an important emotional connection with the patient based on the exercise of detached empathy. During this relationship, the therapist's diagnosis of illness shapes the way the individual understands his or her condition. Since definitions of illness are informed by prevailing cultural norms and expectations, the assignment of the sick role contains the potential for motivating the reintegration of the patient into the wider social system.[48]

Parsons believed that the exercise of social control through permissive therapeutics would be effective as long as there prevailed an 'institutionalized consensus' with respect to 'what constitutes "moral integrity" in our society'. He believed that such a consensus existed, since without 'it the degree of stability which our society has shown could not be understood'.[49] While this may have been so during the 1950s, when Parsons was writing, it can no longer be taken for granted that there is a consensus on what constitutes 'moral integrity' in society. Indeed, society's embrace of the value of non-judgementalism is itself symptomatic of the unravelling of a moral consensus.

By the 1960s, many observers were noting the expansion of non-judgemental attitudes to non-clinical spheres of life. 'To be 'non-judgemental' has become an almost religious tenet' remarked a commentator in the 1962 edition of the *Northwestern University Law Review*. The commentary warned that 'some are non-judgemental to the degree that they are in danger of losing all moral sense and ordinary judgement', and that concepts of 'personal responsibility, of right and wrong' were undermined by non-judgemental attitudes.[50]

Since the 1970s, the influence of non-judgementalism and the weakening of a moral consensus has had a direct impact on debates about the meaning of illness and health, leading to a blurring of this significant boundary. Parsons assumed that the therapeutic relationship is underpinned by a shared 'positive valuation of health and the negative valuation of illness between therapeutic agent and sick persons'.[51] Yet from the 1970s onwards, definitions of illness have become contested, and a negative valuation of illness is itself a subject of controversy. The reluctance to judge other cultures has mutated into hesitancy to distinguish between 'normal' and 'abnormal' or 'being ill' and 'being well'. Illness is no longer necessarily depicted as a temporary interlude before returning to health and can now constitute a defining feature of an individual's identity. 'For some, the patient career may be a permanent way of life, with a self-supporting network of friends, activities, doctors, and treatments', observes Elaine Showalter.[52]

Indeed, identities associated with illness are often cast in a positive light. One study of women's experience with fibromyalgia asserts that the illness can create intimacy and kinship, as it 'provides one with an opportunity to recognize oneself'. Another study of cancer-related identity speculates about how this illness can be a 'potentially positive experience'.[53] The valorisation of the 'positive' features of illness calls into question the original conceptualisation of the sick role as a temporary episode, which should be overcome. When the sick role is experienced as an affirmation of identity, it is likely to assume a more durable character. Terms like 'cancer survivor' and 'recovering alcoholic' testify to a growing tendency to represent illness as constituting a long-term influence on identity.

Changing attitudes towards illness and identity are most strikingly expressed through a growing tendency to embrace the sick role. In Britain and the US, the institutionalisation of permissive therapeutics has led to the extension of the experiences that now warrant exemptions from normal standards of accountability.[54] It has fostered a climate that is hospitable to the continuous widening of the definition of illness: particularly when it comes to psychiatric and psychological disorders, where the proliferation of diagnostic categories indicates that a growing range of experiences are interpreted through the prism of a medical diagnosis. There has been a massive increase in the number of officially diagnosed mental disorders. In 1917, the American Psychiatric Association recognised 59 disorders. The number rose to 128 in 1959. Since that time, there has been a veritable explosion of disorders rising to 350 in 2000. As the problems of everyday life continued to be framed through the language of illness the numbers of disorders continue to expand.

The legitimisation of permissiveness within the therapeutic relationship has created the potential for its expansion into other spheres of life. In this way, the permissive qualities of therapeutics have reinforced the cultural influence of non-judgementalism. Once permissiveness is granted to some individuals some of the time, it becomes difficult to contain other demands for exemption from the prevailing normative order. As the social commentator Christopher Lasch concluded in the late 1970s, 'inappropriately extended beyond the consulting room . . . therapeutic morality encourages a permanent suspension of the moral sense'.[55] People who are sick cannot be expected to exercise critical judgement or to accept moral responsibility for their actions. And when this attitude is extended 'beyond the consulting room' it becomes not simply a treatment for the ill but a guide for individual behaviour. That is why some of the promoters of therapy regard it as not only necessary to cure the ill but as indispensable to the conduct of healthy relationships and normal life. 'Therapy is too good to be limited to the sick' wrote Erving and Miriam Polster, two American psychologists, in 1973.[56]

Non-judgementalism and its application through the medium of permissive therapeutics has important implications for understanding the transformation of the sick role. It blurs the line that divides the state of illness from that of being well and potentially provides everyone with access to exemptions from the prevailing normative order. When even the boundary that separates health and illness is called into question, the disorienting influence of the loss of judgement becomes all too evident. The blurring of the boundary between illness and normality was the topic of a medical conference on *Preventing Overdiagnosis* in Denmark in 2018. Opening the conference, Iona Heath asked 'why are we so afraid of being the normal?'[57] Is it any surprise that with the blurring of the boundary between illness and normality the usage of the word abnormal is increasingly criticised for being too judgemental?[58]

Notes

1 Dunn (1998) p. 12.
2 Held (2003) pp. 189–190.
3 Beck (2005) p. 230.
4 See Wuthnow (1989) p. 70.
5 Beck (2002) p. 19.
6 Ochoa Espejo (2018) p. 71.
7 See Brubaker (1992).
8 Delsol (2003) p. 74.
9 Burrill (1966) p. 245.

10 See Acts 17:22.

11 Wuthnow (1989) p. 75.

12 Wuthnow (1989) p. 75.

13 See Judgement: OED Third Edition, December 2013.

14 See 'judgementalism | judgementalism, n', *OED Online*, March 2019. Oxford University Press. www.oed.com.chain.kent.ac.uk/view/Entry/394283 (accessed May 14, 2019).

15 See Graph charting the usage of the word judgementalism. <iframe name="ngram_chart" src="https://books.google.com/ngrams/interactive_chart?content=judgementalism&year_start=1800&year_end=2000&corpus=15&smoothing=3&share=&direct_url=t1%3B%2Cjudgementalism%3B%2Cc0"width=900height=500marginwidth=0marginheight=0hspace=0 vspace=0 frameborder=0 scrolling=no></iframe>.

16 2005 *Guardian* 18 July 1.18/8.

17 Trilling (1957) p. 234.

18 Wolfe (1998) p. 54.

19 Elshtain, J.K. (1994) 'Judge Not', *First Things*, October, p. 38.

20 www.youtube.com/watch?v=wV1FrqwZyKw.

21 Arendt (2006) pp. 217–218.

22 Merlau-Ponty (1974) p. 116.

23 Midgley (2017).

24 Bauman (1996) p. 32. The term adiaphorous means something that is neither good or bad. It conveys the meaning of indifferent or neutral. For Bauman, adiaphorization refers to systems and procedures that help to detach the evaluation of issues from the domain of morality. It implies the institutionalisation of moral indifference.

25 See Nicholson (2008) p. 57.

26 See Nicholson (2008) p. 82.

27 Herskovits (1958) p. 270.

28 Nicholson (2008) pp. 68–69.

29 Moran (2015) pp. 97–98.

30 Herskovits (1951) p. 22.

31 Cited in Herskovits (1951) p. 22.

32 Benedict (1989) p. 273.

33 See Moran (2015) p. 97.

34 See Moran (2015) p. 97.

35 Trilling (1957) p. 234.

36 See, *The Virginia Quarterly Review*, Volume 72, 1925, p. 488. https://books.google.it/books?id=eH20IXJRjJQC&q="nonjudgemental"&dq="nonjudgemental"&hl=en&sa=X&ved=0ahUKEwj-gaC5np.

37 Witmer (1934) p. 67.

38 Family Service Association of America, News Letter, Volumes 10–14, p. 26. https://books.google.co.uk/books?id=VPscAQAAMAAJ.

39 Rauch (1993) p. 6.

40 Sennett (2003) p. 98.

41 Holmes (1993) p. 234.

42 Smith (2011).

43 Smith (2011) p. 24.

44 Twenge (2017) p. 139.

45 Kluckhohn (1950) p. 246.

46 Parsons (1965) p. 317.

47 Parsons (1978) pp. 77–78.

48 For a discussion of the sick role in a wider cultural setting, see Furedi (2002) chapter 4.

49 Parsons (1965) pp. 323–324.

50 See *Northwestern University Law Review* (1962), vol. 57, pp. 23 & 27. https://books.google.it/books?id=JysvAAAAIAAJ&q=%22nonjudgemental%22&dq=%22nonjudgemental%22&hl=en&sa=X&ved=0ahUKEwjw4a_G7KriAhUsMuwKHYjKDlU4ChDoAQhHMAc.

51 Parsons (1978) p. 76.
52 Showalter (1997) p. 19.
53 See Soderberg, Lundman, and Norberg (1999) p. 584 and Zebrack (2000) p. 241.
54 See Fox (1977) p. 15.
55 Lasch (1979) p. 389.
56 Cited in Dineen (1999) p. 233.
57 See https://blogs.bmj.com/bmj/2018/08/20/helen-macdonald-overdiagnosis-and-the-fear-of-being-normal/.
58 See for example Saul McLeod (2018) 'Abnormal Psychology', *Simply Psychology*, 5 August, https://www.simplypsychology.org/abnormal-psychology.html.

3

UNMASKING OPENNESS

The value of non-judgementalism is closely allied to that of openness. These two values mutually reinforce one another to challenge and diminish conventional moral and symbolic boundaries. Openness has become the medium through which the contemporary sensibility of boundarylessness has come to influence people's imagination. In recent years, it has become radicalised to the point where the very act of closing evokes suspicion.[1] The term 'behind closed doors' is often used to draw attention to secretive, furtive, dishonest or conspiratorial behaviour, while in educational settings, 'closed doors' have become literally prohibited and a metaphor for mistrust. In contrast, the act of opening up something to public scrutiny is likely to enjoy cultural acclaim. In the name of upholding openness, borders and boundaries are disregarded, especially if they are seen to protect a closed society.

The aim of this chapter is to reflect on the meaning and consequence of the mutation of openness from a term of description into an important value. It argues that the advocacy of openness directs its wrath against pre-political community life. The term pre-political refers to the ties of family and networks based on a community of intergenerational links and affiliations. The corollary of the value preference for openness is the disparagement of communities, which take their boundaries seriously. Advocates of openness frequently assume that they have a right and a duty to open up communities that they regard as exclusive and closed. They regard boundaries as impediments to the realisation of an Open World.

The radicalisation of openness

In the everyday vernacular, or what the philosopher Christopher McMahon describes as 'common sense morality', openness is accorded a positive value.

Yet it is far from evident what is 'morally valuable openness', and what kind of behaviour this term implies.[2] Historically, openness was regarded as a state that served as the polar opposite of secrecy or deception; the extent to which it is still used in that sense is shown by the prominent status enjoyed by the ideal of 'transparency'. The mere act of using the word 'open' as an adjective to describe a noun helps bequeath the latter with positive attributes: as indicated by the proliferation of terms such as 'open source', 'open education', 'open skies' 'open sharing', and 'open society'.

However, openness has also acquired a different connotation, which is its resistance to the temptation to judge. In popular culture, openness supposedly rejects preconceived notions, refuses to possess durable commitments and ideas, and does not abide by fixed points and permanent boundaries. Implicitly openness is praised because of its claim to have freed itself from the burden of judgement.

The endowment of openness with positive qualities, and judgement with negative ones, has acquired the status of a self-evident truth in common-sense morality. Openness and non-judgementalism mutually disparage the drawing of lines. Though the relationship between these two terms is rarely explored, it is often highlighted in self-help manuals and motivational literature, where they are used interchangeably. One headline promoting mindfulness asserts that 'Without Judgement: How Mindfulness Leads to being More Open-Minded',[3] while the article's author explains: Keeping an open mind, even for the most free-spirited among us, is harder than it sounds. Our minds have evolved to identify, discern, and judge in order to make sense of the world around us. In some instances, the two words are fused together: one advocate of this ideal exhorts people to cultivate 'nonjudgemental openness'.[4] Others explain that 'openness to experience represents the tendency to view ideas, events, and experiences in a nonjudgemental and interested manner'.[5] The author of a book on lifestyle medicine defines openness as 'acceptance, tolerance, open-heartedness, and being nonjudgemental'.[6]

The transformation of openness into a core value, and its widespread adoption by companies, private and public sector organisations, the self-help industry, educational institutions and websites occurred because it resonates with a hospitable cultural climate. As one astute observer points out, 'if there is one term that might be chosen to characterize the intellectual and moral climate of the present day, it would be the word "openness"'.[7] Yet the ideal of openness emerged unannounced, and the cultural authority it enjoys is rarely explicitly acknowledged.

One of the most insightful interpretation of the idealisation of openness is provided by the Buddhist commentator Bhikku Bodhi. He contends that this ideal has permeated contemporary culture so extensively 'that it now seems almost as an innate human disposition'. Bodhi argues that the popularisation of openness is 'historically rooted in the widespread decline of belief structures centered upon a transcendent goal of human life and an objectively grounded scale of values', and that 'the philosophy of openness takes all truth to be relative, all values personal and subjective'.[8] One reason why Bodhi has been motivated to question and contest the authority of openness is because the sentiments it expresses are widely echoed by advocates of different types of meditation, who claim that they are consistent with Buddhist ideals. Taking exception to the attempt to assimilate the ideal of openness, Bodhi points to the 'gaping difference' between non-judgemental openness and classical Buddhism:

> whereas the school of openness bids us to drop our discriminations, judgements and restraints in order to immerse ourselves in the dynamic flow of immediate experience, the Buddha prescribes an attitude toward experience that arises from carefully wrought judgements, employs precise discriminations, and issues in detachment and restraint. This attitude, the classical Buddhist counterfoil to the modern program of openness, might be summed up by one word found everywhere in the ancient texts. That word is heedfulness *(appamada)*.[9]

The attitude of heedful scrutiny advocated previously recognises the importance of careful discrimination and judgement. Contrary to the claims of many lifestyle and self-help advocates of openness, Buddhism upholds the value of judgement and discrimination and the willingness to draw moral boundaries.

In principle, non-judgemental openness is not the only form that openness can take. There is much to be admired about openness as an attitude towards life, a disposition towards experience, and as a character trait. Genuine openness is open to judgement. It is the transformation of openness into a value that is intolerant of judgement that is problematic, turning it into an apology for avoiding moral choice and responsibility. The politicisation of openness threatens to deprive it of its critical and creative content. One of the first observers to present a systematic challenge to the conformist trajectory driving the politicisation of openness was the American classicist and philosopher Alan Bloom. In his controversial 1987 bestseller *The Closing of the American Mind: How Higher Education Has Failed Democracy and Impoverished the Souls of Today's Students*, Bloom drew attention to the cultural hegemony of non-judgemental openness over intellectual life in higher education.[10]

Throughout *The Closing of the American Mind*, Bloom made a distinction between what he interpreted as a positive and negative form of openness, writing that:

> Openness used to be the virtue that permitted us to seek the good by using reason. It now means accepting everything and denying reason's power. The unrestrained and thoughtless pursuit of openness, without recognizing the inherent political, social, or cultural problem of openness as the goal of nature, has rendered openness meaningless.[11]

For Bloom, genuine openness had as its premise an awareness of the need to make distinctions between right and wrong and true and false. In contrast, the refusal to judge denied the 'possibility of knowing good and bad' and therefore suppressed 'true openness'.[12]

In his polemic against the transformation of openness into a doctrine of evasion, Bloom's main target was the powerful influence of relativism over campus life. Bloom attempted to uphold the necessity of making distinctions between competing cultures and their values. He feared that the transformation of openness into an end in itself would diminish the capacity of students to reason, discriminate, and engage in the intellectual quest for the truth.

The convergence of openness and non-judgementalism

Universities have played an important role in providing intellectual support for the borderless sensibility. But, though the turn towards the openness of indifference is most pronounced in the Academy, it is by no means confined to this institution. Bloom and others have tended to blame the ethos of relativism for the loss of intellectual support for the authority of moral judgement. However, the influence of relativistic thought ought to be interpreted as an outcome of society's alienation from the practice of drawing lines in *all* domains of human experience.

The questioning of the value of judgement coincided with the emergence of a mood of moral malaise within Western society in the aftermath of the First World War. It was during this climate of disillusionment and pessimism that the concept of openness began to gain traction. At that point in time, the catastrophic consequences of that war were often linked to the clandestine diplomacy and political culture that prevailed in the early part of the 20th century. This sentiment was forcefully voiced by the Labour politician Arthur Ponsonby in 1915:

> The stuffy hot-house atmosphere of diplomacy must be cleansed by the fresh air of publicity. The spiders of intrigue which have woven undisturbed their tangled webs in secret must be chased out of darkness into the open light of day.[13]

The call for open diplomacy coincided with a palpable sense of unease towards a world divided into competing, and sometimes conflicting, nation states. The reaction of many intellectuals and policymakers to the Great War took the form of looking for solutions beyond the national borders and investing hope in international institutions such as the League of Nations. Yet back then, the demand for openness was principally directed at the problems associated with secrecy – rather than, as in our time, the act of judgement.

In the dark and troubled times of the 1930s, the philosopher Henri Bergson formulated the concept of 'open society' to signify his commitment to shifting focus from the terrain of the national to a wider cosmopolitan constituency.[14] Bergson was critical of a 'closed society' with its 'closed system of law and religion'. He claimed that closed societies – which he saw as the characteristic feature of most communities – continually prepared for war and argued for an open society that was oriented towards the ethos of 'moral universalism'. In Bergson's case, the idea of an open society was not explicitly linked to a sensibility of non-judgementalism; indeed, he would probably be surprised and dismayed by the subsequent turn that this sentiment has taken. As a conservative, Christian philosopher, Bergson had no problems with judgement; his aim was to go beyond the loyalties of tribe and nation towards a more open future.[15]

The concept of the open society was popularised by the philosopher Karl Popper in the 1940s. His classic study, *The Open Society and Its Enemies*, positively contrasted openness to what he perceived as the tribalist mentality of community and national consciousness. Reacting to the disastrous outcome of the First World War and the subsequent rise of totalitarian states, Popper came to fear and despise both national and ideological attachments. He regarded the nations as closed societies whose borders needed to be transcended and rendered irrelevant by more open internationally minded institutions. To serve this end, Popper defended empires and imperialism as far more enlightened institutions than those representing tribalistic closed societies.

Popper's defence of imperialism is most explicit in his discussion of Ancient Greece. He adopted a positive view of the non-national imperialism of the Athenian empire, which he favourably contrasted to the tribalist political system of Sparta. Characterising 'certain of the imperialist measures introduced by Athens' as 'rather liberal', he explained that his 'favourable view of Athenian imperialism can be supported by comparing it with Spartan methods of handling foreign affairs'.[16] Popper hoped that 'tribalist exclusiveness and self-sufficiency could be superseded by some form of imperialism'.

Popper's idea of 'open society' was linked to a newly developed, technocratic version of cosmopolitanism that looked towards global institutions to save humanity from the closed communities that they allegedly inhabited. Unlike Kant's account of cosmopolitanism, Popper's version rejected national attachments and was deeply suspicious of the exercise of national sovereignty.[17] He condemned nationalism as a 'dreadful heresy'.[18] This was a view shared by many post-war liberals in the aftermath of the Second World War, who blamed extreme nationalism for this terrible episode in human history and invested their hopes in international forms of governance. During the following decades, others expanded Popper's concept of open society, and it acquired more radical dimensions. Marshall McLuhan's influential 1964 study *The Global Village* captured the borderless sensibility that excited the imagination of a section of Western society's cultural elites. From the 1980s onwards, new varieties of cosmopolitan ideas tended to converge with boundaryless sentiments. In the contemporary era, the globalist Open Society Foundations offer a crusading institutional expression of this sensibility

Advocates of boundarylessness often drew inspiration from the apparent success of the European Union in eliminating border controls between most of its member states. One of the leading proponents of the cosmopolitan project, the German sociologist Ulrich Beck, claimed that the 'defining characteristic of the European project was its "radical openness"'.[19] A similar argument was made by the former President of the European Commission, Jose Manuel Barroso, who declared that for Europe, openness is a 'congenital condition' that has been an 'integral part of our values since the beginning of the integration process'.[20] Beck stated that the 'cosmopolitan outlook' was founded on a 'global sense, a sense of boundarylessness'.[21] Though he recognised that the sense of boundarylessness created 'anguish' to those who lost their fixed reference points in life, he welcomed what he characterised as its 'reflexive awareness of ambivalences in a milieu of blurring differentiations and cultural contradictions'.[22] Beck's concept of cosmopolitanism did not merely pertain to national borders, but also to the symbolic boundaries that guided people within the domestic sphere. He applauded the coming of an age 'when apparently fixed differentiations and dichotomies become sterile'.[23]

The tendency to regard fixed differentiations and cultural and conceptual dichotomies as outdated relics is often justified on the grounds that everything has become fluid and transitory in a dynamic, rapidly changing world. Critics of 'bounded' forms of thinking delight in inventing new metaphors to highlight the inability of borders to contain the supposedly omnipotent forces of globalisation. As one academic, Liam O'Dowd observes, 'in the rush to capture the "novel" and nebulous qualities of the new global order and its associated borders, social scientists have reached for a profusion of metaphors, scapes, networks, flows, and fluids to illuminate the growing ease with which capital, information, goods, services, and people cross state boundaries'.[24]

Beck developed the concept of 'methodological cosmopolitanism' to refocus attention from what he perceived as the boundary-fixated consciousness of those who seek reassurance from the familiar lines drawn through the traditions of the nationally bounded imagination. Beck wrote that the 'basic concepts of "modern society" – *household, family, class, democracy, domination, state, economy, the public sphere, politics,* and so on' need 'to be released from the fixations of methodological nationalism and redefined and reconceptualized in the context of methodological cosmopolitanism'.[25] What Beck describes as the 'fixations of methodological nationalism' refers to the taken-for-granted meanings that have gained definition through the guidance provided by symbolic boundaries.

Cosmopolitan boundarylessness is frequently represented as a response to the powerful forces unleashed by globalisation. However, the causal link drawn between globalisation and the rise of a borderless sensibility is far too simplistic to account for the estrangement of society from symbolic boundaries. The questioning of borders and symbolic boundaries predates the rise of globalism. The adoption of globalisation as an all-purpose explanation for diverse forms of cultural and social developments leads to deterministic and objectivist conclusions that invariably minimise the significance of developments in the domain of morality. The loss of authority of judgement and society's estrangement from drawing boundaries are reinforced by current global trends but are not the result of them. Nor does globalism abolish people's aspiration for the security provided by borders: as many commentators have pointed out, globalism is as likely to create a demand for *glocalism* and for a place of belonging as it does for its opposite.

Rather, the commanding influence of boundarylessness derives from the convergence of the influence of the value of openness with the cultural validation of non-judgementalism. The convergence of these two trends occurred in the 1960s, when a variety of otherwise disparate cultural and social trends provided the conditions for non-judgementalism to flourish. As noted in the previous chapter, up to this point the concept of non-judgemental tended to be confined to the therapeutic and social work professions. The spread of the imperative to be 'non-judgemental' to education, cultural institutions, and popular culture resulted from the rapid erosion of moral authority associated with the tumultuous Sixties, where traditional values, institutions, and social conventions became subject to explicit questioning and rejection. As the historian Eric Hobsbawm explains, during this period: 'The old moral vocabulary of rights and duties, mutual obligation, sin and virtue, sacrifice, conscience, rewards, penalties, could no longer be translated into the new language of desired gratification'. According to Hobsbawm, the 'capacity' of moral values to 'structure human life vanished'. The main response to this development was the emergence of a variety of standpoints, from free-market consumerism to postmodernism, which 'tried to sidestep the problem of judgement and values altogether'.[26]

Hostility towards closed communities

The corollary of the value preference for openness is the disparagement of closed communities. Although concepts such as 'open' and 'closed' societies, or methodological cosmopolitanism and methodological nationalism, are presented as objective and neutral categories, they are underwritten by a palpable sense of contempt for communities that are culturally bounded to a territory. Supporters of the ideal of an open society also disparage those who take seriously the status of borders. The cosmopolitan philosopher Jürgen Habermas adopts a tone of unadulterated contempt when he dismisses what he characterises as the 'caricature of national macrosubjects shutting themselves off from each other and blocking any cross-border democratic will-formation'. Predictably, such people are described as the adherents of 'right-wing populism'.[27] Beck regards national borders as the conveyors of the 'morality of exclusion'.[28] Commenting on the 'denigration of borders' by contemporary social theorists, the political scientist Sergei Prozorov draws attention to their alienation from and discomfort with boundaries.[29] Borders are represented as 'dividers of humanity and as expressions of particularisms'; they 'dominate, exclude, and exploit' and carry with them 'a legacy of congealed coercion and violence'.[30]

In an age of non-judgementalism, the unrestrained manner with which negative judgements are flung at supporters of borders and boundaries requires an explanation. Their bitter hostility is visceral and characteristically militant; the kind of response that is usually targeted at an established foe. When Beck characterised 'anticosmopolitan nationalism' as the enemy, he followed the path of Popper and other anti-traditionalist intellectuals and commentators who regard traditionally based pre-political communities and relationships as irrational relics. Pre-political solidarity – ties of kinship, family, friendship, religion, and community membership – are dismissed as semi-archaic links that stand in the way of openness. From their perspective, the influence of these outdated loyalties and affiliations has become even more dangerous in the contemporary era.

The adoption of a combative approach is particularly fierce in relation to what is considered to be a closed society's worst sin: a national sensibility. Beck, along with the British sociologist Anthony Giddens, contends that 'nationalism has become the worst enemy of Europe's nations'.[31] The sentiment is echoed by Habermas, who states that the 'long shadow cast by nationalism continues to obscure the present'. Habermas welcomes the 'cunning of economic reason' for assisting cross-border interactions and for corroding national boundaries, but recognises that in the end his cosmopolitan vision requires that the 'national public spheres gradually *open themselves up to each other*'.[32] Habermas understands that communities do not open themselves up spontaneously, which is why he has devoted himself to the promotion and institutionalisation of a cosmopolitan political culture that will undermine the capacity of communities to remain closed.

Unable to reconcile the pre-political relations and traditions with civic affiliations, border critics mistakenly regard ties of family, religion, culture, and community as potential threats to the workings of a liberal democratic society. Such ties – whether they are intergenerational or community-based – are censured as far too restrictive and exclusive. Even the civic ties of citizenship, which bring people together in a common political membership, are often dismissed on the grounds that they are too restrictive. According to some commentators, national citizenship is not a genuinely open concept because it is not available to everyone inhabiting the earth. Consequently, the *demos*, which has underpinned the workings of democratic societies, is sometimes characterised as complicit in the perpetuation of a closed society. That is why supporters of the concept of an open society tend to adopt a pragmatic or instrumental attitude towards democracy – if not an outright critique. Writing in this vein, one exponent of Popper's views praised him for shifting the 'locus of debate in political philosophy from democracy to openness'.[33]

Fundamentally, the critique of a closed society is based on a disavowal of pre-political bonds. The call to 'openness' is frequently linked to the project of undermining the relations that define and bind people together in their community. In principle, democratically inclined people prefer a society that is open to people making choices and exercising their freedom to a society that is closed to public participation and decision-making. However, for many advocates of openness, the problem with a closed society is not the absence of choice but the influence of pre-existing loyalties. Such organic bonds are frequently regarded with suspicion by intellectuals estranged from their communities. For example, Bergson, writing back in the 1950s, feared that the 'natural' impulses prevailing in communities would lead to aggressive and conflict-oriented behaviour. He outlined his pessimistic view of closed communities in the following terms:

> The closed society is that whose members hold together, caring nothing for the rest of humanity, on the alert for attack and defence, bound, in fact, to a perpetual readiness for battle. Such is human society fresh from the hands of nature. Man was made for this society[34]

Bergson warned that the natural working out of human instinct 'would be far more likely to prompt societies to struggle against one another than to unite to make up humanity'.[35] His pessimistic account of the human spirit anticipates the suspicion that advocates of open society have regarding the 'natural impulses' driving democratic decision-making. As we explain in the next chapter, the anti-democratic spirit animating the open border movement is founded on its mistrust of people.

Bergson's pessimistic account of a closed society was shared by Popper. In his discussion of a closed society, Popper communicates an uninhibited sense of disdain for organic ties, depicting closed societies as a collectivist hive in which its members are not 'confronted with personal decisions'. He wrote that a 'closed society resembles a herd or a tribe in being a semi-organic unit whose members are held together by semi-biological ties – kinship'. In such circumstances, the tribe becomes everything, 'without which the individual is nothing at all'. According to his view, a closed society is a world dominated by magic and superstitious taboo, where rational reflection is conspicuous by its absence.[36]

Popper regarded the borders surrounding a closed society as far from inviolable. He believed that if a society is not able to make the transition from a tribalist to an open one, others are entitled to intervene and bring about regime change. His self-conscious defence of imperialist intervention, discussed prior, was justified on the ground that this was necessary for human progress. As one commentator on Popper's concept of open society explained:

> Open societies are non-tribal societies, they can arise only if individuals are ready to fight for their individual and egoistic interests and break up the bonds and ligatures of tribal societies. If the people of Athens's neighbour cities were unable to break up the bonds of their tribal societies themselves, Athens was justified, according to Popper, in military interventions that helped break up tribal societies.[37]

Popper justified his support for intervention in the affairs of another community as a 'defence of the imperialism of democracy'.[38] His acclamation of a progressive form of imperialism indicated that the concept of open society also provided its practitioners with the warrant to *open up* other societies – whether they liked it or not. From this perspective, borders did not possess any positive moral status: they simply got in the way of those spreading the ideology of openness. Today, similar arguments are used by cosmopolitan partisans of European federalism and by Open Society guided transnational institutions to promote regime change.

Guy Verhofstadt, the Belgian Member of the European Parliament and leading advocate of European federalism, captured the spirit of empire-building openness when he asserted that 'the world of tomorrow is not a world order based on nations states' but one 'that is based on empires'.[39]

Popper's lack of empathy for pre-political affiliations and loyalties was founded upon his conviction that the conflicts that dominated the world in the first half of the 20th century were fuelled by an irrational tribalist mentality. When Popper wrote *The Open Society and its Enemies*, his main target was what he perceived as the tribal nationalism that fuelled wars. In subsequent decades, opponents of closed societies have broadened out their critique to all forms of pre-political bonds, which have come to be regarded as potentially harmful and exclusionary. Advocates of a transnational worldview constantly question the significance of shared traits and of family and community ties. They argue that pre-political 'conceptions of solidarity based on largely involuntary or fixed characteristics such as nationality, gender, ethnicity, or social status' have little moral worth.[40] According to one account, 'indeed, just because two individuals share the same trait, their common characteristic does not provide any clues about the circumstances and ways in which they should act in solidarity with each other' – rather, such forms of solidarity 'run the risk of excluding outsiders'.[41]

Hostility towards closed communities has a long history. As Blake Smith explains, historically the term 'tribalist' was hurled at the 'obstinate Hebrews' who remained resistant to religious or cultural conversion. Smith wrote that by the turn of the 20th century, tribalism was 'not so much a concept but a slur'. Since Popper's appropriation of the term, tribalism tends to be applied to people who, because they take their community loyalties seriously, constitute a threat to a tolerant, open society.[42] Thus, Carl Bildt, the former Chair of the European Council on Foreign Relations, states that 'with the blurring of the old battle lines, politics is gradually being reshaped into a contest between advocates of open, globalized societies and defenders of inward-looking tribalism'.[43]

The dismissive attitudes of the globalist elites towards inward-looking tribalists convey a sense of superiority towards people who are implicitly designated as their moral inferiors. 'The populists, nationalists, stupid nationalists, they are in love with their own countries', declared a bemused European Commission President, Jean-Clause Juncker in May 2019.[44] Juncker's incomprehension of how anyone could love their country was no doubt a genuine response of someone who regards spontaneous loyalties to community and to the borders that surround it as an irritating feature of life.

Since Popper's defence of the 'imperialism of democracy', the project of opening up pre-political communities and institutions that are based on distinct ties of membership and exposing them to boundaryless values has acquired significant momentum. That is why, despite the multiculturalist celebration of difference, the assertion of a sense of difference between a member of a community and someone who is alien to it is often condemned as a form of discrimination. As Chantal Delsol notes, 'to discriminate originally meant *to distinguish*', yet has now 'acquired a pejorative connotation: to distinguish is itself immoral'.[45] This pejorative representation of discrimination confuses the differential role and effect of drawing distinctions in the political and the private spheres. As Arendt explained, in the political sphere, where the principle of equality must prevail, there is no place for discriminating between people: all must receive equal treatment under the law. Matters are different in the private sphere, however, where people need to be able to discriminate between people on the basis of personal preference. Arendt also argued that discrimination has a place in the social sphere, where the right to discriminate serves as the basis for free association and group formation.[46]

One consequence of rebranding discrimination as a pejorative term is to legitimate its policing and regulation. It also legitimates the opening up and the policing of the private sphere. As we note in Chapter 5, the opening up of the pre-political domain assists the erosion of the line between the public and the private spheres. The act of opening up encourages the power of surveillance, which always contains the potential for damaging what has been opened up.

The devaluation of the status of citizenship

The opening up of pre-political communities is in part motivated by the objective of dissolving the distinctions and demarcations based on the traditions that have organically evolved. The project of opening up such communities is not simply directed at ancient tribal affiliations but also at the foundations on which modern and civic notions of citizenship rest. Since a person is a citizen of a specific nation and bounded to its territory, national citizenship fails to meet the criteria of radical openness. Citizenship based on birth and culturally based affiliations and loyalties is particularly decried. But even the status of achieving citizenship through voluntarily committing to a common civic identity – such as when immigrants are accorded such status – is criticised by some proponents of open borders as exclusionary.

Hostility towards borders adopts a peculiarly outraged tone when confronted with arguments that uphold the privileged political status of the citizen. The authority of citizenship, which has played a foundational role in the emergence of representative democracy, is now widely contested, and the distinction between citizen and non-citizen is frequently condemned as unjust and exclusionary. Implicitly, and in some cases explicitly, these arguments are directed at the normative foundation of a territorially based system of democracy.

Those who question the unique status of citizenship rely on two separate but interconnected arguments. The first is that, like borders, citizenship has lost much of its relevance in a complex postnational world. The second is that it is morally wrong to treat citizens differently to those who do not possess this status.

Has national citizenship become irrelevant? This claim is based on the proposition that the forces of globalisation have rendered boundaries porous and undermined the power of national institutions. Consequently, suggests one version of this argument, 'the future of citizenship must therefore be extracted from its location in the nation state'.[47] Another version proclaims that because of the supposed irrelevance of national borders and attachments, 'citizenship is becoming increasingly denationalized', and old forms of citizenships have been displaced by new ones, such as 'global citizenship', 'transnational citizenship' or 'postnational citizenship'.[48] The invention of the new metaphors of global citizenship are justified on the ground that citizenship is 'no longer unequivocally anchored in national political collectivities'.[49]

Another version of the argument for unbounding citizenship from its territorial foundation is the assertion that people's attachment to citizenship has, in any case, been weakened by new and more significant modes of self-identity. According to one proponent of this view, citizenship only 'represents one of the individual's several identities' and does not automatically trump others.[50] Others develop this line of argument by suggesting that with the pluralisation of identity, citizenship acquires a modest role in people's lives:

> Many analysts, including analysts of postnational citizenship, have compellingly argued that people locate their fundamental identities in, and solidarities with, a variety of communities that are neither defined nor circumscribed by nation-state boundaries. Affiliations based on ethnicity, class, gender, religion, nationality, and political commitment – whether within or across state borders – are often, and increasingly, experienced as primary.[51]

The 'pluralisation of identity' argument aims to empty citizenship of its authoritative content by providing this as evidence that national citizenship no longer has relevance for people's lives. It prepares the way for eroding the distinction between citizen and others.

Although arguments about the corrosive impact of globalisation and the pluralisation identity purport to rely on empirical evidence, they should be seen as what the legal scholar Linda Bosniak describes as *aspirational claims*: that is, a 'desire rather than fact'.[52] The inventors of postnational or transnational citizenship are not simply dealing with the facts of a rapidly changing world but offering an interpretation that validates their aspiration for the opening up of a territorially bounded reality. Take the following observation made by the International Relations professor Andrew Linklater, that 'the weakening of the old bonds linking citizens to the state creates unprecedented opportunities for new forms of political community attuned to the principles of cosmopolitan democracy and transnational citizenship'.[53] This statement conveys a sense of triumphalism about the 'unprecedented opportunities' available, for the ascendancy of 'transnational citizenship'. It refers to 'the weakening of the old bonds' as not just simply a statement of fact, but as a desirable and positive development that will assist the project of transnationalism.

The meaning of citizenship is fundamentally altered when it becomes deterritorialised. Though they contain a rhetorical connection to citizenship, the recently invented metaphors of global, cosmopolitan, or transnational citizenship possess only a shallow similarity with one that is nationally bounded. As one study points out: 'if the distinction between citizen and alien erodes, and the boundary defining the national community consequently is blurred, the civil connection between state and society becomes frayed'.[54] Without that civil connection, citizenship becomes depoliticised and transformed into a merely administrative category.

Metaphors that attempt to reinvent citizenship on a non-national basis serve to not only erode an important symbolic boundary but also confuse the fundamental distinction between citizen and non-citizen. The French sociologist and philosopher Jean Baudrillard refers to the promiscuous construction of metaphors as integral to the trend of destabilising 'differential fields and distinct objects'. What he characterises as the 'contamination' of concepts leads to a situation where distinctions and conceptual differences are made to disappear by a 'trans' informed metaphor. He noted that with this loss of specificity 'economics becomes transeconomics, aesthetics becomes transaesthetics, sex becomes transsexuality'.[55] Transparency, too, has become an influential value that validates the destabilisation of previously taken-for-granted boundaries between what can and what cannot be seen. Chapter 5 examines the general trend towards the deployment of contamination concepts, and in particular how the mutation of the term 'political' into a diffuse metaphor – as in 'the personal is political' – erodes the boundary between the public and the private spheres.

Despite their aspirations, arguments that rely on conjunctural factors such as the impact of globalisation or economic liberalisation do not fundamentally challenge the principle on which national citizenship rests. However, a second line of argument directly calls into question the moral standing of citizenship, proclaiming that the distinction between citizens and others is morally wrong. This claim asserts that citizenship is based on an accident of birth, and that on that account people should not possess privileges and resources that are denied to others. Implicitly, this line of attack does not merely contest the formal status of the citizen but also of any form of community membership that accords it privileges that are not available to those outside of the community. The rights enjoyed by people living in a village or a specific urban community are tacitly decried as exclusionary and unjust.

The political scientist Joseph Carens argues that a political community that treats people differentially on the grounds of birth is morally arbitrary and wrong.[56] According to this worldview, discriminating between citizen and noncitizen is akin to discrimination on the grounds of race or sex; therefore, people living in a particular nation state should have no special rights to the territory they inhabit. Citizens and foreigners alike should enjoy the same privileges, and the people who were born in a nation should possess the same rights as a recently arrived migrant. Cosmopolitan and global justice arguments against 'state-based restrictions on immigration and rights of citizenship' denounce these as 'inherently illegitimate', thereby attacking the 'legitimacy of national border controls or restrictions on grants of citizenship'.[57] Proponents of this view aim to devalue the boundary between citizen and non-citizen, denationalise the people inhabiting a common geographical space, and deterritorialise citizenship from any special rights and duties.

The delegitimation of the moral status of citizenship is forcefully advocated by the philosopher Seyla Benhabib. She offers a cosmopolitan critique of national citizenship, proposing one that views 'each individual as equally entitled to moral respect and concern'. Benhabib argues that 'legally, cosmopolitanism considers each individual as a legal person entitled to the protection of basic human rights in virtue of their moral personality and not on account of their citizenship or other membership status'.[58] From this standpoint, what matters are individuals who apparently do not belong to any particular pre-political community, and who do not possess any specific ties of solidarity that distinguishes them from others. Their rights are underwritten by a transnational humanitarian ethos, which apparently trumps the status possessed by a citizen of a nation.

Benhabib's insistence that what matters are 'individuals and not people' echoes a recurring theme deployed by those who advocate the opening up of closed societies. Popper believed that the defining feature of an open society was the prominent role assumed by the individual, the pursuit of individual interest, and individualism. In a closed society, by contrast, there are no individuals – only the tribe and the people. Popper's open society is one where pre-political bonds and influences have lost much of their meaning. Detached from organic links to a community, individuals become 'freed' of any of the cultural, religious or communal attachments that previously gave meaning to existence. Popper explained that 'as a consequence of its loss of organic character, an open society may become, by degrees, what I should like to term an "abstract society"'. He explained that life in an abstract society may lead to the loss of the 'character of a concrete or real group of men, or of a system of such real groups'.[59] In other words, in an abstract society, individuals lose their distinct community and cultural qualities. Elaborating on the de-culturalization of individual life, Popper suggested that:

> We could conceive of a society in which men practically never meet face to face – in which all business is conducted by individuals in isolation who communicate by typed letters or by telegrams, and who go about in closed motor-cars. (Artificial insemination would allow even propagation without a personal element.) Such a fictitious society might be called a "completely abstract or depersonalized society". Now the interesting point is that our modern society resembles in many of its aspects such a completely abstract society.[60]

Popper had no inhibitions about painting a picture of a society where individuals existed in isolation from one another, devoid of organic bonds and obligations. Indeed, he regarded this as merely an extension of the modern society of his time. Although there were downsides – 'There are many people living in a modern society who have no, or extremely few, intimate personal contacts, who live in anonymity and isolation, and consequently in unhappiness' – Popper felt that, on balance, the gains outweighed the losses because 'personal relationships of a new kind can arise where they can be freely entered into, instead of being determined by the accidents of birth; and with this, a new individualism arise'.[61] When the project of abstracting people from their particular circumstances is accomplished, they turn into cosmopolitan citizens. As Delsol wrote in connection with the project of promoting world citizenship: 'it is always a question of dis-incarnating humanity, of detaching man from his territorial and temporal roots, of making him abstract, of saturating him with indetermination'.[62]

Throughout the modern era, philosophers and commentators have warned of the alienating and depersonalising turn of capitalist society. Max Weber used the term 'rationalisation' to capture the trends that reinforce the abstract character of human relations. However, unlike Popper, who celebrated the emergence of an impersonal social order, Weber and other social commentators were worried about its dehumanising impact.[63] Perversely, despite its celebration of the individual, the practice of abstracting people from their particularity leads to the loss of an individual's singularity. The advocacy of openness often coexists with a sense of intolerance towards the singularity of the individual.

Most opponents of borders and national citizenship do not go as far as Popper in their celebration of the abstract individual, recognising that the price that humanity pays for the depersonalisation and fragmentation of social life is often intolerably high. However, they match Popper's aspiration to subordinate the rights of the people to that of the abstract individual, and their ideal is a global citizen whose outlook is not burdened by 'the accidents of birth' and community ties.

In recent decades, the idealisation of an abstract humanity is most systematically expressed through the concept of 'human rights'. The narrative of human rights presents itself as a doctrine that places the interests of the whole of humanity above those of specific nations and communities. By projecting human rights as fundamental, those enacted by national institutions possess a secondary character. From a transnational cosmopolitan perspective, the rights of citizenship ought not possess any advantages over those rights to which all humans are entitled. Advocates of the regime of human rights explicitly argue that that their laws self-consciously efface the distinction between nations and between citizens and non-citizens. As Saskia Sassen argues:

> Human rights are not dependent on nationality, unlike political, social, and civil rights, which are predicated on the distinction between national and alien. Human rights override such distinctions and hence can be seen as potentially contesting state sovereignty and devaluing citizenship.[64]

Sassen contends that with the ascendancy of human rights institutions and laws and the growth of mass immigration, a 'shift of rights of individuals regardless of nationality has occurred'. She adds that 'in accumulating social, civic, and even some political rights in countries of residence, immigrants have diluted the meaning of citizenship and the specialness of the claims that citizens can make on the state'.[65] Mass immigration, and the rights that human rights conventions assign to migrants, are seen by cosmopolitan thinkers as a welcome instrument for diminishing the integrity of national sovereignty.

In reality, however, the cosmopolitan denationalisation of citizenship empties it of both meaning and content. The principle and exercise of citizenship is fundamental to the workings of a democratic society. Citizens possess important political rights and also have responsibilities and duties towards other members of their community. Though the possession of citizenship through birth may seem arbitrary, nevertheless it should be seen as an inheritance that a citizen shares with others. That common inheritance amongst members of a nation state provides the foundation for solidarity between members of a community.

Citizenship is essentially a civic institution, and its legacy is inherited by everyone who is born into it, including the children of families of former immigrants. Identification with the nation helps citizens – old and new – acquire a sense of intergenerational continuity, which provides a bond that offers a sense of permanence and confidence. Historically, democrats of all shades of opinion recognised the importance of intergenerational continuity for civic society to flourish. Indeed, without the bonds supplied by intergenerational and other forms of community ties, it is difficult to establish a stable democratic polity. As the political theorist Bernard Yack explains, 'contingencies of shared memory and identity' are the foundations on which 'individual rights and political freedoms are exercised'.[66] Solidarity between people and the flourishing of a regime of social justice requires that individuals understand the boundaries within which they engage with one another. If we are to 'talk sense about social justice we must know what the relevant social and geographical boundaries are', notes the political theorist Margaret Canovan,[67] cautioning critics of national identity that:

> nations are not just common worlds; they are inherited common worlds, sustained by the facts of birth and the mythology of blood . . . this natal element in political allegiance is crucially important, and is regularly forgotten by political theorists anxious to recommend a non-national version of political community.[68]

As Arendt explained, the inheritance of a common world binds people together in a manner that allows them to identify with one another and with their public institutions. This forging of a relationship facilitates citizens to solidarise with one another and take responsibility for the welfare and future of their society.

Criticism of national sovereignty and the status of citizenship is often made through appealing to the superiority of universal and humanitarian values. However, universalism becomes a caricature of itself when it is transformed into a metaphysical force that stands above the prevailing institutions through which human beings make sense of the world. Humanity does not live above or beyond the boundaries and institutions it created through great struggle and effort.

Whatever the motives behind the project of deterritorialising citizenship and weakening national sovereignty, it represents a grave threat to democracy and public life. Whatever one thinks of national borders, there can be no democratic public life outside their confines. It is only as citizens interacting with one another, within a clearly geographically bounded entity, that democratic decision-making can work. The *demos* has always existed in a bounded space. The nation state and its boundaries are not an obstacle to the development of the spirit of democracy – on the contrary, they are necessary for its realisation. Solidarity, trust, and the willingness to distribute social goods are accomplishments that are best achieved through a clearly bounded common world where people understand their duties and obligations to one another. As Sarah Strong explains:

> If we take seriously the demands of political equality at the core of democracy, we see democratic reasons for defining democracy's boundaries according to the territorial boundaries of states. One key implication of my argument is that the modern territorial state is a normatively desirable – and not simply the *de facto* – basis for defining democracy's boundaries. Because of the territorial state's role in securing the basic conditions of democracy, territorial boundaries should have priority in defining the boundaries of democracy.[69]

Identification with people born into a common world is the main way that solidarity can acquire a dynamic public character. People exercising citizenship rights have interests that are specific to their circumstances and which provide the foundation of their solidarity. If they were to dispossess themselves of those interests, they would unwittingly destroy the public space within which they are able to act as responsible citizens. Paradoxically, the best protection for refugees is provided by nation states, where citizens feel confident about their role and where, as a result, they are able to extend the solidarity they achieved to people beyond their borders.

Notes

1 One prominent exception is the therapeutic act of closure.
2 McMahon (1990) p. 29.
3 Caroline Contillo (2016) 'How mindfulness leads to being more open minded', *Idealist*, 9 August, https://idealistcareers.org/without-judgement-mindfulness-leads-open-minded/.
4 https://energy-n-elements.com/blog/nonjudgemental-openness.
5 Ngnoumen and Langer (2014) p. 32.
6 Rippe (2017) p. 61.
7 Bodhi, B. (1991) 'A note openness', *Buddhist Publication Society*, no. 17. www.bps.lk/olib/nl/nl017.pdf.

8 Bodhi (1991).
9 Bodhi (1991).
10 See Bloom (1987).
11 Bloom (1987) p. 38.
12 Bloom (1987) p. 39.
13 Cited in Götz, N. (2014) p. 11.
14 See Götz (2014) p. 12.
15 See the discussion in Baugh (2016) pp. 352–366.
16 Popper (2003) pp. 194–195.
17 Popper's views on democracy are discussed in Gerson (2019) pp. 208–228.
18 Popper (2012) p. 120.
19 Beck (2003) p. 33.
20 See José Manuel Durão Barroso (2007) President of the European Commission Europe: an open society in a globalised world. International Forum, "The economy and the open society", Milan, 8 May, http://europa.eu/rapid/press-release_SPEECH-07-293_en.htm.
21 Beck (2006) p. 3.
22 Beck (2006) p. 3.
23 Beck (2006) p. 3.
24 O'Dowd (2010) p. 1039.
25 Beck (2005) p. 50.
26 One important exception is Hobbsbawm (2004) pp. 338–339.
27 Habermas (2016) p. 48.
28 Beck (2002) p. 19.
29 See Prozorov (2008).
30 O'Dowd (2010) p. 1039.
31 See Ulrich Beck and Anthony Giddens (2005) 'Nationalism has now become the enemy of Europe's nations', *The Guardian* 4 October, https://www.theguardian.com/politics/2005/oct/04/eu.world.
32 Habermas (2016) pp. 47–48.
33 Jarvie (2003) p. 73.
34 Bergson (1956) p. 266.
35 Bergson (1956) p. 234.
36 Popper (2003) pp. 4, 185 & 186.
37 Steinworth (2006) p. 244.
38 According to Steinworth (2006) p. 245.
39 Cited in https://blogs.spectator.co.uk/2019/09/watch-guy-verhofstadt-on-the-worlds-empires/.
40 See Wachinger, M. (2018) 'EU solidarity between social cohesion and active commitment', *EUVisions*, 25 November, www.euvisions.eu/eu-solidarity-between-social-cohesion-and-active-commitment/.
41 See Wachinger, M. (2018) 'EU solidarity between social cohesion and active commitment', *EUVisions*, 25 November, www.euvisions.eu/eu-solidarity-between-social-cohesion-and-active-commitment/.
42 See Smith, B. (2018) 'Who's afraid of tribalism?', *Quilette*, 1 June.
43 See www.weforum.org/agenda/2016/02/why-populism-is-on-the-rise-aecfc0ba-3f2b-4c03-8369-2f8247b74172/.
44 See Zoya Sheftalovich (2019) 'Juncker lashes out at "stupid nationalist"', *Poliotico*, 23 May, https://www.politico.eu/article/juncker-lashes-out-at-stupid-nationalists/.
45 Delsol (2015) p. 78.
46 See Arendt (1959).
47 Turner (1993) p. 14.
48 Bosniak (1999) p. 449.
49 This is the view of the sociologist Yasemin Soysal, cited in Bosniak (1999) p. 454.
50 Parekh (2006).
51 Bosniak (1999) p. 505.

52 Bosniak (1999) p. 524.
53 Linklater (2007) p. 93.
54 See Jacobson (1997) p. 6.
55 Baudrillard (1993) pp. 7 & 8.
56 See Carens (1987).
57 Ober (2017) pp. 168–169.
58 Benhabib (2016) pp. 113–114.
59 Popper (2003) pp. 186 & 187.
60 Popper (2003) p. 187.
61 Popper (2003) p. 187.
62 Delsol (2015) p. 85.
63 See the discussion in Furedi (2013) pp. 318–322.
64 Sassen (1996) p. 92.
65 Sassen (1996) pp. 92, 95 & 96.
66 Yack (2012) p. 37.
67 Canovan (1996) p. 28.
68 Canovan (1999) p. 108.
69 Song (2012) p. 62.

4

THE CHALLENGE TO SOVEREIGNTY, DEMOCRACY AND CITIZENSHIP

At first sight, it appears that the debate about the rights and wrongs of mass migration and the legitimacy of national border controls is all about who is included and who is excluded in a given territory. Yet there is much more at stake than whether or not a nation state has the right to control its borders. The logic of limitlessness and of the unbounding of human life, discussed in previous chapters, are integral to a transnational cultural outlook that does not only call into question national borders but also fundamental political categories such as sovereignty (national, popular, and individual), citizenship, and democracy. Consequently, critics of national borders are also suspicious of democracy, especially in its majoritarian form. They regard sovereignty as an outdated myth if not always a coercive instrument of exclusion. They denigrate the status of citizenship as endowing individuals with an unfair advantage over those people who do not possess it. As we noted in the previous chapter, the ideology of openness negates the singularity of the individual and unbounds them from their cultural norms. Open border advocates decry the idea of a people as a self-serving mystification designed to artificially divide the human race.

Arguments supporting transnational cosmopolitan ideals invariably claim that territorial borders – in particular those dividing nations – are artificial, accidental, or arbitrary creations. Such borders are said to be in a constant state of flux and groups of academic commentators now use the term 'bordering' to signify what some describe as a 'processual turn'.[1] The term bordering serves a boundary-blurring concept that transforms fixed boundaries into a constantly evolving and fluid one. This chapter questions the project of delegitimating territorial borders. It argues that what is at stake in this debate is not simply the status of territorial borders but the value of citizenship and ultimately of the role of democracy.

Historically, cosmopolitanism represented a positive aspiration for the realisation of the universalist ideals of humanism. Cosmopolitanism recognised that people are not simply defined by their particularity as members of a distinct cultural community, they also share a common humanity. It believed that through going beyond the immediacy of our particularity we are all the more able to understand what it is that makes us human and also grasp the moral duties we have towards members of our species. Regrettably, in recent times cosmopolitanism has been transformed from a universal moral outlook into a dogmatic anti-community ideology. The contemporary radically revised version of this outlook claims that cosmopolitanism means not just going beyond the nation but also rejecting the institutions and borders that support it. As we discuss in this chapter, the distinctive feature of today's version of cosmopolitanism or transnationalism is its hostility to national sovereignty and to the bounding of citizens to their national institutions. Contemporary cosmopolitanism has lost touch with both its religious origins and its debt to the Western Enlightenment. Unlike the Kantian account of cosmopolitanism, it has become a negative ideology that does not quite believe in its aim of establishing a world government. What it fervently supposes is that the nation is a curse, its citizens cannot be trusted, and that democracy is a mixed blessing. It loathes the boundedness of communal and political life.

The project of emptying territorial borders of moral significance

Critics of national borders constantly draw attention to their historically contingent character. They frequently refer to national borders as an *invention* in order to underline their claim that there is nothing natural or normal about the drawing of territorial lines.

In one sense, the claim that borders and boundaries are human inventions is absolutely right. For indeed, just about anything that is important to the social, political, or cultural life of a community can be said to be a human invention. This point was already clear to ancient Greeks, who drew a clear distinction between natural laws and forces – *physis* – and humanly constructed laws and customs – *nomos*. They understood that laws and customs were culturally specific, transient, and subject to human modification.[2] Over 2500 years ago, they possessed a sense of history and understood that the accomplishments of human convention were subject to variation and change.

Unlike the boundary-blurring missionaries of the current era, the Greeks understood that just because an institution was an invention, it did not mean that its establishment and existence was random or that it lacked moral significance. Because morality itself is the accomplishment of human beings struggling to give meaning to their lives and provide their community with clarity about who they are and how to lead a good life, it is, to use the idiom of our time, an 'invention'. However, morality like most invented human conventions – including the borders and boundaries that guide our lives – is not a random or arbitrary accomplishment. Morality and the signposts through which its ideals are communicated is organically linked to what occurred in previous times. It is the outcome of the history of a community. Similarly, so-called inventions, such as nation states and their borders, did not emerge through an accident. They have a past, and their survival depends – among other factors – on the meaning they possess for people. Institutions and borders that are literarily a result of an ahistorical act of invention are likely to be contested soon and may not endure for long.

Arguably it is the feeble sensibility of historical consciousness in our time that fosters a climate that regards the foundational political categories of Western societies as transient and arbitrary inventions. This tendency dominates academic literature on territorial borders. Commentators on this subject have adopted the patronising habit of informing their readers that borders dividing territories and especially nation states did not always exist in the past. The absence of territorial borders in say, antiquity, is used as an argument to highlight the artificial and presumably transient role of boundaries today. Writing in this vein, Professor Christopher Bertram observed:

> Much popular and political thinking about immigration assumes that an international order based on dividing the world into nation states, in which places belong to peoples and each individual has their naturally allotted locations, is the normal order of things.[3]

The aim of Bertram's observation is to remind his readers that the division of the world into nation states is not 'normal'. He claims that 'nation states are recent historical creations' and the belief that they are normal apparently 'distorts our thinking about human migration and mobility'.[4]

Anyone reading Bertram would imagine that borders were invented yesterday. He claims that the 'invention of a world order based around them is within living memory'. He must possess a very long memory, as most scholars take the view that 'borders (defined as state limits) were "invented" in 1648, with the signing of the Treaties of Westphalia'.[5] Though borders are an invention, they are far from recent. They have been integral to the development of the modern world and the fact that throughout the centuries they constituted such important markers for the conduct of community life suggests that they have had a very real meaning for people.

As it happens, the claim that a particular phenomenon is a recent 'invention' does not constitute a serious argument against its legitimacy. Many of the most important customs and institutions that shape life in the contemporary world are recent inventions. The ideal of tolerance or of human and sexual equality or even the recognition of the status of childhood are relatively recent inventions. Very few critics of invented borders are likely to argue that because sexual equality was not practised in ancient times it is not normal or morally meaningful. The refusal to depict the outcome of a historical invention as 'normal' appears to apply only to phenomenon that are the target of opposition.

Another argument used to deny the moral status of borders and boundaries is to characterise them as accidental or arbitrary. Professor Martha Nussbaum's argument for a cosmopolitan as opposed to a national focus for education highlights the supposedly accidental origins of borders. She observed: 'An education that takes national boundaries as morally salient too often reinforces this kind of irrationality by lending what is an accident of history a false moral weight and glory'.[6] For Nussbaum, not only is the act of taking national borders seriously irrational, it also smacks of 'false moral weight and glory'. The emphasis that cosmopolitan commentators attach to the accidental origins of borders is complemented by a view of humans that ascribes to their community affiliations an insignificant and random quality. Indifferent to the particularity of an individual and his cultural connections, cosmopolitan campaigners dismiss these attributes as of little import. 'The accident of where one is born is just that, an accident; any human being might have been born in any nation' declared Nussbaum.[7]

As it happens, a human being has by definition already been born and into a particular community and not just any nation. Yes, human beings are not responsible for the circumstances of their birth. But once they are born, they become biologically and culturally part of their family and also the citizens of their community and nation. It is through the bonds that attach them to these institutions that people develop their moral sensibility and their individuality. As the historian Gertrude Himmelfarb explained, 'the givens of life: parents, ancestors, family, race, religion, heritage, culture, tradition, community – and nationality' are not the '"accidental" attributes of the individual'.[8] Individuals can leave their homes and move to another part of the globe and adopt a new identity but what they cannot do is to be born again 'in any nation'.

The cosmopolitan emphasis on the arbitrary character of someone's birth seeks to render an individual indeterminate and abstract. It seeks to eradicate the singularity of individuals by abstracting them from place and time. Through reducing people to their abstract and biological qualities the humanising moment of what Arendt characterised as natality is overlooked. As Delsol reminds us it is important to understand that 'unlike animals, we are born twice'. She added, 'The unformed human who appears at biological birth must still be humanized. This only occurs through the mediation of a culture, one that is inscribed in space and time'.[9] Through learning a particular language and becoming acquainted with a community's moral norms, human being become humanised. But not as humans in the abstract but as individuals who are immersed in the particular space that they inhabit.

What Nussbaum really means when she characterises national boundaries as 'morally arbitrary' is that they have no intrinsic value. This belittling of a national border makes perfect sense from a transnational worldview that regards the nation state as an obstacle to human progress. Once borders and a sense of nation become morally arbitrary then so does the distinction between people who are its citizens and those who are not. Hence Nussbaum's preference for what she calls 'world citizenship' rather than national citizenship as 'the focus for civic education'.[10]

As is the case with national borders, transnational commentators regard citizenship as also morally arbitrary. It too is often portrayed as the outcome of a historical accident. Joseph Carens argues for open borders and rejects the line that divides citizens from non-citizens. He contends that 'birthplace and parentage are natural contingencies that are "arbitrary" from a moral point of view'.[11] Since citizens of a nation did not choose their place of birth, there is no moral basis for enjoying the privileges associated with their status. For Carens, the place where one is born is an entirely random matter that has no intrinsic moral significance. He suggests that a place of birth and the ties that bind people to a given territory should not provide them with rights that are not possessed by any of the inhabitants of the world.

According to the outlook of transnationalism, just as borders have no moral significance so the people living within them have no legitimate distinct moral claims towards one another that do not apply to all humans. Beck takes the view that the duty and responsibility that members of a national community have towards one and other makes little sense. 'Why do we have to recognize a special moral responsibility towards other people just because, by accident, they have the same nationality?', he asks.[12] He also poses the rhetorical question of 'why should they be free of any moral sensibility towards other people for the sole reason that they happened to be born on the other side of the national fence?' In other words, the ties that bind citizens together ought not impose any special duties that do not also apply to people living 'on the other side of the national fence'.

In one sense, borders can be construed as simply a 'national fence'. It is after all used as an administrative convenience that marks out the limits of a particular territory. In its administrative capacity or in its role of managing the movement of people, borders need not possess any moral significance. But national borders are more than an administrative convenience. They also serve as symbolic boundaries that delineate communities and help people understand 'who we are' and 'who we are not'. Moreover, it is within demarcated territorial spaces that people forge the moral attitudes and relations that govern their lives. Meaningful spaces exist within demarcated symbolic boundaries. And, it is within demarcated spaces that individuals and groups cultivate their moral sensibility. As Ochoa Espejo noted, borders are morally relevant because 'there are genuine moral differences between people living on either side of a territorial border, and their territorial presence justifies differences in their rights and their obligations'.[13] How these moral differences between people are seen and what significance is attached to them in the way that rights and obligations are linked to them is contingent on the attitudes and policies adopted by regimes of border management. But even the most administratively neutral of border management cannot nullify the pre-existing moral sensibility of people.

The sense of belonging to a particular people and of being bounded to a common space constitutes an important source of solidarity and possesses a moral significance for members of a national community. The consciousness of solidarity and the quality of common attachments acquire greater moral depth when as Miller noted, 'the political community conceives of itself as extended in time, indeed often as reaching back into antiquity'.[14] Duties and responsibilities owed to one another based on such connections are seen as both an inheritance from the past and a legacy to be passed on to future generations.

From a transnational perspective, it is essential to deny the moral significance of borders in order to promote its wider objective of delegitimating the status of the nation and the sovereignty of its people. The unbounding of foundational political categories such as sovereignty, nation, citizenship, and democracy depends on emptying borders of moral content. Yet, in a roundabout way, the claim that borders are not 'morally salient' is implicitly and sometimes explicitly contradicted in the narrative of many transnational theorists. Far from morally neutral, in this narrative, borders are portrayed as immoral and violent. If they genuinely believed that borders are not morally salient than it is unlikely that they would devote so much energy to condemning them! Typically, the project of delegitimating borders ignores their meaning for the people who inhabit within the territory they demarcate and one-sidedly adopts the standpoint of those prevented from crossing into it.

The moral condemnation of national borders alleges that the demarcation of territorial space unjustly excludes the 'other'. The distinction between citizen and non-citizen is frequently portrayed as unfair and immoral. 'Categories of citizen and noncitizen render invisible the fact that national wealth comes from those who are seen as outside the national patrimony', argues one opponent of what she calls the 'categories of difference'.[15]

Borders are also questioned on the ground that they constitute a space of violence. Michel Agier, in his influential book, *Borderlands, Towards an Anthropology of the Cosmopolitan Condition*, warns of a trend towards the 'hardening and violence of borders'.[16] Others go a step further and portray the violence of borders as not simply a trend but a fundamental dimension of the territorialisation of space. The post-Marxist French philosopher Étienne Balibar asserts that the process of territorialisation which categorises individuals into different groups and citizens is possible only if others are 'violently or peacefully removed, coercively or voluntarily destroyed'.[17] Bertram echoes Balibar when he describes state borders as 'places of violence and coercion'.[18] This narrative conflates the existence of borders with the violence that has recently flared up when migrants have attempted to cross it. It then makes a conceptual leap from this eruption of violence to characterising borders as defined by it.

The most uncompromising and ambitious attempt to delegitimate borders and the political categories associated with national sovereignty and citizenship is to be found in the works of the Italian philosopher Giorgio Agamben. According to Agamben, the exclusionary imperative unleashed by borders initiates a process whereby migrants – who he characterises as refugees – exist outside of the normal domain of politics. They become objects of humanitarianism and become a 'mass phenomenon' instead of 'individual cases'. Agamben depicts the camps where migrants exist as an institution that by its very existence exposes the immorality of borders and of national sovereignty. To dramatise this point, he refers to the state of exception that empowered the German Nazi regime to create camps where 'everything is possible' as the paradigmatic model of all camps. Hinting at the similarity between the German concentration camps and the migrant detention camps of today, Agamben noted that 'whoever entered the camp moved into a zone of indistinction between the outside and inside, exception and rule, licit and illicit in which the very concepts of subjective right and juridical protection no longer made sense'.[19]

Agamben asserts that the state of exception that prevails in borderland camps calls into question the traditional categories of political life. Referring to the Nuremberg laws on citizenship, he reminds his reader that 'it is significant that the camps appear together with new laws on citizenship and the denationalisation of citizens'.[20] There is more than a hint of a connection between the category of a camp, the abolishment of politics and ultimately of its inhabitants. 'There is no return from camps to classical politics' warns Agamben.[21] In his writing, the camp serves as a standalone metaphor that connects borders and the regulation of the movement of migrants with the death camps of the Holocaust. In this way the Nazi concentration camps lose their unique and historically specific quality and become an early version of a 21st century migrant detention centre. Accordingly, the category of citizenship becomes racialised and its practice constitutes a potential threat to the lives that it excluded.

Agamben's arguments are communicated in an opaque language that is unlikely to resonate with a popular readership. Yet his moral condemnation of the 'violence' of sovereignty and citizenship is spontaneously echoed by critics of borders and border controls. During the summer of 2019, protestors claimed that American detention centres holding Mexican migrants were concentration camps. Congresswoman Alexandria Ocasio Cortez wrote that 'the U.S. is running concentration camps on our southern border, and that is exactly what they are'.[22] Although this comment provoked an outraged response from many Americans, others felt entirely comfortable about harnessing the moral power of human revulsion against the Holocaust to support their argument in the dispute about border controls.

The very attempt to associate borders and the control of migrants with the haunting memory of the Nazi concentration camp indicates that territorial divisions are far from morally insignificant. That the Holocaust, which serves as the contemporary symbol of evil, has been weaponised in the crusade against borders indicates that the controversies over boundaries are fundamentally rooted in the realm of morality.

Eliminating fixed points and destabilising political categories

The academic literature on borders has become increasingly drawn towards questioning the fixity and stability of borders. Commentators assert that globalisation has both diminished and rendered borders more fragile and uncertain. They often pluralise the meaning of a border and insist that since they are proliferating within a national territory, they render conventional borders less significant. Some use the term *fluid*, others the term *decentred* while still others write about the *uncertain* condition of borders. The lack of fixity of borders is highlighted through the claim that bordering is a process of becoming.

The very shift from borders to bordering underlines attempts to call into question the reality of fixed or territorial borders by framing boundaries as indeterminate and fluid processes.[23] The association of borders with spatial fixity is all but lost in the writings of cosmopolitan commentators. 'The border is a process rather than a fixed line; it is constituted in new and changing relations between cores and peripheries, and is the site of political contestations where power and culture interact' observed the sociologist Gerard Delanty.[24] The fixed points that serve as symbolic and physical signposts all but disappear when the blurring of the lines that divide territories is the premise for the concept of borders as a process.

Agier wrote that globalisation 'multiplies and expands' borders, 'while rendering them more fragile and uncertain'.[25] He sees borderlands as 'in the process of making' for it is in his words 'continuously both remade and challenged'.[26] He stresses the uncertainty that surrounds 'any border' and adopts an approach that seeks to 'decentre' this phenomenon. His approach to the study of borders is far from neutral. He observed that 'the instability of borders, their shifting (between local, national and global contexts) or constant renegotiation is an immediate cause for rejoicing'.[27] It appears that the reason why Agier rejoices at the prospect of borders losing their stability is because he prefers the attributes of fluidity to the fixity of territories.

Agier describes the 'ordinary cosmopolitan condition' as one of a 'global and hybrid world'. Hybridity with its promise of blurring lines between cultures and peoples promotes a vision of the world that negates the fixity of concepts through which societies make sense of the world. His model of a hybrid world is one that 'includes uncertain places, uncertain times, uncertain identities that are ambiguous, incomplete or optional, indeterminate or in-between situations, uncertain relationships'.[28] Agier does not so much oppose borders. His criticism is directed at those who refuse to acknowledge the realities of an uncertain world and take fixed lines too seriously. It appears that everything is transient and fluid except for the state of uncertainty. The absolutisation of uncertainty by cosmopolitan commentators indicates it serves as a rhetorical weapon wielded against meaningful boundaries.

Judging by the idioms of transience, uncertainty, and fragility used to describe the state of borders, it is difficult to imagine that they can endure for long. It is as if national borders are an ugly fantasy that can be easily wished away. Beck prefers the metaphor of fluidity to refer to borders. He wrote of a 'new metaphor of the fluid that flows: neither boundaries nor relations mark the difference between one place and another'. In this fluid state, 'sometimes boundaries come and go, while relations transform themselves without fracture'.[29] Beck's ideal is a 'boundaryless organization', one that is 'fluid and adaptive'.[30] He also contends that the dualism implied by a fixed border is rendered superfluous through his 'pluralization of borders'. He explains that this works for 'such fundamental dualisms as the border between nature and society, subject and object, life and death, We and the Others, war and peace'.[31]

The destabilisation of fundamental dualisms is integral to a cosmopolitan project that regards the political ideals and institutions of the nation state as obstacles to be overcome. This point is put succinctly by Chris Rumford when he stated that 'opportunities are cosmopolitan when they cannot be reduced to a binary, an either/or, an us/them dichotomy'. Rumford added that cultural encounters 'blur the distinction between us and them'.[32] The avoidance of dichotomous intellectual categories and the blurring of distinctions are key features of the transnational outlook towards borders and symbolic boundaries. This outlook permeates the so-called spatial turn of cosmopolitan social science.

The spatial turn of social science accomplishes the blurring of the border line by deterritorialising physical space and reducing it to its common denominator of de-cultured territory. This approach elevates the role of global networks and organisations and treats them as of a greater moral weight than national territories. Rumford wrote that:

> The new spatiality of politics has also seen a shift from state-centric approaches to a concern with other, non-territorial spaces: public spheres, cosmopolitan communities, global civil societies, non-proximate or virtual communities, and transnational or global networks, none of which can be bordered in conventional ways. The new spatiality of politics has also become associated with a 'world in motion' ushered in by globalization and consisting of flows, fluids, networks and a whole plethora of mobilities.[33]

Typically, advocates of the spatial focus on cosmopolitan communities inflate the significance of transnational organisations in order to substantiate the case for the blurring of the fixity of national boundaries. What appears to matter for them is to elevate the value of space beyond the national territory.

The spatial turn allows for the disappearance of the distinction between the domestic and the international. Paradoxically just as the borders dividing nations lose their meaning, they reappear in a pluralised form throughout society. Rumford stated that 'whereas borders were once singular and only existed at the boundary of polities, they are now multiple and are dispersed throughout societies'. He also claimed that with the rise of international organisations and other global networks 'political space can no longer be equated with that of the nation-state'.[34] The diminution of the significance of national territory coexists with a call for the re-conceptualisation of political categories as transnational ones. The radical Italian post-Marxists Michael Hardt and Antonio Negri have opted for a global form of sovereignty which has no central locus of territorial power and which is not bounded by fixed borders. This fantasy of a global, borderless Empire is one that is shared by the more radical section of cosmopolitan activists.[35]

The contemporary example that most approximates Hardt and Negri's idealisation of borderless movements is what the French political scientist Oliver Roy has characterised as the 'deterritorialisation of Islam'.[36] In this instance, radical uprooted Islamists struggle for the establishment of an unbounded *Unmah* that stands above and beyond any territorially embedded community. It is not a common territory but common conviction that sets the boundary of the *Unmah*. One of the main appeals of the Islamic State was its destruction of borders.[37] Should this project succeed, it would confirm Arendt's warning that the establishment of an unbounded world government would 'not be the climax of world politics, but quite literally its end'.

Hardt and Negri also wish to detach the concept of a people from its association with the nation state. Following the project of pluralising borders, they wish to eliminate the bond between people and their cultural and political affiliations. They advocate the use of the term *multitude* on the grounds that it transcends the national territory-based loyalties of different groups of people. They claim that 'the multitude is composed of innumerable internal differences that can never be reduced to a unity or a single identity – different cultures, races, ethnicities, genders, sexual orientations; different forms of labour; different ways of living; different views of the world; and different desires'.[38] Their rejection of a unitary conception of people reflects the suspicion that many cosmopolitan commentators have adopted toward the *demos*. As far as they are concerned, the *demos* is far too wedded to the ways of its cultural community and therefore is far too likely to take pre-existing territorial distinctions seriously.

Detaching the *demos* from the nation state

One reason why advocates of cosmopolitanism prefer a global multitude to a nationally rooted *demos* is because it can be conceived as a borderless mass which is supposedly indifferent to forms of solidarity that are both bounded and underwritten by a common culture. Their preference is for a heterogeneous mass rather than a people who have been socialised into a common but particular culture. Hence the detachment of the people from the nation is one of the priorities of cosmopolitan politics.

The clearest formulation of a preference for detaching the people from the nation is to be found in arguments supporting transnational citizenship. Until recently, citizenship as an essential element of democracy within a nation state was a core moral concept of the modern political vocabulary. In recent times, the boundary between citizens and non-citizens has been contested by cosmopolitan critics striving to establish support for a world or a transnational citizenship. As is the case in the discussion on borders, transnational ideologues argue that there is no clear border between citizens and others. They regard the category of citizen as fluid. To substantiate the lack of fixity of the concept of the citizen they seek to pluralise it and suggest that there are multiple forms of citizens. They insist that the bounded nation is not a suitable site for the exercise of citizenship. And finally, as we discussed previously, cosmopolitan advocates dismiss citizenship as exclusionary and morally indefensible.

It appears that the application of the boundary blurring concept of fluidity is mandatory in relation to every dimension of the human condition. A study predictably titled, *Ambiguous citizenship in an age of global migration*, is sympathetic to what it calls 'the emergent field of critical citizenship studies' which 'focuses on the need to think about citizenship beyond presence and instead as process'.[39] Through the usage of an indeterminate and self-consciously ambiguous rhetoric, the concept of citizenship loses its distinct meaning. Instead it becomes a process, which the author of *Ambiguous citizenship* claims is 'linked to the idea of rupture and difference'.

Once a concept has been subjected to its rebranding as a process, it will re-emerge as an abstract entity that exists in the state of transient fragmentation. Not surprisingly, what we end up with is a proliferation of citizenships. From this standpoint, what we have is 'the production of different form of citizenship'; such as the irregular citizen, the illegal citizen, the undocumented citizen, or the alien citizen. The merit of this pluralisation of citizenship is that it avoids the 'ongoing differentiation of citizens from non-citizens'.[40] Supporters of the denationalisation of citizenship have also coined terms, such as 'global citizenship', 'transnational citizenship', and 'postnational citizenship'.[41]

It appears that the main virtue of producing multiple citizenship is to negate the one distinction that has mattered in the modern era, which is that between a citizen and a non-citizen.

Transnational supporters of ambiguity and fluidity are not entirely consistent in the methodology they adopt. They are happy to render symbolic boundaries and core concepts like citizenship fluid and fragmented. However, they apply a different standard to their own worldview. To take one example; Aoileann Ní Mhurchú, author of *Ambiguous citizenship,* writes that:

> By highlighting the precarious boundaries between 'citizen' and 'migrant' here, it should be recognised that 'citizenship' has never been, nor will ever be, a fully bounded and coherent category which opposes itself to 'non-citizenship'. Rather 'citizen' and 'migrant' are categories which constantly challenge and undermine each other.[42]

There is nothing ambiguous or uncertain about the vehemence with which Mhurchú, claims that citizenship has never been and can never be a 'fully bounded and coherent category'. The author of *Ambiguous citizenship* is unambiguously resolute in affirming this point. This contention is all the more startling because an unambiguous version of citizenship has for centuries possessed meaning for millions of people.

It is undoubtedly the case that mass migration calls into question the authority of borders. But whether or not there is a 'precarious' boundary between citizen and migrant is not the outcome of the global movement of people but of a political project that calls into question the concept of citizenship. It is difficult to avoid the conclusion that criticisms of a bounded concept of citizenship tend to be motivated by political objectives rather than the pursuit of disinterested scholarship. Commentators like Balibar, who aim to overcome the 'limitations of citizenship' that is 'coextensive with the institution of the nation state', are stating an ideological preference rather than offering a neutral analysis.[43]

As the legal scholar Linda Bosniak noted, arguments advocating the denationalisation of citizenship are motivated by a normative preference for the non- or transnational. Though communicated through the language of scholarship, they often constitute advocacy claims which masquerade as research. Bosniak noted that: notwithstanding the empirical style of most exponents of citizenship's denationalization, the 'postnational citizenship claim cannot be read merely in descriptive terms'. She remarked that, 'it must, instead, be regarded at least as much as a normative claim about citizenship's future shape and direction as a characterization of the current state of the world'.[44]

Undoubtedly, a statistically insignificant section of the Western professional and cultural elite believe that they have become citizens of the world and lead a non-national globalist existence. But the project of denationalising citizenship remains a utopian enterprise. Migrants, no less than long-standing members of stable communities, wish to become citizens of a nation state rather than members of a transnational institution. Advocacy and expressions of political aspirations towards the future is an entirely legitimate enterprise. However, the attempt to represent boundary-busting concepts as empirically rooted facts rather than as a medium for challenging boundaries serves to only confuse matters.

Cosmopolitan critics of citizenship are continually focused on deconstructing the legitimacy of national citizenship. They may be ambivalent and uncertain about many things, but they have no doubt about the need to detach the concept of citizen from the nation. The author of a paper titled 'Citizenship without Community' wants to 'reimagine' a community as "encounters" and "confrontations"' rather than 'that which is contained within a bounded space'. In other words, this is an approach that is devoted to imagining a world without 'bounded citizens'. The author explained that his is a paper which 'argues for an approach that is attentive to ideas of time and seeks to open up an idea of community that avoids the requirement of commonality'.[45] This quest for a community that is distinguished by the absence of commonality indicates its unstated motive is to eliminate the bonds – cultural and national – that give meaning to citizenship.

Not all cosmopolitan critics of bounded citizenship rely on a rhetoric of fluidity and ambiguity to support their cause. Many base their claim on the argument that people are already investing their hope in international institutions and that therefore their behaviour is not bounded by national borders. The sociologist Bryan Turner stated that 'nation-state is not necessarily the most suitable political framework for housing citizenship rights'. Pointing to the case of the European Union, he argued that 'citizens increasingly appeal to supranational entities . . . to satisfy or achieve their (national) citizenship rights'[46]

Since the 1990s, the arguments against the maintenance of the boundary between citizen and non-citizen have tended to rely on the claim that global migration calls into question both the fixity of national borders and the legitimacy of bounded forms of citizenship. Turner concluded that 'the world refugee problem and aboriginal rights questions cannot be easily approached within the framework of (nation-state) citizenship'.[47] Since the early 1990s, when Turner raised the refugee problem as a challenge to the concept of nationally bounded citizenship, there has been a growing tendency to instrumentalise the issue of global migration and use it to undermine the legitimacy of the concept of a citizen.

Global migration and the migrant have an important normative significance for cosmopolitan commentators. The migrant is at once the personification of boundarylessness and often cast in the role of an agent of positive change. Often migrants are represented as the embodiment of the cosmopolitan condition. For cosmopolitan commentators like Agier, the migrant appears as an instrument for the realisation of a cosmopolitan future. 'Who better than the "uprooted" to give us the concrete and empirical trace of this new cosmopolitan condition, and to reflect on the political perspective that it establishes on a common world scale?' he asks.[48] According to this scenario, the uprooted migrant prefigures the unbounded and denationalised masses of the future. If that is indeed the case, then it is understandable why the 'centrality of migration' is key to understanding the 'future of the world'.[49]

One reason for celebrating migration is because it is seen as a challenge to the sovereign subject. Migration weakens the link between citizen and nation and supposedly 'challenges the idea of the sovereign autonomous subject who can be included or excluded from political community as the only way in which being a citizen can be imagined or experienced'.[50] For those who are sceptical or condemn the ideal of the sovereign autonomous subject, mass migration constitutes a welcome antidote to it.

If migration has been turned into an instrument for the realisation of a future cosmopolitan condition, it should not be surprising to discover that the refugee has been cast into the role of the main protagonist in this heady drama. Agamben offers a most consistent version of the newly invented role of the refugee as saviour. He wrote that the refugee has displaced the citizen and that it was only a matter of time before the refugee 'becomes at once the symbolic and real face of a transnational politics to come'.[51] In Agamben's utopian theoretical framework, the refugee successfully dissolves the principal boundaries and distinctions of modern political theory. He claims that the refugee represents such a subversive force because 'by breaking up the identity between man and citizen, between nativity and nationality, the refugee throws into crisis the original fiction of sovereignty'.[52]

In Agamben's theoretical model, the refugee is both the gravedigger of the world of bounded politics and the harbinger of a better future. 'At least until the process of the dissolution of the nation-state and its sovereignty has come to an end, the refugee is the sole category in which it is possible today to perceive the forms and limits of political community to come'.[53] The refugee not only represents the negation of the present, he also helps bring about Agamben's future utopia.

In reality, people do not become refugees because they want to challenge the status of the citizen – indeed many aspire to becoming citizens of a nation. Nor are refugees in the business of challenging the symbolic boundaries that govern Western public life. But Agamben is less interested in real-life refugees than in abstracting their uprooted predicament, normalising it, in order to call into question the legitimacy of citizenship. In Agamben's ideal world, we would all think of ourselves as refugees and regard the state of our unboundedness as a blessing rather than a curse. The question that remains to be considered is what lies behind the cosmopolitan reaction against citizenship.

The problem of democratic pressure

Cosmopolitan animosity towards citizenship is also motivated by a disdain towards the practice of democracy in a national setting. That is why one advocate of cosmopolitan democracy asserted that 'we need to disengage the practice of democracy from its traditional state/society nexus'.[54] The main reason for the preference for cosmopolitan as opposed to national democracy is an absence of trust towards the political behaviour of a national electorate. The cosmopolitan account of democracy aims to insulate decision-making from the pressure of the electorate. Cosmopolitan thinkers regard ordinary people as unlikely to support their global vision. Consequently, their aim is to detach democracy from its national setting. Just as they prefer a form of citizenship without a territorial community, so too do they endorse a version of democracy without a *demos*.

Concern with the influence of democratic pressure is unambiguously stated by Bertram, who wrote that:

> Even within particular states we have seen that the desire of countries to control migration, often under democratic pressure, can have terrible consequences for the liberal, democratic and egalitarian character of those societies, because of the presence on the territory of people who do not fit neatly into the container model of nation states and their citizens.[55]

Bertram, like anyone else, is entitled to disagree with democratic pressure for the control of migration. This is a contentious issue of serious concern to different parties in the debate. He and other opponents of border control ought to have every opportunity to win support for their views. What is truly disturbing about Bertram's view is not his attitude towards borders but his disdain for the working of democracy. He more or less suggests that we should disregard the aspiration of the electorate. Bertram suggests that the issue of migration is too big for a democratic electorate to handle. He concludes that 'we cannot think about the rights and wrongs of migration simply from the perspective of what is in the interest of the electorates of particular states'.[56] So the question left unanswered is 'whose perspective should prevail on the rights and wrongs of migration?' and 'who gets to decide what are its rights and wrongs?' From a transnational perspective, it is clearly not the people of a nation state.

The cosmopolitan imagination regards the concept of a people with open hostility. They dislike a people because it is based on the foundation of pre-political commonality and they are territorially bounded. They are the very opposite to the abstract de-cultured individual favoured by transnationalists.

In previous times, the cosmopolitan utopia was inspired by a vision of realising the potential of the human spirit. In the 21st century, the principal aim of many transnationalists is to curb what they perceive as the danger of democratic pressure. Their vision of democracy is constrained by the fear of majoritarian outcomes. In particular, they support constraints on democratic decision-making because they don't trust the electorate to look after the interests of minorities. This approach is systematically advocated by Jürgen Habermas. Habermas contends that his aim is not to limit democracy but to place a constraint on imperfect majoritarian decisions.[57] For Habermas, democracy is valuable as long as majoritarian decisions do not conflict with the 'rights of minorities'.[58]

Habermas' negative orientation towards majoritarianism is inspired by his suspicion towards the people and the pre-political traditions that influence it. In particular, he wants to liberate the *demos* from its attachment to the nation and hence he argues for what he calls the 'transnationalization of popular sovereignty'.[59] He justifies this argument through claiming that nation state-based sovereignty has become a façade that was 'breached long ago'.[60] In this way, he can actually present his call to deterritorialise popular sovereignty as an expression of radical democracy. However, in practice the Habermasian concept of transnationalised sovereignty actually means the depoliticisation of the *demos*. The transnational institutions that Habermas envisages transform the people into a depoliticised audience, who are relieved of the burden of will-formation. These are transnational institutions that are judicial rather than political in nature and as Habermas noted 'world citizens need not be expected to engage in collective will-formation in the essentially political sense'.[61]

One of the principal strategies advocated for diminishing the influence of majoritarianism is to deterritorialise popular sovereignty. Habermas' version of transnational popular sovereignty aims to achieve precisely this objective. Disingenuously, Habermas claims that popular sovereignty can no longer flourish within a nation state: its future survival requires a transnational solution. He wrote:

> In view of a politically unregulated growth in the complexity of world society which is placing increasingly narrow systemic restrictions on the scope of action of nation states, the requirement to extend political decision

making capabilities beyond national borders follows from the normative meaning of democracy itself.[62]

From this standpoint, a borderless transnational form of popular sovereignty emanates from the 'normative meaning of democracy itself'.

Habermas has been an energetic advocate of an ideological project that aims to distance people from their national communities. One of the ways in which this project is pursued is through the advocacy of identity politics and rights of minorities, which are promoted at the expense of the right of nations to self-determination. He is an enthusiastic proponent of social and cultural identities that stand in opposition to or are decoupled from national sentiments and traditions. His preference is for identities that are 'post-traditional' and 'post-national'. At first sight, Habermas' affinity towards the 'politics of recognition' and its affirmation of diverse identities seems inconsistent with his commitment to a cosmopolitan outlook. However, like many of the current generation of cosmopolitan figures, his worldview has little in common with the classical Kantian ideal of a cosmopolitan world citizen. His is a negative theory of cosmopolitanism that is principally animated by a dislike for the consciousness of nationhood rather than a positive utopian ideal of world citizenship.

But how can the influence of traditional values be diminished? Habermas clearly understands that traditional ideals that touch on religion, nation, and family life cannot be simply abolished or transcended. Consequently, he opts for an approach that encourages a climate of scepticism towards the status and moral authority of the values of tradition. Through encouraging the questioning of people's values and identities, transnationalist theorists hope that this process weakens people's relationship to long-established traditions. Through this strategy, Habermas hopes to cultivate the 'rationalization of collective identities', which is another way of saying that identities will be distanced from their foundation in the traditions of a nation and continually recast on the basis of reason and rational debate. As one of Habermas' co-thinkers explained, such 'identities were most likely to emerge where national traditions had been put decisively into question and where citizens felt acutely ambivalent about affirming historical continuities'.[63]

It is through the denationalisation of individual identities that Habermas hopes to curb the influence of majoritarianism. Liberated from the burden of territory and nation, Habermas and his co-thinkers hope to insulate themselves from majoritarian pressures. His aspiration to curb the influence of a territorially based popular sovereignty corresponds to the growing tendency of the European cultural elites to perceive themselves as deterritorialised.

In reality, the cosmopolitan denationalisation of citizenship not only empties citizenship of any meaning but also deprives politics of real content. Citizenship and its exercise are fundamental to the workings of a democratic society. Citizens possess important political rights and also have responsibilities and duties towards other members of their community. Though the possession of citizenship through birth may seem arbitrary, nevertheless, it should be seen as an inheritance that a citizen shares with others. That common inheritance amongst members of a nation state provides the foundation for solidarity.

Citizenship is essentially a civic institution, and its legacy is inherited by everyone who is born into it, including the children of families of former immigrants. Identification with the nation helps citizens – old and new – acquire a sense of intergenerational continuity. That sense of intergenerational continuity provides a bond that offers a sense of continuity and confidence to a democratic society.

The exercise of democracy is inconceivable without boundaries. Democracy is a form of decision-making by politically equal subjects. Political equality is the precondition for solidarity between citizens and is conditional on the reproduction of such attachments. The forging and maintenance of such attachments occur within a delineated space and would weaken if there were no limits to its extension. As Song explained, bounding the *demos* within the boundaries of a territorial state is a prerequisite for solidarity to flourish. She noted that:

> The state is not simply an instrument of decision-making or a means of securing rights; it has also become the site of solidarity and trust, which motivates participation. Democratic participation and mobilization do not happen in a vacuum, but in relation to a rich network of institutions. Trust plays an important role here. . . . Trust is more likely among citizens who come together within a stable infrastructure of state institutions and who share a sense of solidarity, rooted in a shared political culture, than among individuals who are constantly banding and disbanding in episodic demoi. To the degree that individuals integrate their trust networks into political institutions, the greater the stake people have in the successful functioning of those institutions.[64]

Where trust is lacking, democracy is usually in trouble. Territory also provides a framework within which the people can establish a clear relation with their representatives and hold them to account. When citizens are territorially disconnected from their representatives, democratic accountability loses its force.

Migration recast as an antidote to majoritarian pressures

The one dimension of majoritarianism that is intensely disliked by its 21st century critics is its association with a homogeneous electorate. A homogeneous public, which lacks internal cultural divisions, is more likely to have a more powerful sense of community and place than one that is made up of different cultural groups. That is why cosmopolitan thinkers prefer a heterogeneous space to a homogeneous one. However, the language with which they transmit their dislike of a homogeneous one is one that constantly creates an association between homogeneity and racism and xenophobia. Following Agamben, one of his interpreters observed that 'the refugee's haunting, lawless presence exposes the exclusionary logics of existing political communities and deconstructs the homogeneous unity and cohesion of individual nations as mythologies of Western superiority'.[65] Agamben's migrant as saviour reappears in the current discussion in the role of an instrument against majoritarianism.

Since the 20th century, opponents of immigration argued against migrants by pointing to their supposed corrosive cultural impact on prevailing community life. Anti-immigrant groups have mobilised opposition to the free movement of people on the grounds that mass immigration represents a threat to the American or British or French way of life. Until recently, advocates of immigration tended to reject the very premise of the analysis of their opponents and insisted that their claims of cultural disruptions were exaggerated. In the face of anti-immigrant opposition, they insisted that immigration would not fundamentally alter the character of the host society. Moreover, they claimed that if handled well, the newly arrived migrants would swiftly adapt and embrace the nation's culture.

In recent decades, the terms of the debate have fundamentally altered. Both sides of the debate now acknowledge that the impact of immigration on society is likely to be disruptive and will not leave the prevailing way of life untouched. Indeed, some argue that migrants can help the society renew itself and change itself for the better. The real debate in the current era is whether or not this disruption and the social and cultural consequences of immigration are positive or negative. Opponents of immigration tend to perceive the downside of the mass movement of people on their society. Many supporters of immigration now accept the argument that mass migration will change the character of their society – but now insist that this transformation is on balance a welcome development. From this standpoint, immigration is perceived as positive and a welcome instrument of social engineering. As the French social commentator Pascal Bruckner observed, the migrant is portrayed as 'both the epitome of oppression and the source of our salvation'.[66]

In any discussion of the impact of immigration on the character of society, it is important to consider its implications for a self-determining political community. As Miller points out, 'when immigrants are admitted, their presence will over a period of time change the composition of the citizen body or, in other words the "self" in "self-determination"'. Consequently, it is entirely possible that this could 'significantly change the decisions that the *demos* takes, because immigrants will not simply replicate the indigenous population with respect to their beliefs, values, interests, cultural preferences, and so forth'.[67] For some, such a shift in the composition of a political community may be desirable, but for the original body of citizens, it can mean the diminishing of their capacity to control what happens to their community in the future.

Increasingly, arguments supporting mass migration are not so much focused on the virtues of free movement but on its positive effects on society. These positive effects are frequently communicated through the language of economics.

But increasingly – and this is a relatively new development – they are now valued precisely because of their transformative effects on national culture. This valuation of immigration as an instrument of social engineering underpinned the statement made by the president of the European Commission, Claude Juncker, when he declared that 'borders are the worst invention ever made by politicians'.[68] In this statement, Juncker coupled his condemnation of borders with a call for support for migrants. But he was not simply interested in demonstrating solidarity with migrants. His denunciation of borders was linked to his hostility towards the nation state and movements that supported it. Which is why, in his next breath, Juncker argued that 'we have to fight nationalism [and] block the avenue of populism'. That is another way of indicating his animosity towards majoritarian democracy.

Historically, liberal supporters of open borders were motivated by their valuation of the human aspiration for the freedom of movement and mobility. In the current era, the target of many of those who are hostile to borders is not so much the obstacle they represent to the movement of people but their protection of the nation state and national cultures. It is not the liberal valuation of freedom of movement but the rejection of the status of national sovereignty and of the authority of the nation state that inspired Juncker and other advocates of the transnational worldview.

The social and cultural arguments for the social engineering project promoted by the anti-border lobby are rarely made explicit, and in public debates they tend to be couched in the language of economic benefits. Instead, they state their arguments through the advocacy of diversity. For a significant section of the Western elite, diversity has become a value in its own right because of their estrangement from the values and historical institutions of their own society. From their perspective, diversity is celebrated not simply as an appreciation of cultural difference but because it is seen as inherently superior to the traditions of their own society.

In previous times, advocates of change promoted a political ideology like liberalism, communism, or socialism to bring about desired objectives. In the contemporary era – where social engineering displaced ideology – some opt for diversity as the motor of change. The former American Vice-President Joe Biden expressed this sentiment in a statement welcoming the former Brazilian President Dilma Rousseff to Washington. Biden stated that 'those of us of European stock' will be a minority by 2017 and concluded 'that's a good thing'.[69] But why should a change in the ethnic or cultural composition of a society be a 'good thing' or for that matter a 'bad thing'? Why should a shift in a demographic balance have an important normative content?

Biden answered this question at an earlier speech given in Morocco in December 2014. He explained that the impending minority status of Americans of European stock was a 'good thing' because it would make America into a stronger nation. 'The secret that people don't know is our diversity is the reason for our incredible strength', he stated.[70] Not democracy, not the constitution, not its liberal ethos, not its creativity and entrepreneurship – the secret of America's strength is its diversity!

Of course, a society open to the movement of people is likely to benefit from the mixing of cultures and ideas. But when diversity is transformed into a standalone medium for change, it can turn into a political weapon used to bypass the national will. For Juncker, getting rid of national borders serves the project of promoting a European federal state. Diversity is the antidote to nationalism.

The transformation of the liberal argument for open borders into support for social engineering should make all tolerant people weary of the rhetoric that surrounds migration and diversity. The use of migration as a weapon against national sovereignty has a wholly corrosive consequence of provoking cultural confusion and uncertainty. An enlightened argument for the freedom of movement must also uphold national sovereignty and recognise the authoritative status of the prevailing national culture. To disregard the special status of national institutions and the culture they represent serves as an invitation to a state of permanent confusion and disorientation.

Notes

1 Yuval-Davis, Wemyss, and Cassidy (2019) p. 18.
2 See discussion in Furedi (2013) pp. 38–40.
3 Bertram (2018) p. 9.
4 Bertram (2018) p. 9.
5 Szary (2015) p. 2.
6 Nussbaum (2002) p. 11.
7 Nussbaum (2002) p. 7.
8 Himmelfarb (2002) p. 77.
9 Delsol (2015) p. 84.
10 Nussbaum (2002) p. 11.
11 Carens (1987) p. 261.
12 Beck (2002) p. 20.
13 Ochoa Espejo (2018) p. 72.
14 Miller (2017) p. 27.
15 Glick Schiller (2012) p. 524.
16 Agier (2017) p. 39.
17 Balibar (2004) p. 4.
18 Bertram (2018) p. 34.
19 Agamben, G. (1998) *Homo Sacer: Sovereign Power and Bare Life*, Stanford University Press: Stanford, p. 170.
20 Agamben (1998) p. 175.
21 Agamben (1998) p. 188.
22 David Montero (2019) 'Some Holocaust survivors oppose "concentration camp" comments. But they're also upset by treatment of migrants', *Los Angeles Times*, 28 June, https://www.latimes.com/nation/la-na-concentration-camps-holocaust-immigrants-detention-20190628-story.html.
23 Rumford (2012) p. 247.
24 Delanty (2006) p. 186.
25 Agier (2017) p. 58.
26 Agier (2017) pp. 8 & 9.

27 Agier (2017) p. 44.
28 Agier (2017) p. 8.
29 Beck (2002) p. 25.
30 Beck (2002) p. 19.
31 Beck (2002) p. 19.
32 Rumford (2012) p. 246.
33 Rumford (2006) p. 160.
34 Rumford (2006) p. 160.
35 Hardt and Negri (2000) p. xii.
36 Roy (2004).
37 My colleague Dr Simon Cottee drew my attention to this example.
38 Hardt and Negri (2004) p. xiv.
39 Mhurchú (2014) p. 3.
40 Mhurchú (2014) p. 6.
41 Bosniak (1999) p. 447.
42 Mhurchú (2014) p. 8.
43 See discussion in Agier (2017) p. 73.
44 Bosniak (1999) pp. 452–453.
45 Stephens (2010) p. 31.
46 Turner (1993) p. 178.
47 Turner (1993) p. 178.
48 Agier (2017) p. 76.
49 Agier (2017) p. 76.
50 Mhurchú (2014) p. 19.
51 Cited in Delsol (2015) p. 18.
52 Agamben (1995) p. 117.
53 Agamben (1995) p. 116.
54 See Falk (2002) p. 59.
55 Bertram (2018) p. 121.
56 Bertram (2018) p. 121.
57 Habermas (1996) p. 285.
58 Habermas (1991) p. 261.
59 Habermas, J. (2012) *The Crisis of the European Union: A Response*, Polity Press: Cambridge, p. 11.
60 Habermas (2012) pp. viii–ix.
61 Habermas (2012) p. 65.
62 Habermas (2012) p. 15.
63 See Müller (2006).
64 Song (2012) p. 59.
65 Theodorakis (2014) p. 43.
66 Pascal Bruckner (2019) 'Europe's Virtues Will Be Its Undoing', *Quilette*, 14 September, https://quillette.com/2019/09/14/europes-virtues-will-be-its-undoing/.
67 Miller (2016) p. 62 & 63.
68 Cited in Savage, M. (2016) 'Borders are worst invention ever, declares Juncker', *The Times*, 23 August.
69 Cited in Washington Examiner, www.washingtonexaminer.com/biden-says-whites-a-minority-in-2017-census-says-2044/article/2567351.
70 Paul Beddard (2015) 'Biden says whites a minority in 2017, Census says 2044', *Washington Examiner*, 30 June, http://www.washingtonexaminer.com/biden-says-whites-a-minority-in-2017-census-says-2044/article/2567351.

5

BREACHING THE PUBLIC–PRIVATE BOUNDARY

One of the most significant achievements of the open border movement has been its success in undermining the legitimacy of the boundary separating the public from the private sphere. The erosion of the symbolic boundary between these two domains has had a profound bearing on how people conduct their informal and intimate relationships. It is in this domain that the advocacy of openness, with its indifference to conventional forms of restraints, has had the greatest impact on everyday life. The sensibility of boundarylessness, or what the French social commentator Régis Debray characterises as limitlessness (*l'illimitation*), has prevailed to the point that the internal integrity of the private sphere has become severely compromised.[1]

From the standpoint of the ideology of openness, the private sphere represents an alien, even hostile, territory. Transparency has acquired the status of an officially endorsed ideal that is intolerant of any boundary that protects people from the public gaze. It has become an influential value that validates the destabilisation of previously taken-for-granted boundaries between what can and what cannot be seen. By recasting openness in a technocratic form, transparency has become institutionalised. Whenever policymakers are at a loss for an answer, the demand for more transparency trips off the tongue – exhortations demanding more openness are rarely challenged in the public domain.

Even people's intimate and inner life has ceased to be a no-go area. Advocates of transparency often confuse privacy with secrecy. Yet as the legal scholar Jeffrey Rosen explains, 'secrecy is only a small dimension of privacy'. He tells the story of a colleague who walked in on her daughter's phone conversation and asked, 'are you talking about something secret', to which she replied, 'no – it's private!'[2]

At first sight, there does not appear to be an obvious connection between the physical borders that divide communities and national territories and the symbolic boundary that separates the public from the private sphere. However, perceptions of borders and boundaries are informed by a common cultural orientation. Consequently, the boundaries between public and private can be interpreted as the internal expression of the borders separating nations and communities. Such boundaries are a characteristic feature of the human condition. 'Distinctions between public and private have been and remain fundamental, not incidental or tangential, ordering principles in all known societies save, perhaps the most simple', writes the American political theorist Jean Bethke Elshtain.[3]

It is worth noting that already amongst the ancient Greeks, the law itself was identified with the boundary line between one household and another. The uneasy relationship between households coexisted with a distinction between public and private that was, at the time, not yet fully elaborated. Nevertheless, there was a recognition that the two spheres should be held to account in different ways. This sentiment was famously confirmed by the Athenian leader Pericles, in his famous Funeral Oration, where he stated:

> The freedom which we enjoy in our government extends also to our ordinary life. There, far from exercising a jealous surveillance over each other, we do not feel called upon to be angry with our neighbour for doing what he likes, or even to indulge in those injurious looks which cannot fail to be offensive, although they inflict no positive penalty. But all this ease in our private relations does not make us lawless as citizen.[4]

Pericles's advocacy of a hands-off approach towards home life constituted an important step towards endowing the boundary protecting the household from public gaze with legitimacy.

However, as Arendt remarked, it is to the Romans that we owe 'the full development of the life of hearth and family into an inner and private space'.[5]

The gradual separation of the household from public life acquired more definition with the rise of modernity, when the boundary dividing them acquired greater legal and political recognition. The rise of the nation state, along with the growing influence of the ideal of sovereignty in the 16th and 17th centuries, created the condition for the emergence of the public realm. It was in this historical context that 'the identification of a private domain free from the encroachment of the state emerged as a response to the claims of monarchs, and, in due course, parliaments, to an untrammelled power to make law'.[6]

The distinction between the public and private spheres underpinned the growing trend towards the liberalisation of political and social life. By the middle of the 19th century, it was widely recognised that people's freedom to act in accordance with their conscience and cultivate their capacity for moral autonomy required a space that was genuinely private. The very idea of tolerance had as its premise the conviction that individual conscience and private belief should not be subject to the laws directed at the regulation of public behaviour and views. Throughout most of the 19th and 20th centuries, the maintenance of and respect for the boundary between public and private was integral to the Western political and cultural imagination. As Norbert Elias wrote, 'with the advance of civilization the lives of human beings are increasingly split between an intimate and a public sphere, between secret and public behaviour'.[7]

During the 1930s, the radical right-wing German political philosopher Carl Schmitt criticised the early modern philosopher Thomas Hobbes because he 'incorporated a distinction between inner and outer, private and public, personal faith and outward confession'.[8] Schmitt claimed that the protection afforded to people's inner and private life served to undermine the authority of the state. He asserted that Hobbes's distinction between public and private 'becomes the seed of death that destroys the powerful Leviathan from within and kills the mortal god'.[9] Those with a totalitarian disposition shared Schmitt's concern about the flourishing of a private space. Indeed, one of the distinct characteristics of totalitarian states is its refusal to recognise any limits to its authority to control the conduct of people's personal lives. However, these sentiments did not gain traction in non-totalitarian settings, and the attempt to breach the boundary between the public and the private tended to be associated with the Orwellian spectre of Big Brother.

Although philosophers and social theorists have long debated the relationship between the private and the public spheres and often clashed about which they preferred, it is only in the 1980s that an unprecedented cultural consensus emerged against positive attachments to private life. Previously, even radical thinkers who regarded family life as stultifying still believed that a private life was essential for the moral development of human beings.[10] Gradually, a sense of disillusionment with family life came to pervade the cultural landscape.

By the 1970s, the private sphere, and particularly family life, had acquired overtly negative connotations amongst Western intellectuals and other opinion-formers. Within a decade, these negative sentiments had spread way beyond the confines of academia. The revision of social attitudes towards the private sphere went hand in hand with the emergence of a new consensus that regarded openness and transparency as highly valued ideals. This shift in attitudes represents one of the most important alterations to the value system of Western societies in the past two decades.

Until the late 1970s, the moral status of the private domain was held in high regard, and attempts to breach the boundary separating it from public life were regarded as perilous. Nevertheless, this boundary was continually tested. A leading British lawyer, Louis Blom-Cooper, alerted his readers in 1967 to the challenge faced by those committed to securing the boundary protecting private life:

> An Englishman's home may still be his castle, largely impervious to the infiltration of State authorities. The law, mindful of its task of warding off frontal attacks by the State, has not, however, effectively blocked the inquisitive eyes and ears of individuals seeking a less direct mode of entry.[11]

Despite his concern regarding 'intrusive eyes and ears', Blom-Cooper could still assume in 1967 that an 'Englishman's home may still be his castle'. The inviolability of the home was underwritten by the common law tradition. Its meaning was spelled out in 1760 by William Pitt (the Elder) when he declared:

> The poorest man may in his cottage bid defiance to all the force of the Crown. It may be frail, its roof may shake, the wind may blow through it. The rain may enter. The storms may enter. But the king of England may not enter. All his forces dare not cross the threshold of the ruined tenement.[12]

Yet this ancient liberty was formally quashed in the UK in 2004, by the Labour Government, supported by the Conservative opposition. The Domestic Violence, Crime and Victims Act contains a power to force entry into a home in connection with unpaid fines imposed for criminal offences. Three years later, the law was extended to allow bailiffs to use physical force against householders in order to restrain them.[13]

In more ways than one, Blom-Cooper's world has given way to one in which, all too often, the boundary protecting the private sphere struggles to block off 'inquisitive eyes and ears'. This chapter investigates how, and why, this is so.

Targeting reticence

Historically, the concept of openness was perceived as the antonym of secrecy. The *OED* defines openness as the 'absence of dissimulation, secrecy, or reserve; frankness, candour, sincerity'.[14] While this definition still stands, the meaning of openness has significantly expanded to signify a distinct orientation to life, which distrusts existing limits and boundaries. Increasingly, the term is also used in reference to a personality type: for example, a 'cosmopolitan personality', that is open to the world. As Delsol noted, 'the highest virtue of our time is open-mindedness'.[15] Openness has permeated the *zeitgeist* to the point that it influences public values and individual behaviour. It works as a value that strives to erode the boundary between what is personal and what is public, what can and cannot be seen or heard.

Personal and emotional openness are regarded as cultural ideals and promoted through the media and popular culture. Children are instructed to share their deepest private concerns and anxieties with their classmates and teachers, to get in touch with their own emotions, and readily absorb the emotions of others. This focus on the socialisation of the emotions is one of the principal features of what I characterised as *therapy culture*.[16] More widely, people are continually exhorted to 'express themselves', to 'share', and to 'talk about it'. Individuals who draw attention to their private troubles and publicly air their woes are applauded for their bravery. Once an athlete or a celebrity opens up about a mental health problem or confesses to a personal tragedy, they are awarded the status of a role model.

Whereas the public display of emotionalism was previously stigmatised as an example of the unrestrained behaviour of immature adults, today it is often praised as an expression of maturity. Numerous advocacy groups and academics have launched campaigns designed to encourage those cultural diehards who insist on keeping private matters private to embrace the *zeitgeist* of openness. Twenty-first century public culture has also become suspicious of how people manage their feelings outside the public gaze. The classical virtue of stoicism is frequently dismissed as an obstacle to the achievement of mental health. 'Keeping it in', or refusing to discuss private troubles, is portrayed as a serious character flaw.

In a world where the uninhibited display of emotion is frequently applauded by cultural influencers, privacy and intimacy are often targets of mistrust. Those who seek refuge in their private life go against the grain of the dominant outlook that validates the self through the public display of emotion. Consequently, the project of self-restraint is often caricatured as a dishonest attempt to cover up a variety of emotional deficits; a pathology that denies the true self and intensifies negative and destructive emotions. 'Popular therapies have demonized silence and stoicism, promoting the belief that healthy people talk about themselves', writes the American social critic Wendy Kaminer.[17]

The commanding influence of the ideal of an open personality has been paralleled by the cultural devaluation of the 'stiff upper lip'. This long-standing British metaphor for the demonstration of fortitude in the face of adversity is ridiculed as a symptom of emotional illiteracy rather than endorsed as a model for enduring disappointment and pain. The refusal to acknowledge fear and anxiety publicly is often diagnosed as both the cause, and result, of psychological problems. Writing in this vein, a group of researchers argue that one reason why the UK lags behind other countries in the fight to beat cancer is because of its 'stiff upper lip culture'.[18]

Indeed, the 'stiff upper lip' is routinely condemned and portrayed as a major threat to public health. The younger members of the British Royal Family regularly advise their subjects to abandon their stoic disposition and embrace emotional openness. For example, Prince William states that 'keeping a stiff upper lip can damage health', and that role models should open up about their mental health issues.[19] At times, the promotion of openness acquires the character of a moral crusade against emotional continence. One report, published by the Samaritans charity and reported under the headline 'How the stiff upper lip is making Britons miserable', asserted that 'British people are almost three times as likely to listen to other people sharing their problems than open up about their own'.[20] In recent times, the condition of so-called 'toxic masculinity' is attributed to men's failure to open up and discuss their issues in public. The claim that the 'stiff upper lip is killing men' is frequently communicated by campaigners who portray the reluctance to 'open up' as a marker for suicide. According to one version of this narrative, 'men are three times more likely to take their lives than women in the UK, but until they address their inability to open up, they'll continue to die'. 'If he'd learned to open up a bit more, maybe my dad wouldn't have spent his life avoiding help and would still be here', reflects one journalist, insisting that 'until we address our inability to open up, we'll continue to die early and needlessly'.[21]

The act of opening up is presented, not as a personal option, but as a public duty. Individuals who are not inclined to adopt help-seeking behaviour face considerable pressure to fall in line with prevailing cultural expectations, reinforced by the media and popular culture. Kathleen Lowney's study of American TV talk shows finds that 'guests are chided until they agree to enter therapy or go to a 12-step program or some other support group'.[22] In her fascinating study of the ascendancy of the ideal of transparency, Clare Birchall points out that 'valuing openness was reflected in, and reinforced by twentieth century media content':

> The 1960s saw certain figures contribute to a "culture of confession" in particular such as "celebrity" Evangelist preachers and therapists inviting the public to confess their sins and secrets on air (via radio and then television), and hailing the benefits of doing so (see Wise Bauer, 2008). From the psychoanalytic strand of this confessionary culture, Phil Donahue, and countless others after him, established the talk show genre which relies on the currency of personal revelation. Reality television, which arguably begins with MTV's *The Real World* in 1992, can also be seen as setting new standards for expectations of access and openness.[23]

Popular culture celebrates voyeuristic behaviour. 'How do you feel?' is now the only question that matters on reality TV shows, where the more you disclose, the more you are respected. The imperative of opening up the private sphere informs the entertainment formula of a culture where disclosures of individual troubles masquerade as a public service. 'Sharing problems' has assumed the character of a civic virtue which is affirmed with the obligatory refrain, 'thanks for sharing'. Indeed, contemporary ideals of community seek to achieve a sense of unity through the sharing of what were once private thoughts.

Politicians and public figures can no longer refuse to answer a question on the grounds that 'it is personal'. Through radio and television, the emotional orientation of the public figures defines an event. 'Capturing a sob, seeing tears flow down cheeks, looking into the eyes of the interviewee during tight camera shots merged as critical features of the message and, in some cases, the most important part of the report', writes the sociologist David Altheide in his provocative study of media news in the US.[24] This preoccupation with public figures' feelings has inexorably led to more and more questions being posed about their personal lives

Stripping away the protection of privacy is one way of forcing individuals to become open. As Josh Cohen explains, 'in scientific and media culture alike, nothing unknown can remain thus' – hence, 'neither self nor world can be granted the right to privacy'.[25] The media treats privacy as a condition to be breached for the purpose of entertainment. Millions of people watch *Love Island* or the *X Factor* as they are drawn into the supposed intimate personal lives of the contestants. During the penultimate episode of each series, the contestants' parents come on *Love Island* to offer their verdict on their children's exhibitionist behaviour, often praising their public performance of intimacy for being brave and courageous.

One of the themes promoted through confessional television is that in order to heal, emotionally injured individuals need to let go of 'private wounds by sharing them with others'.[26] The act of 'sharing' – that is, turning private troubles into public stories – strongly resonates with current cultural norms

One casualty of the breached boundary between the public and the private is the valued status of intimacy. During one interview, Andrew McMillan, competing to be the next Oxford Professor of Poetry, boasted that 'retired women at literary festivals will come up and tell me the most intimate details about their husbands or their sex lives'. His interviewer appeared to take the view that this was an admirable accomplishment and observed that McMillan's 'candour can inspire similar soul-baring from fans'.[27] The ability to incite strangers to reveal intimate details of their sex lives is portrayed as a mark of distinction in an open personality. As the ethos of transparency has succeeded in trumping the value of privacy, intimacy has become subject to public exposure. There is a relentless drive to 'normalise', routinise, and demystify the domain of sex. The boundaries that historically shielded intimate relations have becomes less and less effective, to the point where the consumption of pornography is regarded as a taken for granted feature of a modern lifestyle. Pornography has become a culturally, even socially, validated fetish. It totally resonates with the tendency to devalue the private sphere.

Once fiercely defended as a private matter, sex has become a constant topic of public deliberation by supposedly open-minded television hosts, sex educators, and 'agony aunts' – reinforced by the widely held consensus that the open disclosure of emotion has important therapeutic benefits. As the philosopher Thomas Nagel warned, 'once a convention of privacy loses its grip, there is a race to the bottom by competing media of publicity'.[28] The depths to which this race to the bottom now goes was strikingly illustrated by the announcement of a programme aired on the UK's Channel 4 in 2006, devoted to the promotion of masturbation. Once upon a time, masturbation in public was seen as a form of sordid behaviour by sad old men wearing raincoats. Channel 4 and the organisers of Europe's very first 'Masturbate-a-Thon' event rebranded this display of exhibitionism as the ultimate expression of responsible open sexual behaviour. The broadcaster enthusiastically embraced this opportunity to promote yet another of its 'brave', 'pioneering', 'agenda-setting' and 'taboo-breaking' reality shows.

It is worth noting that Channel 4 is not what is euphemistically referred to as an 'adult content provider'. This is the mainstream TV channel that had previously organised a programme on designer vaginas and also a 'Penis Week'. The promoters of this spectacle stated that their objective was to encourage people to 'explore safe sex' and 'talk about masturbation and lift the taboos that still surround the subject by coming to a public place and coming in a public place'. Sexual health charities also promote the message that openly discussing masturbation is an important feature of an overall enlightened sexual etiquette. According to a leaflet produced by the FPA (formerly the Family Planning Association), titled 'Masturbation – Support Notes', talking about it 'encourages safe and non-judgemental environments in which people can explore their sexuality'. Like the widely-celebrated *Vagina Monologues*, the publicity material promoting Channel 4's Masturbate-a-Thon claimed to 'raise awareness of, and dispel the shame and taboos' surrounding this 'natural and safe form of sexual activity'.

Sex education often serves as an instrument for breaking 'taboo' subjects amongst children. A sex education programme rolled out to 214 primary schools in Warwickshire, and directed at children as young as six, offered self-touching lessons to youngsters. The programme offers advice on self-stimulation and advises teachers to tell the children that 'lots of people like to tickle or stroke themselves as it might feel nice'.[29]

In passing, it is worth noting that the term 'breaking taboos' is invariably used to provide cultural validation for the public airing of subjects that were previously discussed in private, if at all. For example, one *Ted Talk* devoted to 'Busting Taboos – one part at a time' was advertised in the following terms:

> Laura Dodsworth photographed & interviewed 300 women and men about their breasts, penises, vulvas and vaginas. By turning her lens on physical taboos, she catalyses a ground-breaking conversation about social taboos and offers a deeply personal perspective on our most private, painful and pleasurable stories.[30]

Yet programmes and initiatives discussing menstruation, the shape of vaginas, the size of penises, masturbation, and so on, are not so much breaking taboos as conforming to the current demand for public exposure of issues that were once considered to be private matters. The main impulse driving this project is the loss of meaning that private life possesses for certain sections of society. The act of public disclosure has turned into a ritual that legitimates a person's moral standing. Cohen observes that this ritual involves the 'public unveiling of the inner self by the camera'. As he explains, 'in the confessional universe, it's never enough merely to believe in the value of the truth', since 'your commitment to truth can be authenticated only by your willingness to share it with any – and everyone'.[31]

The willingness to expose so much of what was once perceived as an intimate act speaks not only to a loss of reticence about prying into people's private affairs, but the sentiment that such reticence is a barrier that should be breached. In the contemporary cultural climate, reticence, like stoicism, tends to be regarded as a relatively unattractive character trait. It is also medicalised as a pathology. A paper published by two professors of communication defines reticence in the following terms:

> When people avoid communication because they believe it is better to remain silent than to risk appearing foolish, we refer to this behavior as reticence. Individuals who are referred to as reticent are people who tend to avoid communication because they believe it is better to remain silent than to risk appearing foolish.[32]

The authors of this definition diagnose reticence as a 'communication problem with cognitive, affective, and behavioural dimension', underwritten by the fear of negative reactions from others. It appears that they, in line with other advocates of openness, have lost sight of people's need for concealment. Contemporary culture tends to regard reticence as a prudish 'hang-up' and overlooks people's need to stay silent in some circumstances and on certain subjects.

Rather than a communication problem, reticent behaviour can be understood as a form of emotional work that aims to maintain the boundary between thoughts that should and shouldn't be divulged in public. Reticence strives to maintain the distinction between the inner and outer dimensions of the exercise of human subjectivity. Precisely because reticence constitutes a psychic reaction to current exhortations to bare the soul, it directly contradicts the ethos of transparency. Yet human relationships and interactions require that from time to time; individuals conceal their feelings and do not respond in the heat of the moment. 'There is much more going on inside us all the time than we are willing to express, and civilization would be impossible if we could all read each other's minds', notes Nagel.[33]

The capacity and willingness to conceal is integral to the development of children's maturity. Through the process of socialisation and the experience gained in interacting with others, children learn the importance of keeping some of their thoughts and feelings to themselves. They quickly realise that their relationship with others would be disrupted if they verbalised every thought and emotion that they felt. Learning to read situations and to make judgement calls is interlinked with the development of the capacity for acting with discretion and reticence.

Reticence has both an important social and individual dimension. As individuals, we rely on reticence to protect our inner life from public scrutiny. Socially, it minimises the potential for the eruption of interpersonal hostility and conflict. In her account of Kant's defence of reticence, Sharron Anderson-Gold explains how reticence plays an important role in the 'moral development of future generations', contending that reticence makes an essential contribution to social life:

> Reticence is important in the context of how we disclose our own personal character to others and in the context of how we respond to the faults of others. In fact, attempts at full disclosure can be morally damaging in

several important ways. By fully disclosing our vulnerabilities to others we may create the moral hazard of encouraging exploitation. And by fully disclosing our faults to others we may accustom others to fault and thus create the impression that vice is 'normal'. Reticence, or the disposition of non-disclosure, can then be a virtue. By not giving public recognition to private failings, in ourselves and others, we support the expectation of public or social virtue.[34]

Contrary to the ethos of transparency, the refusal to disclose our thoughts and emotions is essential for the maintenance of an enlightened moral order. Indeed, as Anderson-Gold writes,

> our current tendency to drag the imperfections of our public servants and celebrities into public view and ridicule them on late-night television would probably strike Kant not so much as a virtuous search for truth and honesty but as an indication of the corrupt state of our own public culture.[35]

The depreciation of reticence represents the loss of meaning of the sensibility of self-limitation. And yet without limitation, the singular qualities of an individual lose their distinct being.

The ridiculing of reticence and stoicism constitutes a threat to the most fundamental of boundaries that assist human flourishing. Far from constituting a limited, outmoded sensibility, striving to protect our inner life from public scrutiny is the precondition for the flourishing a society confronted with the uncertainties of the 21st century.

Kicking the door open

The spirit of limitlessness fuels a mood of suspicion and intolerance towards the private sphere. Calls to breach the boundary between public and private are usually framed through the argument that what happens in informal relations 'behind closed doors' is likely to be damaging. In particular, privacy is indicted because 'it has been used to shield the abuse of women in intimate relationships'.[36] A thriving industry of confessional and misery memoirs continually dwells on the sordid details of domestic violence and child abuse. This pornography of suffering also represents a demand for opening the doors to domestic life.

The tragic reality of domestic violence does not negate the need for the private realm. Arguably those who have suffered such violence need the security offered by privacy even more than their peers. The solution to the problem of domestic violence is the provision of refuges and the kind of assistance that facilitates the victim's acquisition of a measure of control over their life in a different setting.

There has been a dramatic reversal of the way that the private sphere is portrayed in popular culture. Once regarded as a safe refuge from the demands of everyday life, it is now often depicted as a toxic environment in which its inmates vent their destructive emotions at those who are closest to them. Consequently, the argument that people's private lives are a legitimate target for a degree of public scrutiny resonates with a wider outlook. Such sentiments have existed since the 19th century, when groups of social reformers were often repelled by what they saw as the degradation of the home life of the poor.[37] However, such attitudes were confined to the margins of society and tended to be selectively directed at the poorest of the urban poor.[38]

Present-day society retains a resilient strain of respect for privacy and family life. But the commanding cultural impulse is to seek out and 'expose' their harmful effects. Terms such as the 'dark side' of family life invoke a sense of dread about private and invisible relations. Feminist commentators have mounted a trenchant critique of privacy, arguing that in the private sphere, women are rendered invisible, their work becomes unrecognised and devalued, and their lives becomes subject to male violence.

The American legal scholar Catherine MacKinnon has insisted that for 'women, the private is the distinct sphere of intimate violation and abuse, neither free nor particularly personal'.[39] Cultural feminists like MacKinnon are deeply hostile to the idealisation of privacy and regard the boundary that protects it as an instrument of violent oppression. Her argument against according privacy a moral value is uncompromising:

> It is probably not coincidence that the very things feminism regards as central to the subjection of women – the very place, the body; the very relations, heterosexual; the very activities, intercourse and reproduction; and the very feelings, intimate – form the core of what is covered by privacy doctrine. From this perspective, the legal concept of privacy can and has shielded the place of battery, marital rape and women's exploited labour; has preserved the central institutions whereby women are *deprived* of identity, autonomy, control and self-definition; and has protected the primary activity through which male supremacy is expressed and enforce.[40]

MacKinnon's association of intimacy with male depravity and oppression has been widely featured in an ever-growing literature on family violence, which depicts abuse as a normal feature of private life rather than an abhorrent exception.

It is worthy of note, that MacKinnon's condemnation of privacy stands in sharp contrast to the positive value that many women attached to it in the past. In *A Room of One's Own*, Virginia Woolf suggested that without the protection of privacy, women faced significant obstacles to developing their capacity to express themselves.

Suspicion regarding what is likely to happen behind the closed door has become an important motif in contemporary culture. The title of a classic 1980 account of family violence, *Behind Closed Doors: Violence in the American Family*, articulates the degree of mistrust about fundamental private encounters.

One American artist, Justine Nuaman Greif, exhibited a triptych piercing titled 'Behind Closed Doors'. According to one review of this work:

> At first glance, the screen seems to depict Everytown USA, some of the homes are modest; some of the homes and gardens are opulent; all of them seem to be a portrait of tranquillity. It is not until the visitors pull down the faces of each home and read the correlated messages that they are confronted with the realisation of what happens behind closed door. Justine Nauman Greif has created a powerful means of reminding us that each time we retreat to the sanctuary of our own safe environments, we can not forget the thousands of victims in our own communities who are fighting for their lives behind closed doors.[41]

Raising 'awareness' about the danger presented by the closed door is emblematic of the lack of trust that society feels towards intimate relations. Bookshop shelves groan with memoirs such as Jenny Tomlin's *Behind Closed Doors*, with publishers' blurbs revelling in the pathology of the private sphere:

> Jenny grew up in a house where no-one was safe. Born one of five children in the East End, her childhood was spent in squalor and terror. Her father's violent beatings, humiliations, and sexual abuse were part of daily life; her mother – also his sexual victim and savagely beaten – was no source of help.[42]

B. A. Paris's 2016 novel *Behind Closed Doors* portrays privacy as a cloak or a sham, hiding the truth. The closed door allows people to hide their dirty little secrets, and therefore the reality of private life contradicts the way they present themselves in public. Similar themes recur in Susan Sloan's *Behind Closed Doors* (2017) or in E. S. Morrell's *What Really Happens Behind Closed Doors* (2018).

The view that the private sphere is an intensely dangerous place, particularly for women and children, has acquired the status of an incontrovertible truth in media commentary and academic literature. According to one widely-cited study titled *Behind Closed Doors: Violence in Families*:

> What is new and surprising is that the American family and the American home are perhaps as or more violent than any other single American institution or setting (with the exception of the military, and only then in time of war). Americans run the greatest risk of assault, physical injury, and even murder in their own homes by members of their own families.[43]

More radical accounts imply that the private sphere masks the conflict of interest between parents and their children. Bob Franklin, a British campaigner for children's rights, claims that high-profile cases of child abuse have 'exploded the myth of the family as an institution which offered its members security and safety'. Instead of offering protection, the domain of the private is a 'potentially dangerous arena'.[44] If that is indeed the case, it follows that society has a moral duty to dismantle the boundary between the private and the public spheres.

The shift in cultural perceptions of family life are reflected in the contemporary social science literature, where it is virtually impossible to find any systematic defence of privacy and family life.[45] The general approach adopted by most contributions on the subject is to privilege the public over the private on the ground that terrible things occur under the cloak of privacy. It is often suggested that the problem is not the erosion of privacy, but that the state does not intervene enough to protect the vulnerable casualties of family life. The argument that only an ever-vigilant public institution can protect children from adult predators is one of the most frequently used objections against the claim for the autonomy of the private sphere.[46]

The tendency to depict privacy as a 'cloak' or a 'sham' is based on the premise that toxic emotions dominate family life. It assumes that left to their own devices and away from public view, people tend to be dominated by destructive emotions. Men, in particular, are condemned for abusing the privilege of privacy to terrorise women and children. This unflattering representation of intimate relationships constitutes a warning of imminent victimisation. From this standpoint, privacy can have no redeeming features: it becomes an imperative that the private sphere should be opened up to the public gaze and official regulation.

Why privacy is important

Perceptions regarding the distinction between private and public are influenced by what society values. As Weintraub points out, 'debates about how to cut up the social world between public and private are rarely innocent exercises, since they often carry powerful normative implications'.[47] For example, the frequently repeated argument that the innocent has nothing to fear from the official prying eyes conveys a moral sensibility that assigns little intrinsic value to the aspiration for a protected private space. It directly contradicts the celebration of private space captured by the old phrase 'an Englishman's home is his castle'.

It wasn't until the rise of capitalism and modern society in Europe that arguments for the maintenance of a dichotomous sphere of public and private were rigorously formulated. The need to protect the private sphere was forcefully promoted by advocates of classical liberalism, who insisted that what happened in the household was not a matter for state intervention. Since the 16th century, arguments for privacy have been made in a variety of ways. Early claims coupled private with property and the defence of individual conscience. During the past two centuries, the case for the private sphere has evolved and it came to be justified on moral, psychological, and political grounds.

A useful working definition of privacy is provided by Alan Westin in his study, *Privacy And Freedom*: 'Privacy is the claim of individuals, groups, or institutions to determine for themselves when, how, and of what extent information about them is communicated to others'.[48] This definition has as its focus the attempt by individuals to establish a balance between the aspiration for privacy and the desire for disclosure and communication. Historically, this goal was motivated by the exigency of curtailing the power of the state to intrude into people's private activities. The restraint of state intervention into private life remains an important concern. However, arguments for privacy are increasingly focused on the psychological and moral necessity for a retreat from a busy public world, so that, insulated from the immediacy of outside pressures, people can be themselves.

According to Westin, privacy has four important functions for the individual. The first, and arguably most important, is the quest and necessity for personal autonomy. The distinct qualities of an individual can only be cultivated in a protected private space. The development of individuality and autonomy 'requires time for sheltered experimentation and testing of ideas, for preparation and practice in thought and conduct without fear of ridicule or penalty', and for the 'opportunity to alter opinions before making them public'.[49] The capacity to play an effective role as a public citizen presupposes the acquisition of the sense of independence that comes from the struggle to gain a measure of autonomy. Privacy ensures that the distinction between a person's life as an individual and their life as a citizen is maintained. In an important essay published in 1890, 'The Rights of the Citizen – to his own Reputation', E.L. Godkin, the founding editor of *The Nation*, eloquently explained that the existence of a secure private sphere allowed a person to 'draw the line between his life as an individual and his life as a citizen, or in other words, the power of deciding how much or how little the community shall see of him, know of him, beyond which is necessary for the proper discharge of all his duties to his neighbors and to the state'.[50]

The impulse to kick open the door of the private sphere is often underwritten by the tendency to perceive people as abstract individuals who are shorn of their particularity. Josh Cohen contends that privacy is 'subject to unrelenting attack, direct and indirect, gross and subtle, precisely because it guards the strangeness in you that *no power will be able to reach*, that no amount of intrusion from the science or media or state or friends and neighbours can render visible'.[51] That is why those who are sceptical of the value of the private are also dismissive of the value of individual autonomy.

Privacy also serves as an important medium for emotional release. The intensity and uncertainty of life creates a circumstance where periods of privacy are 'required from the pressure of playing social roles'.[52] Constant exposure to conflicting social demands would be unbearable if people could not move off-stage and drop their social mask in order to try to be themselves. Privacy provides a space where people can deviate from, even violate, some of the prevailing social norms. Another dimension of this release is the ability to manage bodily and sexual functions and behaviour without being monitored.

The third important function of privacy is the space it provides for the act of self-evaluation. Through self-evaluation, individuals are able to reflect, integrate, and give meaning to their experience. Self-evaluation can only be conducted in privacy. Westin argues that 'the evaluative function of privacy 'has a "major moral dimension" as it allows for the "exercise of conscience" through which the individual "repossesses himself"'.[53] Arendt wrote eloquently of the 'silent dialogue of myself with myself'. It is through our capacity to cultivate this inner voice that we begin to understand our place in the world.

Fourthly, privacy allows for limited and protected communication. Limited communication is essential for the harmony and stability of social interaction. Total openness would create confusion and conflict. At the same time, privacy allows for the sharing of confidences, which in turn encourages the consolidation of friendships and intimate relationships. Limited communication sets boundaries between the most intimate and the most public of social situations. Limited or protected communication is also necessary for relationships with professionals offering advice. The prohibition of public disclosure is assumed in relationships with doctors, lawyers, or priests. Privacy is required to ensure that knowledge of our pain and distress is not used against us by people who have become aware of our vulnerabilities.

One point that is often overlooked is that the quality of public life is closely connected to people's ability to freely conduct their private life. Privacy allows for the possibility of solitude and the development of self-consciousness and personal dignity; qualities which prepare an individual to reveal who they are and what they think in public.

A tolerant state respects the distinction between public and private spheres because it recognises that the ability to expose, in some contexts, parts of our identity that we may conceal in others is indispensable for freedom. Privacy and protected communication are prerequisites for the forging of the close bonds and ties through which people establish relations of intimate trust, allowing us to reveal parts of ourselves to friends, family members, or lovers that we withhold from the rest of the world. From this perspective, privacy should not be interpreted as either good or bad but simply as necessary.

The need to protect people's attempt to find themselves or to be themselves underscores the necessity for a domain of life that is distinct from the workings of public life. Liberal theory is premised on the assumption that it is both desirable and necessary for individuals to have a life that is separate from the one they conduct in public as citizens. It was thought that without the existence of the private sphere, the totalising dynamic of state activity would be difficult to contain. Its consequence would be the subjection of individual pursuits to a bureaucratic imperative, which would in turn lead to the politicisation of every dimension of human existence. Such a development would not only diminish the flourishing of personal autonomy – it would also disorient public life from its pursuit of the common good. Experience shows that whenever the state seeks to politicise private life and attempts to abolish the boundary protecting it – for example, in the Cultural Revolution in China – public life itself becomes depoliticised.

The protection of the private realm is essential for the conduct of a healthy public life. Privacy is essential for exercising our capacity to make something of ourselves. It is within the confines of the private realm that people can reflect, test out ideas on their intimates, develop their political capacities, and acquire the moral resources necessary for the conduct of public life.

There is little doubt that private life can sometimes be unpleasant, violent, and degrading. Privacy can provide a space for the exercise of destructive and oppressive behaviour. But these negative aspects of private life do not provide a coherent argument for eradicating the private sphere altogether, any more than the existence of street crime is an argument for eliminating the public sphere. Today's casual dismissal of the private sphere denigrates one of the most important sites of human experience. The separation of the public and private spheres has been essential for the emergence of the modern individual. The aspiration for autonomy and identity cannot be entirely resolved in the public sphere. The private sphere not only provides a potential space for reflection but also for the development of personality. Intimate relationships require privacy if they are not to disintegrate under the pressure of public scrutiny. Whatever problems might exist in the private sphere, it is the prerequisite for the exercise of freedom.

The need for maintaining boundaries

The breaching of the boundary between public and private constitutes a problem for both of these arenas. Neither realm is meaningful without the other. The stability of the private sphere assists the smooth conduct of public life. 'The public-private boundary keeps the public domain free of disruptive material' and 'it also keeps the private domain free of insupportable controls', concludes Nagel.[54] In this sense, the boundary itself plays an important role in the construction of a dynamic interaction between two poles of human life, setting limits to how much public exposure an individual can put up with.

There are several reasons why boundaries, like that separating the public from the private, are essential for the conduct of everyday life. The Canadian sociologist Erving Goffman has written eloquently about how people fiercely guard their personal boundaries to manage their encounters – not only with strangers, but also with acquaintances and friends. In human encounters, strangers 'maintain boundaries of reticence that other people are forbidden to cross without mutually negotiated consent'.[55] Symbolic boundaries regulate interpersonal relations and protect us from unwanted gaze and attention. Goffman's concept of 'civic inattention' illuminates how we behave in response to the convention that dictates that it is rude to stare at strangers.[56] Symbolic boundaries allow individuals to retain a measure of control over the management of their encounter with strangers as well as people they know.

Symbolic boundaries also delineate a space within which people can come together and develop an understanding of what they have in common. Such boundaries provide guidance and an interpretative framework within which people make choices in line with, and in response to, the expectations of others. It is not surprising that since its emergence, the law has 'always been defined in terms of boundaries and limitations'.[57] The work of anthropologists indicates that virtually all societies set limits on what can and what cannot be seen. As Gurstein explains, 'virtually all known civilization and societies have maintained distinct boundaries between those things that must be hidden and those that are fit to appear before others'.[58]

With the erosion of the line between the private and the public, the need for boundaries is often recast according to a hyper-individualistic personal logic. Consequently, intimacy is often perceived as a form of personal space that must be secured through individuals setting their own boundaries. As we discuss in Chapter 9, the proliferation of self-help advice on how to set your boundary highlights the disorienting impact of the delegitimation of the private sphere.

Human action itself invites the construction of boundaries and limits. Action, with its unpredictable consequences, can have destabilising consequences on the lives of the people affected by it. As Arendt explained, action, 'no matter what its specific content, always establishes relationships and therefore has an inherent tendency to force open all limitations and cut across all boundaries'. The boundless potential of human action requires the establishment of both symbolic and legal restraints, conventions, and norms that set boundaries and limitations:

> The fences inclosing private property and insuring the limitations of each household, the territorial boundaries which protect and make possible the physical identity of a people, and the laws which protect and make possible its political existence, are of such great importance to the stability of human affairs precisely because no such limiting and protecting principles rise out of the activities going on in the realm of human affairs itself.[59]

The limitations inscribed by the law, as well as the physical and symbolic boundaries protecting a community or a nation state, are 'never entirely reliable safeguards against action from without'. However, the boundlessness of action also strives towards the establishment of relationships and conventions that restrain its unpredictability. Arendt pointed out that 'this is why the old virtue of moderation, of keeping within bounds, is indeed one of the political virtues par excellence'.[60] Understanding the creative tension between the boundlessness of action and the prevailing modes of restraint is a constant challenge facing humanity. Normative, symbolic, and legal boundaries offer a medium for the reconciliation of the positive and, at times boundless, aspiration for freedom with the need for predictability and security.

A compelling account of the inescapable necessity for limits is offered by the existentialist philosopher Karl Jaspers in his concept of *Grenzsituation* – 'boundary situations' or 'ultimate situations'.[61] These are situations that we 'cannot evade or change', such as life and death – situations that touch on the boundary of our being. Jaspers argues that despite people's effort to ignore such boundaries, 'men band together in a community in order to limit and ultimately abolish the endless struggle of all against all'.[62]

Conclusion

The waning cultural support for the boundary protecting the private sphere from public scrutiny offers a striking example of the difficulty that society has in grasping the significance of symbolic limits. As is the case with physical borders, those who strive to uphold the integrity of the private sphere find it difficult to counter the cultural influence of the prevailing mood of limitlessness. Arguments in favour of defending the private sphere tend to be technical and focus on the threats posed by technologies of surveillance. They imagine that technical and legal solutions can solve the threat to private life. Thus, they appeal to legal instruments such as Article 8 of the Human Rights Act, which asserts that 'everyone has the right to respect for his private and family life, his home and his correspondence'. Unfortunately, this emphasis on legal and technical solutions overlooks what is principally a cultural problem. The moral and cultural climate of limitlessness cannot be effectively contested through reliance on formal legal instruments. As the social commentator Tim Black explains, 'the idea of privacy has not been legally debased' – it has been 'culturally and politically undermined'.[63]

Yet, the private sphere has also become culturally debased. The most striking illustration of this trend is Western society's acclamation of the ideal of transgression and the identities constructed around it. According to one assessment of this trend, there is a concerted attempt to transgress the boundary protecting the private sphere in order to open up 'new areas of struggle for the establishment of private identities in the public domain'.[64] In this way, forms of behaviour that were historically perceived as private become performed as public acts. As one sympathetic account of this development explains:

> Perhaps the most important aspect of this struggle is the politicization of bodily and sexual expression, that is, legalization as publicly permissible of such behavior that yet recently was considered indecent, socially unacceptable or even punishable. The domain of such expression used to be 'covered' with categories of indecency, perversion and crime.[65]

From this standpoint 'the right to express publicly the peculiarities of one's sexuality' leads to the emergence of the so-called 'sexual citizen'. The performance of transgression becomes a constituent part of sexually based public identities.

A significant body of literature contests the value of transparency. However, with a few important exceptions, critics of transparency rarely challenge the culture of suspicion that has succeeded in rebranding the private sphere as a toxic site of debased, abusive, and violent behaviour. Consequently, periodic outrage against intrusion into some aspects of private life coexists with its casual acceptance in others. While there are numerous commentators prepared to denounce mass snooping by the National Security Agency, serious criticisms of the association of private life with toxic and abusive behaviour are few and far between. If it is accepted that private life is fundamentally toxic, arguments against the snoopers are likely to prove ineffective. As Black reminds us, when Eric Schmidt, Google's CEO, stated in 2009 that 'if you have something that you don't want anyone to know, maybe you shouldn't be doing it in the first place', many people reacted with concern, but 'few were able to defend the need to be hidden from the gaze of indiscriminate others'.[66]

The failure to uphold the moral authority of the boundary between public and private constitutes a fundamental threat to society. Who needs George Orwell's Big Brother when the media is literally invited to gaze into people's inner life? In previous times, totalitarian states were committed to breaching the boundary that protected people's personal life, but they were far less effective in undermining the legitimacy of privacy than the contemporary cultural war waged against it.

The aspiration for limitlessness creates the condition for the flourishing of a soft form of totalitarianism. The suspicion directed at closed doors directly questions the value of human freedom. It does not trust people to exercise their freedom responsibly when they are out of sight. Its denial of the importance of people cultivating their selves in secret is motivated by a preference for the flattened-out conformism of the totalitarian imagery. The French philosopher Jacques Derrida understood the threat posed by the totalitarian instinct fuelling the compulsion to negate secrecy when he told his interviewer that 'I have an impulse of fear and terror in the face of a political space' that 'makes no room for the secret'. He added that 'the demand that everything be paraded in the public square' is a 'glaring sign of the totalitarianization of democracy' and warned that 'if a right to the secret is not maintained, we are in a totalitarian space'.[67]

Once the space for secrecy is lost, the individual's capacity to question, doubt, and act in accordance with their inclinations is undermined. In this area as in others, the flourishing of freedom is inseparable from the maintenance of limits and boundaries.

Notes

1 See Debray (2010).
2 Rosen (2000) p. 210.
3 Elshtain (1993) p. 6.
4 Thucydides (c. 460–c. 400 BCE), in his History of the Peloponnesian War.
5 Arendt (1998) p. 59.
6 See, Wack (2014).
7 Elias (2000) p. 160.
8 See Holmes (1993) pp. 52–53.

9   Cited in Holmes (1993) p. 53.

10 Leading social theorists like Jurgen Habermas, who was critical of what he saw as the sham of privacy and wrote of the 'pseudo-privacy' of family life but did not question the right to privacy as such. See for example the discussion in Wolfe (1997).

11 Blom-Cooper (1967) p. vii.

12 Cited by Phillip Johnson in 'An Englishman's home is no longer his Castle', *The Daily Telegraph*, 11 January 2009, www.telegraph.co.uk/comment/columnists/philipjohnston/4218091/An-Englishmans-home-is-no-longer-his-castle.html.

13 See Phillip Johnson in 'An Englishman's home is no longer his Castle', *The Daily Telegraph*, 11 January 2009, www.telegraph.co.uk/comment/columnists/philipjohnston/4218091/An-Englishmans-home-is-no-longer-his-castle.html.

14 "Openness, n.", *OED Online*, September 2019. Oxford University Press. www.oed.com. chain.kent.ac.uk/view/Entry/131722?redirectedFrom=openness (accessed September 30, 2019).

15 Delsol (2003a) p. 67.

16 See Furedi (2003).

17 See Kaminer, W. (2000) 'I spy', *The American Prospect*, vol. 11, no. 18.

18 Roberts, M. (2013) 'Cancer fight "hampered in UK by stiff upper lip"', *BBC News*, 30 January.

19 Prince William says keeping a stiff upper lip can damage health 18 April 2017, www.bbc.com/news/uk-39625897.

20 John Bingham (2016) 'How the stiff upper lip is making Britons miserable', *The Daily Telegraph*, 23 February, https://www.telegraph.co.uk/news/health/news/12168570/How-the-stuff-upper-lip-is-making-Britons-miserable.html.

21 See Urwin, J. (2014) 'Not opening up kills men', *Vice*, 19 October, www.vice.com/en_us/article/jmbnp7/a-stiff-upper-lip-is-killing-british-men-344.

22 Lowney, K. (1999) *Baring Our Souls: TV Talk Shows and the Religion of Recovery*, Aldine de Gruyter: New York, p. 18.

23 Birchall (2019).

24 Altheide (2002) p. 108.

25 See Cohen, J. (2013) *The Private Life*, Granta: London, p. xvi.

26 Lowney (1999) p. 19.

27 Fane-Saunders, T. (2019) *The Daily Telegraph*, 18 June. 'Andrew McMillan interview: 'Retired women tell me the most intimate details about their sex lives', www.telegraph.co.uk/books/authors/andrew-mcmillan-interview-retired-women-tell-intimate-details/.

28 Nagel (1998) p. 4.

29 See www.dailymail.co.uk/news/article-7490415/Children-young-SIX-given-compulsory-self-touching-lessons.html.

30 Laura Dodsworth, 'Breaking One Taboo at a Time'. https://www.youtube.com/watch?v=BABLrJXOe7A.

31 Cohen (2013) p. 127.

32 Keaten and Kelly (2000) p. 168.

33 Nagel (1998) p. 4.

34 Anderson-Gold (2010) p. 29.

35 Anderson-Gold (2010) p. 41.

36 Balos (2004) p. 79.

37 See Flege (2016).

38 See Manning and Waugh (1866) for an illustration of an early example of the crusade against an 'Englishman's Castle', where cruelty's doer is 'most secure from detection'.

39 MacKinnon (1987) p. 168.

40 MacKinnon (1987) p. 101.

41 See review on www.qwi.net/-tbkkpt/justine.htm.

42 See www.amazon.co.uk/Behind-Closed-Doors-Jenny-Tomlin/dp/0340837926/ref=sr_1_34?keywords=closed+door&qid=1560694843&s=books&sr=1-34.

43 Strauss, Gelles, and Steinmetz (1980) p. 3.

44 Franklin (1995) p. 4.
45 This is paticularly the case within the discipline of the sociology of the family. For an exceptional counterpoint to this trend; see the articles – particularly those of Jean Cohen and Jean Bethke Elshtain- in Weintraub and Kumar (1997).
46 See LaFontaine and Sapford (1993).
47 Weintraub (1997) p. 3.
48 Westin (1967) p. 7.
49 Westin (1967) p. 34.
50 Godkin is cited by Gurstein (1996). Rochelle Gurstein's excellent study of the rise and decline of reticence in the United States offers an important historical context for the discussion in this chapter.
51 Cohen (2013) p. 25.
52 Westin (1967) p. 34.
53 Westin (1967) p. 37.
54 Nagel (1998) p. 20.
55 Rosen (2000) p. 16.
56 See Goffman (1959) p. 128.
57 Arendt (1998) p. 191.
58 Gurstein (1996) pp. 12–13.
59 Arendt (1998) p. 191.
60 Arendt (1998) p. 191.
61 For a discussion of this concept see Grieder (2009) pp. 330–336.
62 Jaspers (1964).
63 Black, T. (2016) 'The Tyranny of transparency', *Spiked*, 26 April, www.spiked-online.com/2016/04/26/the-tyranny-of-transparency/.
64 Rubavičius (2008) p. 74.
65 Rubavičius (2008) p. 74.
66 Rubavičius (2008) p. 74.
67 Derrida and Ferraris (2000) p. 59.

6

POLITICS GOES PERSONAL

The previous chapter explored the disturbing implications of the erosion of the boundary between the public and the private for the conduct of life in the private sphere. In this chapter, we examine the way in which the logic of boundaryless-ness contributes to the unsettling of public life.

The experience of recent decades indicates, once it becomes subject to the public gaze, the private sphere inevitably becomes politicised. The loss of a sense of limits results in confusion about how to distinguish between private matters and those that are a legitimate subject of public concern. The fates of the public and the private spheres are intertwined, and once the distinction between them becomes confused, the integrity of both becomes compromised. Precisely at the historical moment when the private sphere has become politicised, the domain of the public has become increasingly depoliticised.

The tendency to render politics personal is paralleled by its detachment from its historic home in the public sphere. The contamination of concepts, briefly outlined in Chapter 2, is strikingly illustrated in the way that politics is increasingly used to signify concerns and issues that pertain to private matters. The invention of the boundary-blurring concept, *the personal is political*, is paradigmatic in this respect. Once the personal is rendered political, not even the most intimate dimension of human life can remain immune from being dragged into the political net.

One result of this is that the term 'political' has been rendered a rhetorical device that invites attention. Academic and social commentators are busy reflecting on the 'Politics of Pubic Hair'.[1] The prestigious British medical journal, *The Lancet*, holds forth on 'The Politics of Masturbation'.[2] 'The Politics of Menstruation' is the subject of a serious monograph in the journal *Social Problems*. Even body smell has become politicised: according to a feature in the *New Scientist*; 'if you hate body odour, you are more likely to support Trump'.[3] The following list shows some of the bewildering range of ways in which the term 'politics' is deployed to invite public attention to personal matters:

- The Politics of Black Hair
- The Politics of Breast Feeding
- The Politics of Plastic Surgery
- The Politics of Assisted Reproduction
- The Politics of Body Modification
- The Politics of the Body
- The Politics of Body Image
- The Politics of Intimacy
- The Politics of Parenting
- The Politics of Healthy Eating
- The Politics of Obesity

The semantic widening of the term 'politics' trivialises it by emptying it of its classical meaning. Some commentators believe that this represents an advance over its previous 'narrow' focus of politics on public matters. However, this trend towards the politicisation of personal issues inevitably leads to the degradation of the political.

Richard Sennett's *The Fall of Public Man*[4] offers a persuasive account of the emptying-out of public life. Like many observers, Sennett assumes that the main driver of this process is a people's growing tendency to retreat into the private sphere. He believes that society's obsessive preoccupation with the self and self-disclosure goes hand in hand with society's tendency to constitute its regime of control in psychological terms. Sennett's concept of the 'tyrannies of intimacy' refers to a trend whereby the cultivation of narcissistic and egocentric individuals leads to the disintegration of the public sphere and the fall of public man.

Sennett assumes that it is the attraction of the private sphere – its promise of emotional bonds, human warmth and affection, intimacy based on love and friendship – that accounts for the diminishing appeal of public life.[5] However, it is not only people's estrangement from a depersonalised public sphere that leads people to look for a haven in a more personal intimate setting. The declining significance of the public to people's lives is an indirect expression of the erosion of a meaningful boundary separating it from the private sphere.

The displacement of the political

It is increasingly difficult to answer the question of where public life ends and where private life begins. The private lives of political leaders make for a constant topic of discussion and controversy. Public figures are more likely to be judged on their personal attributes, their character, and their appearance than on their views and ideals. Political candidates often rely on their partners and family to promote their image, while a veritable army of political archaeologists devotes itself to the task of digging up their intimate details. In the United States, the school yearbook of a political candidate is carefully scrutinised for evidence of a youthful indiscretion. Comments made on social media by public figures as teenagers are used to embarrass or discredit them later in life. Any 'inappropriate' remark or act will come back to bite a politician. Take the case of Tulsi Gabbard, a Democratic Party Congresswoman from Hawaii, and a candidate in the 2020 American presidential elections. An Iraq War veteran, she made history in 2012 as the first Hindu elected to Congress. Yet she has had to apologise for working with her father in his anti-gay rights organisation when she was a teenager.

Though *ad-hominem* politics – attacking an individual's character to undermine their arguments and appeal – has a long history, it is only in recent times that it has become institutionalised as the normal conduct of political life. The unrestrained determination with which the exposure of a politician's private life is pursued is also unprecedented. One consequence of the relentless personalisation of public life is that political operatives act on the assumption that attacking a person's character and credibility 'may be just as effective as attacking the claim that the person is making'.[6]

Judging political figures according to the standards and ideals used by intimates towards one another invariably distracts from deliberating on matters of public policy, ideals, and values. At times, it appears that the media attaches greater significance to what politicians say in the 'privacy' of their bedroom than in their public pronouncements. During the contest for the leadership of the British Conservative Party in June 2019, the media became transfixed by a private argument between one of the candidates – Boris Johnson – and his partner Carrie Symonds. The couple's heated verbal exchange was surreptitiously recorded by a neighbour and published verbatim by *The Guardian* newspaper. In a different era, this salacious exposure of an intimate conversation would have been condemned as a grotesque invasion of private life; but today, many commentators rebranded it as entirely justified on the grounds of public interest.

The media's attempt to create a scandal around Boris Johnson's character indicates that standards of behaviour traditionally associated with salacious private gossip have become seamlessly internalised by public life. In the Anglo-American sphere in particular, the debate and exploration of important public issues has given way to an almost pornographic fascination with the private problems of public figures. As Zygmunt Bauman observed, increasingly public interest is 'reduced to curiosity about the private lives of public figures, and the art of public life is narrowed to the public display of private affairs and public confessions of private sentiments'. Bauman noted that public issues 'which resist such reduction become all but incomprehensible'.[7]

This development became institutionalised during the Clinton presidency of the 1990s. From the moment Bill Clinton was elected, every aspect of his private life became a subject of media scrutiny. His golf game was scrutinised, his eating habits were ridiculed, and the public was informed that his penis had 'distinguishing characteristics'. The media went to great lengths to dwell on the distinguishing features of Clinton's genitals during the course of Paula Jones' sexual harassment suit against the President. As a matter of public interest, *The Independent* reported that according to Jones, Clinton's 'erect penis is about five inches long, has a circumference of a quarter (a shade less than a 2p coin) and heads off at an angle, presumably rather like a finger bent at the joint'.[8] Preoccupation with Clinton's penis continued well into the 21st century. Fourteen years after *The Independent*'s report, a study of this affair concluded that 'evidence from confidential sources now establishes with near certainty that the alleged "distinguishing characteristic" described by Paula Jones' did not exist 'as an anatomical matter'.[9] Just in case the public did not lose its salacious appetite for Clinton's personal life, during the investigation of his affair with Monica Lewinsky, the independent counsel's 453-page report about his sexual escapades was published on the Internet.

Although the worldwide exposure of Clinton's personal life represents an extreme manifestation of the erosion of privacy, it is symptomatic of a trend that has, if anything, become even more prevalent in the contemporary era. It is also worth noting that Clinton himself was more than ready to expose his private problems and psychological issues to the media and the wider public. Kaminer notes how Clinton and his Vice-President, Al Gore, specialised in telling the world about their private troubles and personal growth stories.[10]

With the fusion of public and private motifs, politicians often appear to be more concerned with managing their personal affairs and image than with engaging with complicated matters of public policy. At the same time, as we discuss later in the chapter, policymakers have become increasingly drawn towards the management of ordinary people's behaviour. Lifestyle matters to do with eating, exercising, or child-rearing are now seen as legitimate topics for policy deliberation and political intervention. Elshtain wrote that the 'insistence that the private world be integrated fully into an overarching public arena' is paralleled by 'an equally vehement demand for what might be called the "privatization" of the public realm with politics falling under its standards, ideals and purposes'.[11]

The dissolution of the boundary between the personal and political invariably unleashes a process where people's private interests are mixed up with those of the public. When the taken-for-granted expectations that individuals have towards each other are exported into the domain of politics, they lose their meaning and force. The rules of conduct that govern relations between lovers, family members, or friends are very different from the formal procedures that ought to regulate public affairs. Informal interaction and spontaneous behaviour generate the kind of unexpected subjective preferences and displays of emotional responses that necessarily complicate the forging of public solidarity and interests. The vocabulary of meanings appropriate to the conduct of private affairs rarely makes sense in the pursuit of public relationships. Politicians who draw attention to an event in their personal life are not merely performing an act of self-disclosure but using the technology of the confessional to produce a desired public image of themselves. When the vocabulary of private life – sincerity, loyalty, authenticity, intimacy, trust – enters the language of political discourse, it both loses its previous meaning and distorts public affairs.

A vibrant political sphere requires that the issues that are the subject of political deliberation are not subjected to the pressures of personal concerns. The expansion of personal matters into the public domain inflicts serious damage on the conduct of political life; what makes the public sphere genuinely public is that it serves as an arena in which citizens from different backgrounds are able to collaborate on the task of addressing and resolving problems of common concern. When personal issues become meshed with those of common concern, politics can become overfamiliar to the point that the common good is lost sight of. Since political decisions affect everyone, they should not be contaminated by private concerns.

Experience indicates that once personal stories and attributes are harnessed to the project of endowing a public figure with credibility, the stakes in the authenticity race are continually raised. Inevitably, politicians' reliance on their personal image serves as an invitation for others to spoil it. That is why so much effort and energy is devoted to cultivating the art of character assassination, and why would-be political candidates have their past carefully scrutinised for unguarded comments and embarrassing episodes. Personal details are carefully assessed to work out whether they constitute political assets or liabilities.

Though some perceive the privatisation of the public realm as an expression of a more inclusive widening of the political sphere, it actually constitutes the debasement of politics. When just about anything can be characterised as political, politics as a sphere for deliberation about competing visions of public interest ceases to exist. Once the conceptual boundary between public and private becomes blurred, there is little resistance to the temptation to project personal issues and preoccupations into the public sphere.

'The personal is political'

The politicisation of the person is the most significant and also the most destabilising outcome of the blurred boundary between public and private. This development, in the 1960s and 1970s, was fuelled by powerful cultural trends. Disappointment with what could be achieved in the public sphere through the politics of interests disposed the counterculture movement to opt for personal solutions to the problems of existence. Changing yourself or realising yourself, expressing yourself or emancipating yourself became rallying calls for young people drawn towards the self-absorbed spirit of the time. For many, the project of changing yourself served as an end in itself. This was the time when former leaders of the 1960s cultural movement – Jerry Rubin, Abbie Hoffman – declared that it was 'more important to get your head together than to move the multitudes'.[12]

Lasch characterised this shift from politics to self-examination as the 'culture of narcissism'. The culture of narcissism fostered a climate where personal feelings were accorded an important political significance. Gradually, the strength of feelings held by an individual or group has come to serve as the functional equivalent of a previous era's depth of political conviction. Public pronouncements are frequently conveyed with an emotional tone, as protestors displaying placards that draw attention to their anger assume that the act of communicating this emotion serves as an argument in and of itself. A placard announcing, 'I am Really Angry About This. We Need to Stop Brexit', carried by protestors on one recent demonstration seeks to transform a person's state of mind into a political statement.[13] Extinction Rebellion protesters explicitly aim to provoke anger in order to gain an audience for their objectives.[14]

In recent times, some feminists have promoted 'female rage' as a political weapon. Books such as *Good and Mad: The Revolutionary Power of Women's Anger* (2018), *Rage Becomes Her: The Power of Women's Anger* (2018), and *Eloquent Rage: A Black Feminist Discovers Her Superpower* (2018) portray anger as a valuable political emotion.[15] Two American academics argue that anger 'serves as a means of social and personal transformation, serving as a way to heal from oppression and exploitation'; they claim to have learned to 'use anger, as means to survive everyday racism' and now understand 'that this rage partially defines us'.[16] In the same vein, an academic supporter of the Black Lives Matter campaigns argues that:

> anger is productive in that it can serve as a unifying discourse that seeks liberation rather than liberal democratic incorporation, and it is disruptive to the hegemony of powerful national narratives premised on the inevitability of racial progress but that actually mask the mechanisms of white supremacy.[17]

Rage is not the only emotion to be promoted as an instrument of public/political communication. Feelings of pain, grief, and suffering offer therapeutic resources for the mobilisation of political causes. Expressions of personal vulnerability compete with one another in an effort to gain access to public sympathy and political resources. The protest movement Extinction Rebellion self-consciously flaunts the vulnerability of its members. Its tactic of achieving mass arrests is justified on the ground that it shows 'how vulnerable we are'.[18] The framing of public issues and political causes through the language of personal feelings is often celebrated on the ground that it signifies a much-needed liberation of the emotions. In reality, public life suffers when causes are justified on the ground of the quantity of personal anger they inspire rather than on the quality of the argument.

Unlike reflective thought, the political mobilisation of feelings has no objective points of reference. It is an unbounded and unrestrained sensibility that lacks the capacity to transform itself into a mutually comprehensible public resource. As Delsol noted, it 'releases its tide without thought' and though it 'often expresses the irruption of fundamental human aspirations', it 'remains deprived of judgement, it rambles aimlessly'.[19] The Italian sociologist Alberto Melucci claims that one of the distinct features of contemporary social movements is that people's participation within movements is no longer a means to an end, but an end in itself. He remarks that, 'participation in collective action is seen to have no value for the individual unless it provides a direct response to personal needs'.[20]

Once personal motivations and problems came to be regarded as the stuff of political activism, people's feelings and emotions could be seen as resources on which activists could draw. In its 1970 manifesto, the feminist San Francisco Redstockings Collective argued, 'Our politics begin with our feelings'. Supporters of a personalised and feelings-oriented movement frequently denounced what they perceived as the rigid separation of the emotional and the rational. The prevailing influence of lifestyle and therapeutic sensibilities played an important role in the crystallisation of the slogan of the personal is political.

The trends discussed prior were given greater definition by a conscious attempt to portray the cultural authority of privacy as an impediment to women's liberation from the regime of male oppression. Carol Hanisch's 1969 essay 'The Personal is Political' helped to popularise this sensibility.[21] The slogan encouraged many feminists to talk about their personal predicament, which they hitherto experienced silently within their private life. Others decried the maintenance of a boundary that associated the public with masculine values, and where men got to decide what was in the public good. They claimed that 'women, bodies, sex, emotions and intimate relationships' were unfairly separated from the political world.[22] Some argued that most intimate relations were actually relations of power, that subjugated women to a life of oppression. Marriage and conventional family life were denounced on the ground that they were a 'prison that sucked all personal freedom and personality away from the women who entered into it'.[23] These criticisms made some valid points about the artificiality of the distinction between the domestic and the public realms. Unfortunately, the problems raised about this distinction extended to calling into question the concepts of the public and the private.

The proliferation of consciousness-raising groups, in which women were encouraged to disclose their most personal and intimate issues, indicated that the private sphere was becoming regarded as a legitimate site for political action. People who were drawn towards the politicisation of the person frequently adopted an outlook that asserted that society's problems could be overcome through changing personal behaviour. Although initially, the politicisation of the personal possessed the relatively limited ambition of giving voice to those cut off from other people facing similar, private predicaments, it soon acquired a momentum that sought the collapse of any significant distinction between the personal and the political realms. Love, sexual intimacy, the ties that bound a family together, and childrearing became targets deemed suitable for politicisation.

Though feminist commentators were the most coherent exponents of the slogan 'the personal is political', its ideals were echoed by a wider section of society caught up in the 'culture of narcissism'. Lasch noted that 'if the sixties were the Age of Aquarius, the age of social commitment and cultural revolution, the seventies soon gained a reputation for self-absorption and political retreat'. The cumulative outcome of this development was **to alter the very meaning of the self**. The previous ideals of the self emphasised the active side of the individual through the exercise of self-control, self-help and above all self-determination. In the sixties, this active orientation was displaced by a passive version of the self – one whose flourishing depended on the validation of others.

There was a noticeable shift from the inner-self and the cultivation of self-understanding to a preoccupation with how the self was perceived by others. The contemporary emphasis on *self-esteem*, which relies on validation from others, indicates an important shift from the private self to one that was publicly oriented and affirmed.

The more that the self became detached from the private sphere and politicised, the more it assumed a public form of identity. The growing influence of identity over public life has subsequently transformed the conduct of politics. As one American commentator explained, 'identity politics, based on sex, sexuality, and, mostly, race and ethnicity, suggests that politics should work not so much to give people things, such as education and jobs, as to give them recognition'.[24]

The politicisation of the person led to the transformation of identity into a political resource. Today, when identity politics has assumed a culturally commanding influence in the Western world, it is useful to recall that its ascendancy is relatively recent. Though concern with the nature of selfhood is a recurrent theme in history, it is only since the late 1960s that it came to be framed through the prism of identity. As Marie Moran explains, in her important study of this topic; identity 'never "mattered" prior to the 1960s because it did not in fact *exist* or operate as a shared political and cultural idea *until* the 1960s'. She continues:

> Until the 1950s, or even the 1960s and 1970s, there was no discussion of sexual identity, ethnic identity, political identity, national identity, corporate identity, brand identity, identity crisis, or 'losing' or 'finding' one's identity.[25]

Once people's intimate lives became subject to political calculations, identity itself could become an issue. In this instance, the unravelling of the boundary between the two spheres of life meant that it became difficult to separate the views held by an individual from their identity as a person. By the turn of the 21st century, advocates of identity politics would come to regard criticisms of their opinions as a direct attack on their persona. Back in the late 1990s, Elshtain explained this development in the following terms:

> Intimate life is pervaded by politics; private life becomes a recommendation or authentication of one's political stance. It follows further that the ante gets upped in political contestation because to argue against a position is to challenge someone's "private" or personal identity.[26]

When one's identity becomes meshed with one's political views, there is little scope for argument about contrasting opinions. Those who question an individual's viewpoint can be perceived as a threat to their very sense of self. In more extreme cases, those who are seriously invested in their political identity can and do experience criticism as a threat to their psychic existence. Some groups have adopted the tactic of attempting to gain sympathy by drawing attention to the life-threatening harm caused by those who question their identity. The use of the term 'deadnaming' by promoters of trans culture is exemplary in this respect. Deadnaming occurs when a person, intentionally or by mistake, calls someone who is transgender by the name they used before they transitioned. It is claimed that deadnaming effectively invalidates the identity of an individual and thereby causes significant psychological harm.[27]

Identity politics personalises public engagement to the point that differences of views become difficult to express 'out loud'. Individuals who begin their statement at a public meeting with the words 'speaking as a woman' or 'from my perspective as a gay man' subliminally warn the audience that any challenge to their point of view will be viewed as an attack on their identity as a woman or a gay man. Such criticism is more likely to be met with an outburst of indignation than with a counter argument. When US Congress Speaker of the House Nancy Pelosi criticised four young Congresswomen, she was attacked by one of them, Alexandria Ocasio-Cortes, for singling out 'newly elected women of color'.[28] Ocasio-Cortes could have drawn attention to her radical politics as the focus of political conflict, but instead chose to highlight her identity to legitimate her stance.

In its more radical forms, identity politics erases entirely the line separating a person and an opinion. Someone who criticises a view put forward by a woman can expect to be denounced for their 'toxic masculinity' or 'male attitude'. People who question the practice of the gender reassignment for children are accused of transphobia. Question someone who complains that their anger is not recognised or validated, and you may be accused of possessing white attitudes. Transgender activists frequently use their identity as a political weapon, accusing those who question their views as propagators of hate.[29] In all these situations, the autonomy of the political sphere becomes a casualty of the blurred boundary between private and public.

Politicised identities possess an inherently insecure orientation towards the world. They are easily offended and invariably outraged by even a hint of disagreement. Differences of opinion are not simply perceived as personal slights but also as an attack on the group identity to which an individual belongs. In this way, the fate of an individual's political identity becomes inextricably linked with the status accorded to the wider group to which they belong. Consequently, individuals associate the realisation of their identity with the affirmation that wider society accords to their group's grievances. That is why, in recent decades, there has been a veritable explosion of identity-led group grievances.

Such grievances often constitute a politicised response to what in the past would have been seen as an act of personal miscommunication, such as an unintended insensitive remark. Take the case of Rebka Bayou, a university student, who complained that in Australia 'discussions around race' stop 'at Islamophobia'. Bayou, who is an Australian-Ethiopian, wanted the insensitive remarks directed at Africans to be treated as comparable to Islamophobia. She noted 'as an Aussie-born Ethiopian, the first kind of micro-aggression I ever came across was the ignorance people have about my cultural background'.[30] Her casual transformation of people's lack of knowledge about Ethiopia into the cultural crime of microaggression indicates that every miscommunication can be recast as a slight to an individual's identity.

The demand that the failure to recognise or understand a different culture should be treated as a serious offence highlights the insecure and unrestrained passions unleashed by the politicisation of identity. A preoccupation with culturally insensitive gestures and remarks often appears to have an obsessive character. Someone in the UK or the US who asks a colleague 'where are you from?' may be denounced for their 'unwitting racism'. According to the movement challenging what they describe as 'everyday racism', such a question may convey the sentiment that 'you do not belong here'.[31]

The heightened sense of personal insecurity, which translates the problems of daily life into a psychological language of harm, is most systematically captured by the recently invented concept of *microaggression*. The term is associated with the publications of counselling psychologist Derald Wing Sue. Sue defines microaggression as 'the brief and commonplace daily verbal, behavioral, and environmental indignities, whether intentional or unintentional, that communicate hostile, derogatory, or negative racial, gender, and sexual orientation, and religious slights and insults to the target person or group'. What's important about this definition is that these indignities need not be the outcome of intentional behaviour: indeed, Sue argues that 'perpetrators of micro-aggressions are often unaware' of the indignities that they inflict on others.[32]

The blurring of the boundary between the personal and the political was a precondition for the invention of the idea of microaggression. The politicisation of the personal set in motion a process whereby the conventional boundaries framing an individual's relation with society lost much of their significance. The distinction between voicing matters of personal subjectivity and rule-based objective pronouncements became less clear. At the same time, society finds it increasingly difficult to differentiate between the articulation of personal feeling and a public view. With the codification of the idea of microaggression, the difference between intentional and unwitting behaviour lost its force. People are not indicted for what they have done, nor for what they said or even what they think they think. They are condemned for sentiments that lie deep in the preconscious thoughts. In this way, the important distinction between the conscious and the unconscious loses its significance. The all-important boundary between intentional and unintentional outcomes ceases to possess any moral significance.

Holding people to account for their unconscious thoughts undermines the status of moral responsibility. An enlightened society recognises that it is difficult, if not impossible, to hold people responsible for the unintended consequences of their actions and words. Intentionality plays an important role in how a civilised society makes judgement about human behaviour. Since the emergence of the liberal ideal of tolerance in the 17th century, enlightened philosophers such as Spinoza and Locke argued that it was wrong to attempt to regulate people's inner thoughts and beliefs. Both made a distinction between belief/thought and action, and this contrast served as a point of departure for the elaboration of the two distinct spheres of private and public.[33] If people are held to account for their unconscious thoughts rather than their conscious actions, the idea of moral responsibility becomes emptied of meaning.

Worse still, the project of drilling into people's inner lives threatens people's capacity to live in accordance with the dictates of their conscience. In the 16th century, Martin Luther's affirmation of people's conscience and inner life undoubtedly played a critical role in freeing the individual from external constraint. And policing people in accordance with what they did and not what they thought is one of the characteristics that distinguishes a free democratic society from a totalitarian one. The casual manner with which advocates of microaggression direct their animosity towards the domain of the unconscious indicates that even the boundary that protects people's inner life has become the target of the impulse of limitlessness.

It's all about me

The contemporary focus on the personal lends public life a subjective and arbitrary character. It is as if personal feelings have become their own cause. In public exchanges, feelings often appear to enjoy greater status than thought. When individuals assert that they feel offended or uncomfortable, they are able to rely on the priority that contemporary culture attaches to feelings in order to close down discussion. On university campuses, students who assert that they feel uncomfortable with being exposed to certain views and images by their lecturers are often assured by college authorities that their feelings will be respected.

The slogan the 'personal is political' has given way to the infantilised rhetoric of 'it's all about me'. The words 'I' and 'me' have become a central feature of the vocabulary of narcissistic protests that characterise the current era. References to the first-person singular in the context of social protest are a relatively new development. But since the slogan of 'Not in My Name', widely used during protests against the 2003 Iraq war, they have become increasingly common. Pictures of individuals holding up a poster stating 'Stop Policing My Body' or 'I regret My Abortion' serve as reminders that politics has become very personal. Protestors chanting 'Not in My Name' or flaunting their #Metoo memes are making a statement about themselves. There is something disturbingly immature about individual protestors signalling their virtue through posting selfies with a placard stating, 'I am angry and I demand respect'.

As protest and individual needs intermesh, feelings and emotions cease to be personal matters. Emotions are mobilised to make a statement of outrage. Criticism and sharply crafted arguments are countered with the statement, 'I am offended'. Unlike the statement 'I disagree', there is no comeback on the assertion 'I am offended'. Disagreement invites an argument, the statement 'I am offended' closes down conversation and debate. This performance of outrage is a central feature of the moral crusade against microaggressions. There are microaggression websites where 'victims' air their grievances, often through holding signs bearing a message of defiance. In 2014, students from Oxford University copied the 'I, Too, Am Harvard' campaign, which highlighted the slights and insults suffered by black students. On the 'I, Too, Am Oxford' website, students from minority ethnic groups are photographed holding small whiteboards – one reads, 'Wow your English is great! Thanks – I was born in London'.

The current sensibility of 'It's all about me' was anticipated in the 1970s by Lasch when he defined the emergent 'culture of narcissism' as 'a disposition to see the world as a mirror, more particularly as a projection of one's own fears and desires'.[34] That is why advocates of identity politics express so much concern about the supposed threats to their persona.

The blurring of boundaries has led to the fusion of the psychological and political, to the point that disappointment with the results of an election are diagnosed as symptoms of mental health problems. In recent times, the term 'political depression' has been invented to describe the reaction of American middle-class people to Donald Trump's election as President of the United States. According to one report, in the San Francisco Bay area, 'election depression' was followed by 'political depression': a mood disorder characterised by 'several psychologists' as being 'commonly marked by nightmares, insomnia, digestive problems, and headaches, with anxiety, jitteriness, chest tightness, and a hallucinatory sense of slow-motion doom'. The report added:

> Sufferers may describe feeling demoralized and powerless, and even a sense of unreality. People have been missing work and school. They have seen relationships impaired and a decline in daily functioning (these are particular red flags for therapists). One woman even described an inability to put her children to sleep on time due to difficulty tearing herself away from the news.[35]

One clinical psychologist suggested that political depression could be a clinical disorder that meets the American Psychiatric Association's criteria for 'depressive disorder'. According to clinical psychologist Robert Lusson, symptoms of political depression 'include a depressed or irritable mood most days for most of the day along with thoughts and feelings of sadness, emptiness or hopelessness', which 'cause significant distress or impairment in social, occupational or other important areas of functioning'.[36] Similar responses have also been reported in the UK following the 2016 Brexit vote, where 'for Britain's pro-EU middle classes, Brexit is akin to a psychological trauma which has left many unable to behave rationally'. Philip Corr, professor of psychology and behavioural economics at the University of London, and clinical psychologist Dr Simon Stuart stated that these responses were what 'psychologists would expect from those suffering from chronic anxiety caused by loss of control and insecurity'.[37]

In October 2019, the *British Medical Journal* reported that anxiety about Brexit may have triggered a patient's psychotic episode. The author of the report, 'Acute transient psychotic disorder precipitated by Brexit vote', claims that 'political events can be a source of significant psychological stress'.[38] According to this report, the mental health of a 40-year-old man deteriorated rapidly following the announcement of the result of Brexit. When disappointment with the outcome of a political contest mutates into a psychological condition, it is evident that politics has become truly personal.

The politics of behaviour

The slogan 'the personal is political' does not merely motivate the outlook of student radicals or movements devoted to the promotion of an identity. With the erosion of the line separating the public and the private spheres, governments and state and civic institutions have become increasingly drawn towards involving themselves in affairs that were once considered citizens' private matters. Policymaking is confined less and less to the issues that used to monopolise the attention of the state – defence, security, public spending – and increasingly drawn towards the management and regulation of people's personal affairs and behaviour. The emergence and institutionalisation of the *politics of behaviour* exists in a symbiotic relationship with the personalisation of politics.

Just as individual emotions have gained an unprecedented significance in public life, so policymakers have become increasingly interested in influencing the private attitudes and behaviour of individuals. That personal issues such as loneliness, happiness, wellbeing, sexual satisfaction, self-esteem, and parental values have become the target of government policy illustrates the extent to which officialdom has become intertwined with the management of private affairs. For example, in early 2018, the British Government decided to devote its attention to dealing with what it characterised as an epidemic of loneliness by appointing Tracey Crouch as the world's first Minister of Loneliness. The official 'loneliness strategy'[39] promised to link up lonely and isolated people with support groups and welfare organisations. The paper outlining this strategy stated that the government would be 'incorporating loneliness into ongoing policy decisions with a view to a loneliness "policy test" being included in departments' plans', and approvingly cited a comment made by one of its advisors:

> This is a serious strategy that's not only going to help people feel more connected in their everyday lives but is also inspiring other Governments

and communities around the world to see loneliness for what it is: a heart-breaking emotion and a major public health issue.[40]

Loneliness may well be a heartbreaking emotion but since when has people's existential pain become the business of government? And if people's emotional life becomes reframed as a public health issue, what important matter is left for private decision-making?

So-called happiness experts insist that public policy should shift its emphasis from economics and wealth creation towards a strategy that enhances the happiness of the population. *The World Happiness Report* seeks to measure the extent to which people perceive themselves to be happy.[41] Advocates promoting this approach assume that influencing and shaping the psychological state of citizens is a legitimate concern of public policy. Like officialdom's objective of tackling loneliness, policies that attempt to increase the state of individual happiness are mental health interventions targeting the citizens' internal lives. Promoters of the politics of happiness claim that 'governments could have more success in improving people's lives if they prioritised improving mental health over traditional top goals such as boosting economic growth'.[42] This point was echoed by former Prime Minister David Cameron when he stated that 'we should be thinking not what is good for putting money in people's pockets but what is good for putting joy in people's hearts'.[43] For Cameron, happiness was nothing less than a central goal of government.[44]

In the UK, the Office for National Statistics regularly reports on the state of people's happiness,[45] and the United Nations publishes an annual happiness survey.[46] Policymakers claim that 'pessimism' contributes to poor educational and job performance, depression, suicide, drug abuse, and a host of other maladies. This sentiment is underpinned by a fashionable dogma that regards mental illness as one of the main causes of social problems. Not surprisingly, many of the leading advocates of the instrumentalisation of happiness are associated with the fields of positive psychology and behavioural economics.

Policies directed at governing people's emotions are not simply about making people feel good about themselves. The policy of instrumentalising happiness implicitly conveys a narrative about how people should behave, encouraging them to adopt attitudes that conform to specific public norms and ideals. Such policies depersonalise feelings and reframe them as emotionally correct public attitudes. Consequently, the instrumentalisation of happiness leads deftly to fashioning this emotion as a political weapon. At a 2016 conference organised by the London School of Economics, the OECD and the Paris School of Economics, Gus O'Donnell, the former UK head of civil service, argued that embedding happiness in public policy would reduce the electoral appeal of populism. O'Donnell stated that both the victory for Brexit in Britain's EU referendum and Donald Trump's success in the US Presidential elections could be 'explained by an analysis of people's wellbeing': the implication being that if people had felt happier they would have voted to stay in the EU and elected Hillary Clinton as President.[47]

Loneliness has also been weaponised politically. 'Loneliness is a political issue – or, at least, it should be', argues one American psychotherapist in *Psychology Today*. The article ends with the conclusion that 'progressives should make alleviating loneliness an important and explicit part of everything they say and every program they propose'.[48]

Freud may have been a little cynical when he suggested that his objective was to 'convert neurotic misery into ordinary unhappiness' – but he understood that true happiness is an ideal that we pursue but rarely achieve. Nor is that a problem. A good life is not always a happy one. People are often justified in being unhappy about their circumstances and surroundings, and discontent with one's lot has historically driven people to confront and overcome the challenges they faced. That is why the Controller in Huxley's *Brave New World* wanted to reduce discontent by feeding the population a diet of 'feelies' and 'scent organs'.

Historically, problems of the emotion were regarded as private matters and not an area with which governments and policy makers should concern themselves. Governments always sought to influence public behaviour, but they tended to rely on local custom, moral norms, and the informal pressures of community life to do so. Democratic societies used to operate according to the unwritten rule that government should not intrude into the domain of people's private lives. This point was at least rhetorically acknowledged in the UK government's 1998 consultation document, *Supporting Families*, which warned that, 'Governments have to be very careful in devising policies that affect our most intimate relationships'.[49]

Yet despite striking this note of caution, the document brazenly proposed intervention into intimate aspects of family life. It outlined plans for a government programme to help individuals prepare for marriage; proposed launching projects aimed at saving marriages; and put forward policies designed to help parents cope with the arrival of a baby. On a more ominous note, the document suggested imposing parenting orders on mothers and fathers deemed to have failed to control their children. Former home secretary Jack Straw stated that the culture of parenting needed to be changed so that 'seeking advice and help' was 'seen not as failure but [as] the actions of concerned and responsible parents'. One of his objectives was to turn parenting into a legitimate sphere for government intervention.[50] And indeed, since the publication of this document, the UK government has adopted an ever-expanding interventionist role in family life.

The loss of restraint when it comes to intervening in people's private lives is one of the most significant developments in public policy over the past two decades. Governments that have become uncertain of their values and purpose have refocused their energies on the management of individual behaviour and the regulation of informal relationships. Increasingly, they have adopted the role of protecting people from themselves and from other members of the public.

Scandinavian societies have been in the forefront of this dynamic. In 1979, Sweden became the first country to criminalise parents who used physical punishment to discipline their children. Since that time, Swedish government has adopted an increasingly interventionist approach towards directing parents how their children ought to be socialised. Thus, in many Swedish nurseries, teachers are encouraged to avoid referring to children's gender, and preschools are organised around the explicit promotion of gender neutrality.

One of the most extreme examples of this kind of government intervention in family life occurred in Scotland in 2018, when school teachers were directed to allow children to change their gender without informing parents. Guidelines endorsed by the Scottish government stated that children as young as three 'should be supported to explore and express their identity'. These guidelines explicitly presume that it is the teacher, not the parent, who should possess the authority to provide the conditions that allow children to transition to another gender. The document, *Supporting Transgender Young People: Guidance for Schools in Scotland*, insists that children must give permission for teachers to alert parents to their decision. These guidelines clearly regard parents as a problem as they might prevent their child from transitioning; hence, they should be kept out of the picture. The Scottish government has also made it clear that if parents oppose their child changing their sex, teachers and school staff should report them to the local authorities.

The Scottish government appears to take the view that not only is the personal political, but that policies should be as personal as possible. In 2014, its *Children and Young People (Scotland) Act* provided provision for a so-called Named Person. The 'Named Person' is a state-assigned professional 'guardian' tasked with overseeing the interests of every child from birth. Protecting children from the effects of bad or abusive parenting is the principal justification for the state assuming a shared responsibility for childrearing.[51] Thankfully this extreme example of state intrusion into the private sphere proved to be too controversial and The Scottish Government was forced to scrap it in 2019.

Of course, governments have always sought to influence public attitudes. But influencing attitudes over issues such as war or capital punishment is very different to today's project of manipulating how individuals behave within the confines of their own homes. Today's interventionism into private life is also very different to previous approaches to social policy. Those who support the colonisation of the private sphere sometimes claim that they are merely following in a progressive tradition that has covered everything from the abolition of child labour to the provision of free milk in schools, and that their policies are designed to anticipate and offset problems that might compromise public health. However, these defenders of the enabling state confuse public health policies that seek to create the conditions for healthy living with public health policies that attempt to manage individual behaviour and manipulate people's emotions.

For example, today's campaigns exhorting people to adopt 'healthier lifestyles' are less about improving our health than indicating how we ought to live. They are motivated very much by what politicians themselves refer to as the 'politics of behaviour': described by former Labour government minister Tessa Jowell as 'one of the most fascinating challenges facing the government'.[52] As

Arnar Arnason notes, 'it is telling that technologies similar to those employed by counselling have now become part and parcel of the way in which the current British government governs its people'. Arnason believes that the government's recent obsession with focus groups and other instruments designed to gauge public opinion represents a quest to 'gain unfettered access to people's subjectivity'.[53]

The politics of behaviour may well provide a provisional solution for a political establishment confused about its role and direction by substituting therapeutic intervention for political direction. Whereas today's cultural elite lacks the confidence to tell people what to believe, it feels quite comfortable instructing them how to feel. As public life becomes emptied of its content, private and personal preoccupations are projected into the public sphere. Consequently, passions that were once stirred by ideological differences are far more likely to be engaged by individual misbehaviour, private troubles, and personality conflicts. In this climate, the practice of individual therapy is seen as indistinguishable from the measures that are required for the 'healing' of society. As one Downing Street policy analyst noted, government plays the role of a therapist exhorting the patient to 'own his anger'.[54]

Politics becomes really personal when it adopts the management of behaviour as a legitimate target of policymaking. The adoption of such techniques was explicitly pursued by David Cameron during his tenure as Prime Minister of the UK. Cameron helped set up an outfit called the *Behavioural Insight Team* in 2010, which was charged with the task of developing policies that could shape people's thoughts, choices, and actions. This team, otherwise known as the 'Nudge Unit', operated on the assumption that attempting politically to convince the electorate of government policies is pointless; subliminal psychological techniques and manipulation were considered more effective than democratic debate and argument. Behavioural management techniques are based on the ideas of American behavioural economist Richard Thaler, who believes that since people often fail to act rationally and in their own interests, they can only benefit from being nudged in the 'right' direction by governments and experts – and taking measures to thwart people from acting in other ways.

The casual manner in which the advocates of nudge dismiss people's right to behave in accordance with their intuition and instincts exposes their soft authoritarian ambitions. When Britain's former Deputy Prime Minister Nick Clegg casually remarked that his government's nudge unit 'could change the way citizens think', he spoke a language usually associated with a totalitarian propaganda agency. Since when has it been a democratic government's brief to wage an ideological crusade to alter its citizens' thoughts? According to Clegg's vision, governing is not so much about realising people's aspirations as it is about changing those aspirations so that they correspond to the worldview of the government.

Since its inception, the Nudge Unit has acquired significant global influence. Its expertise is widely used by international organisations such as the World Bank. It has offices in the US, Canada, Australia, New Zealand, and Singapore and provides advice to governments throughout the world.[55] It appears that the personalisation of politics has acquired global interest.

But nudge is not some benign technique. It assumes for the state the role of a therapist and relegates the public to the status of a patient. Such policies promote the colonisation of private life, as personal conduct becomes the target of officially endorsed attempts to manipulate citizens' emotions and behaviour.

Remoulding the way people think and act requires a significant erosion of their right to assent to, or reject, policies, presupposing the elimination of a two-way discussion between citizens and their rulers. This was indeed the objective outlined in the British Cabinet Office paper *Mindspace: Influencing Behaviour through Public Policy*: an approach that relied on citizens 'not fully' realising 'that their behaviour is being changed – or at least how it is being changed'.[56]

The advocates of nudge choose to describe their approach as 'libertarian paternalism'. Of course, paternalistic behaviour is entirely appropriate in relation to young children. Most parents understand that there is little point in arguing with a toddler; it is far better simply to use childrearing techniques that will encourage children to act in accordance with their parents' desires. Parents are responsible for their children and therefore expected to have some authority and control over their behaviour. Infants lack experience and, more important, they lack the capacity for autonomy and moral independence. But things are fundamentally different when it comes to the relationship between government and adults. When similar techniques are used in relation to adults, we see the corrosion, and ultimately the corruption, of public life. The erosion of the boundary between adult and child in matters of public life ultimately constitutes the moral disenfranchisement of the citizen. Individuals are no longer seen as morally autonomous citizens, but as biologically mature children who need to be tricked into doing what is in their best interest.

Conclusion

There are many ways of conceptualising the relation between the public and the private spheres. For the Greeks and Romans, it was the public sphere that really mattered; they regarded the private as a clearly inferior domain that was subject to the forces of necessity. In the 20th century, the private sphere came into its own, and many regarded it as a refuge in an increasingly depersonalised world. But however these two spheres were conceptualised, it was recognised that they were interrelated but also distinct. Historical experience showed that the boundary dividing the two spheres can be contested and can alter; but if the boundary itself becomes blurred, the quality of both public and private life will suffer.

The main theme of this chapter was the way in which the politicisation of the person and the politics of behaviour impacts on social life. Superficially, it seems that everything has become political. But once politics becomes unbounded from its legitimate home in the public sphere and can be arbitrarily attached to just about anything, its very essence is altered. Democracy, which for centuries had a meaning that centred on the idea of government by the people, has become detached from popular sovereignty. Now, the term is often used as a free-floating signifier of a positive attribute. The term 'democratisation' is now applied to institutions and relations that have nothing to do with how society is governed. People advocate the democratisation of the family, the democratisation of medicine, and the democratisation of science. A quick Google search will find references to the democratisation of data, knowledge, information, internet, education, technology, luxury, history, culture, AI, and finance – and many, many others.

Once politics becomes deprived of its inner content, democracy loses its relationship to any fixed points and becomes a caricature of itself. That is why the Head of Politics at Cambridge University could call for children as young as six to be given the vote. Professor David Runciman advocated this proposal on the ground that young people were 'massively outnumbered' by the elderly and that this created a democratic crisis that had to be put right.[57] The infantilisation of politics outlined here is but one manifestation of the disintegration of the conceptual boundary between adults and children. As we shall see in the next chapter, confusion about what's private and what's public coincides with the unravelling of the line separating childhood from adulthood.

Notes

1 Kristin Blinne 'The Hair Down There: Untangling Pubic Hair Politics'. https://www. academia.edu/12937413/The_Hair_Down_There_Untangling_Pubic_Hair_Politics.
2 www.thelancet.com/journals/lancet/article/PIIS0140-6736(95)90436-0/fulltext.
3 Jessica Hamzelou, 'If you hate bad body odour, you're more likely to support Trump', New Scientist, 28 February 2018. https://www.newscientist.com/article/2162285-if-you-hate-bad-body-odour-youre-more-likely-to-support-trump/.
4 Sennett (2017).
5 Sennett (2017) p. 5.
6 See Martino, E. (2018) '"You're fake news" the unfortunate reality of the ad hominem', Quillete, 27 February, https://quillette.com/2018/02/27/youre-fake-news-unfortunate-reality-ad-hominem/.
7 Bauman (2013) p. 67.
8 John Carlin (2017) 'No moles, no growths, but Clinton has blemishes', The Independent, 16 November, https://www.independent.co.uk/news/no-moles-no-growths-but-clinton-has-his-blemishes-1294429.html.
9 Gormley, K. (2011) The Death of American Virtue: Clinton vs. Starr, Broadway Books: New York. Fascination with this tawdry affair continues to be of public interest. See www.vox.com/2016/10/9/13221670/paula-jones-kathleen-willey-bill-clinton-sexual-harassment-accusations.
10 Kaminer, W. (2002) 'Jesus and the politicians', Free InquiryMagazine, vol. 20, no. 2, 29 June.
11 Elshtain (1993) p. 4.
12 Cited in Lasch (1979) p. 14.
13 See www.gettyimages.ae/detail/news-photo/people-hold-a-placard-saying-im-really-quite-angry-about-news-photo/1052624724.
14 Ben Smee (2019) 'Extinction Rebellion: hitting a nerve at Australia's climate flashpoint', The Guardian, 10 August, https://www.theguardian.com/environment/2019/aug/11/extinction-rebellion-hitting-a-nerve-at-australias-climate-flashpoint.

15 See Traister (2018), Chemaly (2018), and Cooper (2018).

16 Rodriguez and Boahene (2012) p. 450.

17 Thompson (2017) p. 457.

18 Tom Parfitt (2019) 'Extinction Rebellion activists blockade BBC offices as police chief attacks "irresponsible" protests', *The Independent*, 11 October, https://www.indepen dent.co.uk/news/uk/home-news/extinction-rebellion-protests-bbc-news-climate-change-london-arrests-police-a9151891.html.

19 Delsol (2003a).

20 Melucci (1989) p. 49.

21 See Carol Hanisch (1969) 'The Personal Is Political'. http://www.carolhanisch.org/CHwritings/PIP.html.

22 Holmes (2000) pp. 305–306.

23 Saxonhouse (2015) p. 565.

24 Purdy (1999) p. 64.

25 Moran (2018), www.historicalmaterialism.org/articles/identity-and-identity-politics.

26 Elshtain (1993) p. 171.

27 See www.huffpost.com/entry/deadnaming-a-trans-person-is-violenceso-why-does_b_58cc58cce4b0e0d348b3434b.

28 Natalie Andrews (2019) 'Racial Issues Rise to Surface in Dispute Between Pelosi, House Freshman', *The Wall Street Journal*, 11 July, https://www.wsj.com/articles/racial-issues-rise-to-surface-in-dispute-between-pelosi-house-freshmen-11562878423.

29 Jo Bartosch (2019) 'Twitter's War On Outspoken Women', *Spiked*; 21 March, https://www.spiked-online.com/2019/03/21/twitters-war-on-outspoken-women/.

30 Rebka Bayou (2016) 'Stereotyping Africans is everywhere, but Australians are particularly clueless', *The Guardian*, https://www.theguardian.com/commentisfree/2016/mar/08/stereotyping-of-africans-is-everywhere-but-australians-are-particularly-clueless.

31 See my discussion of this point in Furedi (2017) pp. 120–121.

32 Sue, Bucceri, Lin, Nadal, and Torino (2007) p. 271.

33 See Furedi (2011) pp. 38–39.

34 Lasch (1985) p. 33.

35 Zahara, M. and Miller, H. (2017) 'Politics-related depression: Is it real?', 3 March, www.nationalreview.com/2017/03/political-depression-doctors-explain/.

36 See Lusson, R. (2017) 'Political depression', *Huffpost*, 13 January, www.huffpost.com/entry/political-depression_b_5879574ae4b077a19d180dbe.

37 'Britain's middle class anxiety disorder', www.politico.eu/article/brexit-anxiety-disorder-britain-middle-class/.

38 See Muhammed Zia Ul Haq Katshu (2019) 'Acute transient psychotic disorder precipitated by Brexit vote', *BMJ Case Reports*, vol. 12, issue 10. https://casereports.bmj.com/content/12/10/e232363.

39 See www.gov.uk/government/news/pm-launches-governments-first-loneliness-strategy.

40 Cited in www.gov.uk/government/news/pm-launches-governments-first-loneliness-strategy.

41 *World Happiness Report 2019*, https://worldhappiness.report/ed/2019/#read.

42 Tamsin Rutter (2016) 'New Research Boosts Crusade To Embed Happiness In Public Policy', *Global Government Forum*, 15 December, https://www.globalgovernmentforum.com/new-research-boosts-crusade-to-embed-happiness-in-public-policy/.

43 Cited in Mark Easton (2006) 'The Politics of happiness', *BBC Home*, 22 May, http://news.bbc.co.uk/2/hi/programmes/happiness_formula/4809828.stm.

44 Frank Furedi (2006) 'Politicians, economists, teachers. Why are they so desperate to make us happy?', *The Daily Telegraph*, 7 May, https://www.telegraph.co.uk/comment/personal-view/3624819/Politicians-economists-teachers-why-are-they-so-desperate-to-make-us-happy.html.

45 See Sam Rigby (2017) 'The UK's happiness levels have hit a high despite Brexit and terrorist attacks', *Quartz*, 7 November, https://qz.com/1122305/uk-happiness-ons-survey-population-has-highest-levels-of-well-being-since-2011/.

46 www.aol.co.uk/news/2019/03/20/ita-s-official-a-the-uk-is-getting-happier-un-report-claims/?guccounter=1&guce_referrer=aHR0cHM6Ly93d3cuZ29vZ2xlLmN vbS88&guce_referrer_sig=AQAAAI4Vwbb_FnIVBX7XK_HcpARyfz8hEyAqgabJb hYfcRgzgF08Oqcy5BGTlPv2VXCLLNAJUxBeYyA9F-1Gzh8v6BMQwWCydl hJnCor_0E4pYhWpQHi4rslc9hgj_-V54TFysqvWylfx60y7Pgs60ipVeXtC6BAYJen_-VGS-FvsGXa.

47 Tamsin Rutter (2016) 'New Research Boosts Crusade To Embed Happiness In Public Policy', *Global Government Forum*, 15 December, https://www.globalgovernmentforum. com/new-research-boosts-crusade-to-embed-happiness-in-public-policy/.

48 Michael Bader (2015) 'The Politics of Loneliness', *Psychology Today*, 23 December, https://www.psychologytoday.com/us/blog/what-is-he-thinking/201512/the-politics-loneliness.

49 Home Office, Supporting Families: A Consultation Document, p. 30, 1998, London.

50 'Draft speech for the Home Secretary: Launch of the lords and commons family and child protection group's report "family matters", 23 July 1998.

51 On the Named Person, see Waiton (2016).

52 See Jowell, T. (2004) 'Politics of behaviour', *The Observer*, 21 November.

53 Arnason (2000) p. 194.

54 Cited by Wintour, P. (2005) 'Voters act like teenagers says no 10 policy analyst', *The Guardian*, 22 December.

55 www.theguardian.com/politics/2018/nov/10/nudge-unit-pushed-way-private-sector-behavioural-insights-team.

56 See www.instituteforgovernment.org.uk/publications/mindspace.

57 Matthew Weaver (2016) 'Give six year olds the vote says Cambridge University academic', *The Guardian*, 6 December, https://www.theguardian.com/politics/2018/dec/06/give-six-year-olds-the-vote-says-cambridge-university-academic.

7

BORDERLINE IDENTITY CRISIS

The significance of boundaries for the development of identity is not confined to collective entities like the community or the nation. The development of individual identity is mediated through the boundaries that communities establish to mark the different stages of the life course. From birth onwards, children develop within the confines set by their parents and adult society. Their successful transition to adolescence and, later, young adulthood, requires clarity about the meaning of the psychological boundaries between the life stages. Blurring these boundaries gives rise to a condition often referred to as an 'identity crisis'.

The concept of identity crisis was pioneered by the psychiatrist Erik Erikson, writing in the 1950s. It has now become a widely used term and seen to afflict not just teenagers but also adults, right through to old age. Terms such as 'mid-life crisis' and even 'quarter-life crisis' speak to a condition of identity confusion. A dominant feature of 21st-century Western society is the unparalleled obsession with identity, revealed in the proliferation of so-called identity groups and the seriousness with which they protect, uphold, and flaunt their respective identities.

This chapter examines the relationship between the boundaryless spirit of our time, and the confusions it has created for the conduct of intergenerational relations. Just as boundaries are essential for the emergence of national identity, so they are indispensable for the development of the identity of a human being. Individuals' capacity to answer the question 'who am I?' depends on the clarity with which society communicates its expectations and ideals to children. Such ideals outline the moral boundaries within which human development occurs. As children understand the meaning of these boundaries, they become prepared to make the transition from one stage of their life to another. Ideally, in this way, children are able to form an identity of their selves that harmonises their needs with those of society. As Raymond Martin and John Barresi note in their study of the history of personal identity:

> Ego identity requires knowing who you are and how you fit into society. It requires forming for yourself an identity of self that satisfies both your own internal needs and those of society. The task is easier if the society already has a clear role that you are expected to fill and respects you for filling it, and you have good role models. It helps also if there is a clear boundary between childhood and adulthood supported by "rites of passage". Under such conditions, there is little reason for an adolescent to experience a "crisis" in making the transition from childhood to adulthood.[1]

In the absence of clear signposts, the boundary between childhood and adulthood becomes blurred, and everyone – adolescents and adults alike – becomes confused about their roles.

Typically, commentators who are hostile to national borders also underestimate or misunderstand the significance of the boundaries that are essential for the cultivation of individual identity. Agier writes that an 'obsession with borders' should be understood as an 'obsession with identity'.[2] He is right to highlight the connection between boundaries and identity – regrettably, however, he associates these obsessions only with a conservative 'identity-based resistance' to the current state of fluidity.[3] That is why he can draw the conclusion that the instability of borders is 'an immediate cause for rejoicing'.[4] Agier overlooks the fact that obsession with identity is far more prevalent amongst individuals who are self-consciously hostile to any form of conservatism, and that since the late 20th century, identity politics has more or less displaced the worldviews that previously defined left-wing politics.

One of the arguments frequently directed at national borders is that in a globalised and mobile world, people have embraced multiple identities and therefore attach far less significance to the place of their birth. The ideology of limitlessness in relation to borders is translated into the language of unbounded identities in relation to individual behaviour. Having dismissed borders as an artificial invention, the globalist imagination idealises an identity that is unconnected to all the customs and institutions of the past. Nikos Papastergiadis argues that a shift in a 'strict equation of identity and place' has created a situation of fluidity 'where no fixed identity or exclusive place of belonging is determined in advance'.[5] It may well be the case that identity formation has acquired an apparently free-floating and uncertain quality. But if it has, it is not because boundaries have become less significant than in previous times, but because Western cultures struggle to give meaning to them.

Sociologists write of a post-traditional world were the self is 'made' rather than passively inherited. The proliferation of new identities, and the ease with which some individuals change their identity, is undoubtedly an important feature of contemporary life. Greater choice and freedom to decide how one wants to live can greatly assist human flourishing. However, when the development of the self is not guided by its community's ideals and expectations, the formation of identity runs into serious trouble. Far from being an unambiguous blessing, the proliferation and multiplication of identities should be diagnosed as symptoms of confusion, brought on by a loss of solidarity and of human connections. As discussed later in this chapter, one of the most grievous outcomes of this is the difficulty that many young people have in making the transition to adulthood.

Regardless of the preference adopted towards the choosing of identity, the question of its relation to boundaries cannot be avoided. Without a sense of limits, identity becomes unstable, threatening to undermine an individual's sense of self. Boundaries and identities interweave with one another and exist in a mutually interactive relationship. The classification of identities, such as child, adolescent, or adult, rely on distinctions maintained through boundaries, reproduced through the process of socialisation, and institutionalised through the elaboration of distinct roles.

Since the 1950s, the institutions, conventions, and the traditions which helped both legitimate and enforce generational distinctions have been losing clarity and force. This development was first noted in the United States. In a 1954 study, the sociologists Hans Gerth and C. Wright Mills observed that Western societies did not have a 'generally understood and clearly demarcated "threshold" between childhood and adulthood'. One reason was that 'religious rites such as "confirmation" remain segmental, as they do not coincide with the transition from school years to employment and marriage'.[6] In the decades following the publication of this study, the absence of a clear demarcation between childhood and adulthood gradually became associated with identity confusion.

The psychoanalyst Martha Wolfenstein, in her influential 1951 essay 'The emergence of fun morality', observed an important shift in the expectations that American society had about adulthood. Wolfenstein claimed that whereas having fun was once a taboo in adult culture, it had now become obligatory. This new 'fun morality' challenged previous moral and psychological boundaries and signalled the idea that 'not having fun is not merely an occasion for regret but involved a loss of self-esteem'. One outcome of this development was that 'boundaries formerly maintained between play and work break down'.[7] The importation of play into the realm of adulthood provided evidence that the line dividing the generations was being redrawn.

The sociological classic *The Homeless Mind*, published in the early 1970s, observed that the modern identity had become 'peculiarly open', though it was still rooted in stable elements of socialisation. The authors concluded that the 'open ended' quality of 'modern identity engenders psychological strains and makes the individual peculiarly vulnerable to the shifting definitions of others'. They also believed that consequently 'modern man is afflicted with a permanent identity crisis, a condition conducive to considerable nervousness'.[8] It is worth noting that at this point in time, commentaries on identity tended to underline its problematic features – and its unbounded, unstable character was rarely celebrated for its fluidity.

Erik Erikson, who both innovated and popularised the idea of an identity crisis, drew attention to the growing tendency for the private matter of identity to become a public issue. As the boundary between people's inner and outer lives became blurred, so the question of individual identity appeared to acquire an explosive political dimension. In his discussion of the youth rebellion of the 1960s, Erikson noted that 'we are witnessing an exacerbated "identity-consciousness"':

> For whereas twenty years ago we gingerly suggested that some young people might be suffering from a more or less unconscious identity conflict, a certain type tells us in no uncertain terms, and with the dramatic outer display of what we once considered to be inner secrets, that yes, indeed, they have an identity conflict – and they wear it on their sleeves.[9]

Writing in 1968, Erikson pointed to the 'outer display' of what was previously perceived as an 'inner secret'. Today, however, the identity conflicts of the 1960s appear relatively restrained and benign; what Erikson perceived as the dramatic display of inner secrets has become commonplace and unremarkable. Why? Because society's estrangement from boundedness has created a world where people are continually expressing the concern that they lack a clear sense of identity.

The erosion of the boundary between children and adults

Clarity regarding the distinction between children and adults is of fundamental necessity for resolving the normal identity crisis faced by adolescents and for allowing them to make a successful transition to adulthood. Currently, a diminished sense of adult responsibility coexists with a profound sense of ambiguity about what it means to be an adult. Matters are complicated by the feeble sense of valuation for adulthood and the identities associated with it. A reluctance to assume the responsibilities associated with growing up has become a feature of 21st-century society. The phenomenon of infantilisation, identified by social commentators such as Christopher Lasch in the 1970s, has gained significant momentum during the subsequent decades.

The infantilisation of adulthood represents one of the most damaging outcomes of Western culture's inability to take symbolic boundaries seriously. As Erikson explained, identity formation requires that adults provide young people with a model of what it means to be a grown-up person. Adults with integrated identities provide a contrast to those who have not yet arrived at this point. In the absence of adults 'in possession of such integrity, young people in need of an identity can neither rebel nor obey';[10] they become disoriented by the disjointed signals that are communicated to them. Without the clear signposts provided by adult society, young people often find it difficult to make the transition to adulthood; indeed, the negativity that contemporary culture often projects onto maturity leads many young people to retrench and hold onto their adolescent identity into their late twenties and even early thirties.

Social scientists in more recent years have invented the term 'emerging adulthood', which allegedly lasts between ages 18 and 29, to capture this new preadult phase in people's lives.[11] Commentaries often present this as an inevitable consequence of a rapidly changing uncertain world. Yet it is better understood as a consequence of the gradual unravelling of the psychological and moral boundaries that helped solidify the conventional distinction between children and adults. In an insightful contribution to this discussion, the criminologist Keith Hayward argues that 'rather than anything as significant as a new life stage, what is actually happening is the erosion of established ones'.[12] To capture the dynamic of this development, Hayward has innovated the concept of *life stage dissolution*. The most significant manifestation of the dissolution of life stage is what Hayward depicts as a bidirectional process of 'adultification' and 'infantilisation'. The principal cultural feature of this bidirectional process is the attribution of moral equivalence between children and adults, and the cultivation of immaturity amongst grown-up people.

Western culture has demonstrated a relatively feeble capacity to prepare the young for the world of adulthood. Instead of acknowledging the scale of this problem, society has responded by acquiescing to it. The cultural significance of maturity has been devalued and disparaged. In the Anglo-American world, wisdom has ceased to be associated with adulthood; the child has become an object of veneration, their supposed perspicacity favourably contrasted with the outdated sentiments of the old. As adulthood became detached from moral authority, it can no longer provide a positive model to which young people can aspire. In such circumstances, the dynamic of intergenerational transaction, through which identities are forged, is undermined.

To understand the problem posed by 'life stage dissolution' and its contribution to the transition from adolescence to adulthood, it is useful to consider Erikson's contribution to our understanding of the working of an identity crisis. Although the term conveys the notion of a serious psychological condition, it originally alluded to a normal moment in the process of adolescent development. As Erikson explained back in the 1960s, identity crisis 'no longer connotes impending catastrophe'; it is 'now being accepted as designating a necessary turning point, a crucial moment, when development must move one way or another, marshalling resources of growth, recovery, and further differentiation'.[13] For Erikson, the problem was not so much with the 'normative "identity crisis"' of adolescence but the 'undue prolongation' of overcoming it or 'regression' to a previous phase of development.[14]

Erikson advanced a model of an eight-stage life cycle of psychosocial development, where each stage confronted the individual with different psychosocial challenges that had to be overcome in order to proceed. During the fifth stage of development, which coincides with adolescence, the individual is confronted by a crisis incurred by the tension between confusion and identity. In normal circumstances, the process of identity formation is for the most part unconscious – except when inner conditions and outer circumstances combine to aggravate a painful, or elated, 'identity consciousness'. Identity consciousness crystallises amongst individuals who remain unclear about who they are.

Although it is principally a psychological accomplishment, an adolescent's ability to successfully overcome an identity crisis is contingent on the cultural support provided by adult society. Erikson explained that though the developmental process through which people acquire their identity is '*at the core of an individual*', it is also '*in the core of his communal culture*'.[15] Erikson ceaselessly drew attention to the responsibility that the adult world bore for the successful development of young people's identity. He believed that for adolescents to 'let go of the safe and secure childhood', they needed to depend on the 'reliability of those he must let go of, and those who will 'RECEIVE HIM''.[16]

Developmental transition depends on well-established symbolic boundaries and on conventions and rituals that assist young people to understand the meaning and significance of the boundary they are about cross. Erikson claimed that:

> Ritual confirmations, initiations, and indoctrinations only enhance an indispensable process by which healthy societies stow traditional strengths on the new generations and thereby bind to themselves the strength of youth. Societies thus verify the new individual and are themselves historically verified.[17]

From this perspective, the development of individual identity depends on the support which the young individual receives from the 'collective sense of identity characterising the social groups significant to him: his class, his nation, his culture'.[18]

Adults play a central role in guiding young people to develop their identity and make the transition to a new stage in their life. But what happens when adults become estranged from this responsibility and lack the maturity required to offer guidance to young people? In the late 1960s, Erikson remarked on the adoption of infantilised forms of behaviour by sections of adult society, going so far as to suggest that parents often appear to their children as 'overgrown boys and girls'.[19] He pointedly remarked that 'we must not overlook what appears to be a certain abrogation of responsibility on the part of the older generation in providing those forceful ideals which must antecede identity formation in the next generation – if only so that youth can rebel against a well-defined set of older values'.[20]

Erikson's warning highlighted a trend that has acquired far greater prominence today. Since the late 1960s, the moral status of adulthood has steadily depreciated, leading to an erosion of parental authority and that of other adults. This results from a lack of clarity about where to draw the line between adulthood and childhood. The argument that children as young as six should have the right to vote – noted in the previous chapter – is but one illustration of the tendency to treat children as if they are adults. The adulation directed by adult society at Greta Thunberg, the 16-year-old face of the climate change 'school strikes' movement, is paradigmatic in this respect. The old adage of 'out of the mouths of babes' no doubt led to her nomination for the Nobel Peace Prize.[21]

There are many influences that contribute to the lack of clarity about where to draw the line between the generations. Probably the most corrosive is Western society's depreciation of adulthood in general, and adult authority in particular. The idealisation of the children involved in the 'school strikes' movement is justified on the ground that adults have failed to take responsibility for dealing with the problem of the environment. 'Adults are failing us on climate change, that's why I am striking', is the bold headline of a post on the Friends of the Earth website.[22]

Significant sections of the cultural elite support a reversal in roles that assigns children the authority to educate apparently irresponsible adults. As Thunberg explained in her lecture to the United Nations climate change summit in December 2018. 'Since our leaders are behaving like children, we will have to take the responsibility they should have taken long ago', she said. 'We have to understand what the older generation has dealt to us, what mess they have created that we have to clean up and live with'.[23] A similar message was communicated by the prominent British Green crusader Jonathan Porritt, when he informed children that 'your parents and grandparents have made a mess of looking after the Earth', adding: 'They may deny it, but they are stealing your future'.[24] Youngsters have been more than ready to respond to these invitations to mistrust their elders. Posters stating 'You'll Die of Old Age, We'll Die of Climate Change' or 'I Am Ditching School Because You Are Ditching Our Future' point the finger of blame at slothful adults who are supposedly responsible for the early deaths of their offspring. On an anti-Brexit demonstration in London, a placard screaming 'Adults Ruin Everything. Stop Brexit' captures this spirit of adult-blaming.[25]

The sociologist Jennie Bristow offers a compelling account of the 'Generation Wars' and the defensive response of the adult world to the insults hurled at it.[26] It has become fashionable for politicians to praise the guidance and insights of children – at least outwardly. Time and again, public figures lecture their audiences to 'listen to the youth'. Parenting experts and child professionals have deified the 'children's voice', and new forms of pedagogy call for the elimination of the distinction between teachers and pupil in favour of the boundary-diluting concept of a 'learner'. To minimise the distinction between pupil and teacher, some schools refer to the latter as 'lead learners'.

Challenges to the moral authority of adults invariably question the conventional boundary that separates the generations. If indeed adults lack the maturity and wisdom to deal with the problems of society, why should they be in a position to exercise authority over children? The loss of adult authority has important implications for the development of people's identity. Knowing what it means to be an adult, and acquiring the aspiration to become one, is essential for acquiring the confidence to enter the realm of maturity. The crossing of this boundary becomes far more difficult in the absence of adult leadership.

Infantilisation – the dissolution of generational boundaries

Lamentably, confusions about the meaning of adulthood have led many biologically mature individuals to cross the line back into childhood. The appeal of being 'forever young' exercises an important influence on people in their twenties and early thirties, who believe that it is mandatory to be 'cool'. Parents, teachers, and other adults involved with children have gone out of their way to attempt to become young people's friends rather than their guides and mentors. Some commentators welcome this development as evidence of intergenerational fluidity – but on closer inspection, fluidity turns into a form of regression back to a life stage where maturity and generational responsibility is not demanded.

Andrew Calcutt's book *Arrested Development* suggests that the reluctance to grow up is connected to the cultural devaluation of adulthood.[27] According to Calcutt, Western culture celebrates the Peter Pan-like aspiration to immaturity. The fun morality that Wolfenstein described in 1951 has acquired an unprecedented impact in the current era. When an essay titled 'The Death of Adulthood in American Culture' was published in *The New York Times* in 2014, most readers had little trouble grasping its message.[28] In today's popular culture, adulthood is rarely associated with positive qualities or virtues. A significant section of adult society now openly questions its responsibility for giving guidance and direction to the younger generations.

The abandonment of responsibility for children's socialisation is in some cases presented as an enlightened form of parenting. Some parents claim that it is wrong to impose their values on their youngsters, and that it is far better that they should decide them for themselves. In recent years, some mothers and fathers have opted for what is fashionably called 'gender-neutral parenting', giving their child a neutral name and dressing them ambiguously so that no one will presume to know the youngster's gender. The premise of this reckless form of childrearing is that it should be up to a child to decide how she or he wants to be identified later in life. In a different era, imposing upon a child the responsibility for their identity formation in this way would have been characterised as an act of negligence.

The disassociation of adulthood from responsibility for the younger generations is paralleled by a loss of clarity about what being an adult even *means*. The historic aspiration to grow up has given way to attitudes that are deeply ambivalent about adulthood.[29] Grown-up men and women who have embraced the spirit of extended adolescence are not only encouraged to celebrate their playful side but also to regard adulthood with a mixture of suspicion and contempt. Today's version of adulthood is rarely associated with positive connotations but is frequently depicted as a stultifying period of conformism. The contrast between our culture's affirmation of being young and its awkwardness towards grown-ups is striking. To all intents and purposes, culture has become youth culture.

The adoption of an adolescent imagination by men and women is driven by their estrangement from ideals associated with maturity. People have never completely accepted the loss of their youth. But the infantilisation of our current culture is different to past attempts to slow down the inexorable process of ageing. Our grandparents wanted to appear young and attractive but not necessarily to behave like children. Twenty-first century society finds it difficult to endow adulthood with purposeful meaning. In this regard, our self-conscious cultivation of immaturity is very much a response to the emptying out of adult identity.

Our society is full of lost boys and girls hanging out at the edge of adulthood. Yet we find it difficult even to give them a name. The absence of a readily-recognised word to describe these infantilised adults demonstrates the unease with which this phenomenon is greeted. Advertisers and toy manufacturers have invented the term 'kidult' to describe this segment of the market. Another word sometimes used to describe these 20- to 35-year-olds is 'adultescent', generally defined as someone who refuses to settle down and make commitments, and who would rather go on partying into middle age. Nonetheless, the lack of clarity about the border between the generations is now widely recognised. So when the title of an essay in *The Atlantic asks* 'When Are You Really An Adult?', it follows up its rhetorical question with the statement 'in an age when the line between childhood and adulthood is blurrier then ever, what is it that makes people grow up?'[30] Typically, the essay does not provide an answer – merely leaving the reader with the clear impression of whatever adulthood is, it is a drag. According to the author, 'being an adult isn't always a desirable thing': 'independence can become loneliness' and 'responsibility can become stress'.

The sense of despair that surrounds adult identity helps explain why contemporary culture struggles to maintain a line between adulthood and childhood. Childishness is idealised for the very simple reason that many despair at the thought of living the alternative. Maturity, responsibility, and commitment are only feebly affirmed by contemporary culture.

The vanishing of adult authority

The reluctance to draw and enforce a line between adults and children is a symptom of the same borderless sensibility that exists in relation to the physical and symbolic boundaries discussed in previous chapters. Adults are not simply biologically mature people: they possess the moral capacity to exercise responsibility and embrace their duty to the young. As the *OED* reminds us, adulthood implies the possession of characteristics 'befitting an adult' as 'opposed to a child'. This moral contrast assumes that those possessing the characteristic 'befitting an adult' bear a significant measure of responsibility for the guidance and wellbeing of younger generations.

The actions of adults should be viewed as a collective response to social necessity, not a collection of arbitrary responses by individual grown-ups acting in terms of their self-generated personality traits. Adult responsibility should be conceptualised as a species of *collective responsibility* for the future wellbeing of the younger generations. This is a *shared responsibility*, since neither an individual on their own, nor a single institution such as the family or the school, can be expected to successfully cultivate the desired attributes in young people. The development of moral virtues and character has as its premise the exercise of adult responsibility.

The responsibility of adulthood is not simply directed at one's own children. This point was stressed by Erikson, who explained that adults are not obliged to have children, but that 'one participates otherwise in the establishment, the guidance, and the enrichment of the living generation and the world it inherits'. He declared that

> the right (or the obligation) to have fewer children (or none) can only be a liberated one if it means a greater personal and communal responsibility for all those born, and the application of parental concerns to the preservation of what enhances the whole cycle of life.[31]

Arguing that one of the psychosocial tasks of adults is to care for the young, Erikson conceptualised this task through the idea of *generativity*: 'the concern in establishing and guiding the next generation'.[32] Generativity contains the moral obligation to give 'without the expectation of return', speaking to a relation of mutual dependence between generations and helping to establish a connection between them.

The exercise of adult responsibility requires that the distinction between adult and child is taken seriously. Historically, this distinction was underwritten and enforced through the workings of adult authority. Yet today, just as the demarcation between the private and the public spheres, or that imposed by national borders, is contested, so too are the distinctions drawn through the exercise of adult authority. Authority is frequently denounced as authoritarian, with self-appointed children's advocates suggesting that there should be a relationship of equality between children and adults. Supporters of 'children's rights' suggest that the family ought to be democratised, and that the young should be equal decision-makers within this institution.

The erosion of adult authority has evolved alongside the moral depreciation of adulthood. One of the first accounts of the dissolution of adult authority is to be found in David Riesman's sociological classic, *The Lonely Crowd*. Published in 1950, this study drew attention to adults' loss of belief in their own authoritative status, resulting in the emergence of doubts 'as to how to bring up children'. Riesman also noted that 'parents no longer feel themselves superior to the children'.[33] Almost two decades later, in his 1969 Preface to a new edition of the book, the author noted that the unravelling of adult authority had greatly accelerated:

> Since 1950 the decline in the weight and authority of adults chronicled in *The Lonely Crowd* has proceeded even further. Now attending high school and college are the children of the mistrustful parents who felt themselves revealed in books like *The Lonely Crowd*. The loss of inner confidence among adults is a worldwide phenomenon, reflecting rapid change in technology and values. Margaret Mead has spoken of native-born American parents feeling like immigrants in the country of the young. The young react to the loss of adult legitimacy with even greater mistrust, confusion, and rebellion.[34]

The corrosive impact of the loss of adult authority on the development of young people was of great concern to Hannah Arendt, also writing in the 1950s. Arendt drew attention to the 'gradual breakdown of the one form of authority' which existed in 'all historically known societies, the authority of parents over children, of teachers over pupils and, generally of the elders over the young'.[35] She observed:

> the most significant symptom of the crisis, indicating its depth and seriousness, is that it has spread to such pre-political areas as child-rearing and education, where authority in the widest sense has always been accepted as a natural necessity, obviously required as much by natural needs, the helplessness of the child, as by political necessity, the continuity of an established civilization which can be assured only if those who are newcomers by birth are guided through a pre-established world into which they are born as strangers.[36]

Today, acrimonious debates over childrearing, health, lifestyles, and the conduct of personal relationships indicate the extent to which the contestation of moral authority dominates the pre-political spheres of everyday life. Arendt recognised that once adult authority was put to question, the blurring of the moral boundary between the generations was inevitable.

Instead of exercising adult authority, many biologically mature individuals are, to use a newly-invented phrase, 'adulting'. Adulting is a term applied to the practices and forms of behaviour of biologically mature people who occasionally go through the motion of doing grown-up stuff.[37] People who do not quite regard themselves as adults are practising adulting when they carry out tasks such as cooking a meal, cleaning their rooms, or helping their grandmother to visit a doctor. Adulting is about playing at being an adult. In New York, I see men in their early forties sporting a T-shirt that declares, 'I Can't Adult Today'.[38] That behaving in an adult-like fashion is presented as a jokey lifestyle option highlights the precarious status of adult authority.

Socialisation without boundaries

The loss of the meaning of boundaries has acquired an intensely disturbing form in the domain of childrearing. Mothers and fathers understand that children cannot be properly socialised unless they learn to draw lines, respect their authority, and adhere to certain rules. Maintaining and enforcing such lines is particularly important with young children, and testing boundaries is an integral part of a child's development. Young children constantly seek attention and find it difficult to accept family rules about when to go to bed or when to stop their online activities. Contemporary parenting culture provides little guidance to parents who are attempting to establish clear boundaries for their children, instead encouraging them to be flexible and to avoid being too disciplinary. It advises parents to avoid responding to their rebellious child with an unequivocal 'NO'; rather, they should 'negotiate' with their child. In these conditions, it is not surprising that parents are often at a loss to know how to set boundaries for their children.

There is a veritable industry of parenting advice on the art of setting boundaries. Such texts often convey the impression that parents are too insecure to get on with the job of boundary setting. With a tone of reassurance, one parenting expert explains that 'setting boundaries doesn't make you a mean or unfair parent, even if your child says that to you at the time, out of anger'.[39] The constant flow of banal advice informing parents that it is OK to set boundaries serves as a testimony of the widely held view that holding the line is a difficult accomplishment[40] and invariably treats boundary-setting as a technical skill that mothers and fathers need to learn. Yet authoritative parenting is not a technical accomplishment.

The socialisation of the young requires adults who are confident in their authority and in their ability to transmit the norms and values of their community. When adult authority is feeble, the development of young people's identity lacks the cultural support required to make the transition to adulthood. Erikson did not systematically develop his argument on the relationship between value transmission through socialisation and its contribution to the resolution of the crisis of identity, but he made several allusions to its significance, writing of a 'normative identity crisis' facing adolescents and emphasising the ethics of adult responsibility for socialising young people.[41] Yet despite its importance in guiding intergenerational relations, the issue of socialisation and its relation to the manifestation of identity crisis is rarely explored as a problem worthy of investigation in its own right.

Over the past century, Western societies have found it increasingly difficult to socialise young people into the values of the previous generations. In the face of extraordinary technological and social changes, older generations lost confidence in the values into which they were acculturated, and society has found it difficult to provide its adult members with a compelling narrative for socialisation. When Erikson posed the question 'what really, is an adult?' he drew attention to the importance of resolving the identity crisis of adolescence through a satisfactory account of adulthood.[42] For socialisation to occur successfully, adults must be able to draw on a system of child training that is culturally rooted in the experience of previous generations. Erikson remarked that the values with which children are trained 'persist because the cultural ethos continues to consider them "natural" and does not admit of alternatives'. He observed that:

> They persist because they have become an essential part of the individual's sense of identity, which he must preserve as a core of sanity and efficiency. But values do not persist unless they work, economically, psychologically, and spiritually; and I argue that to this end they must continue to be anchored, generation after generation, in early child training; while child training, to remain consistent, must be embedded in a system of continued economic and cultural synthesis.[43]

Through transmitting the values of the past, socialisation is integral to an intergenerational transaction whereby moral norms are communicated by authoritative adults to the young.

One of the by-products of the de-authorisation of adulthood has been a loss of clarity about what values to transmit to children. One often hears educators openly acknowledge that, since they have lost confidence about the values into which they were socialised, they are not sure what ideals they should impart to their children. The absence of a consensus on the narrative of adulthood enhances the difficulty for young people to adopt 'grown-up' attitudes to life.

The inability of the current regime of socialisation to help the young negotiate the boundary that they must cross to develop their moral and intellectual capacities does not only pertain to adolescents. In a fascinating study on what she calls the *iGen* generation – those born after 1995 – the psychologist Jean Twenge drew the conclusion that it was not merely the achievement of *adulthood* that was delayed, but also the length of time it took to reach *adolescence*.

Drawing on a series of surveys, Twenge concludes that 'childhood has lengthened' so that teenagers were being treated as children and 'more protected by parents than they once were'. The entire stage of development from 'childhood to adolescence to adulthood' has slowed down, and consequently, the meaning of adolescence has altered. 'Adolescence is now an extension of childhood rather than the beginning of adulthood', argues Twenge.[44] Typically, the young people interviewed by Twenge claimed that they preferred childhood to adulthood because was there was no need to assume the responsibilities connected with growing up.

One reason why teenagers, and even young people in their twenties, find it difficult to let go of the security of childhood is because they have not been provided with the moral resources necessary to adopt the habits of independent behaviour. In our previous discussion on the commanding influence of non-judgementalism, we noted that it runs in parallel with the sensibility of boundarylessness and openness. Outwardly, this sensibility appears to liberate individuals from the demands placed on them by adult authority and the conventions of wider society. But without acquiring the habit of judgement, the young find it difficult to cross the border into adulthood. Instead of being freed from the limits posed by borders, they can only avoid and delay the day when they have to cross them. This problem of judgement is confirmed by the research carried out by scholars from the University of Notre Dame. The authors of *Lost in Transition: The Dark Side of Emerging Adulthood* conclude that the making of moral judgements 'seems almost inconceivable to most emerging adults today'.[45] Having been left bereft of the capacity to negotiate moral boundaries, many young people find the invitation to maturity easy to ignore.

The consequences of not preparing young people to undertake the journey into adulthood is played out on a daily basis on the campuses of Anglo-American universities, where the age-old distinction between school children and university students is fast losing its meaning. In effect, the infantilisation of university students has become institutionalised. College administrators often treat students as if they are biologically mature children rather than as young men and women and assume that they require therapeutic support to make the transition from high school to the university.[46]

In some instances, the infantilisation of university students has become a caricature of itself. Many universities provide anxious undergraduates facing exams with soft toys and pets to stroke in designated chill-out rooms. Harvard Medical School and Yale Law School both have resident therapy dogs in their libraries. At the University of Canberra in Australia, pre-exam stress relief activities include a petting zoo, bubble wrap popping, balloon bursting, and a session titled 'How can you be stressed when you pat a goat?'

Most influential explanations of the emotional fragility of current university students blame new social and economic factors, such as the rapid pace of change or economic insecurity faced by undergraduates. Invariably such accounts overlook the deeper cause of this infantilisation, which lies in society's inability to educate young people in the values of the past. As Erikson explained, the identity confusions of the young can be overcome by a form of socialisation that provides meaning, noting that parents 'must be able to represent to the child a deep, an almost somatic conviction that there is meaning to what they are doing'. Erikson took the view that the problem was not that young people were frustrated, but that they were not provided with the cultural support essential for dealing with it, writing that 'ultimately children become neurotic not from frustrations' but from 'lack or loss of societal meaning in these frustrations'.[47]

Today's society has accepted the dissolution of life stage boundaries and their consequences as a fact of life. This sentiment was forcefully communicated by Neil Howe and William Strauss in their 2003 report *Millennials Go to College*, which stated that the current cohort of students find it difficult to flourish in the less structured environment of higher education. They added that 'the millennial generation is far more closely tied to their parents' than the students that preceded them, and that they insist on a 'secure and regulated environment'.

In effect, the situation described by Howe and Strauss is one where university students continue to carry on with modes of behaviour that they practised in schools – and this is accepted by wider adult society as just the way things are.

The estrangement from boundaries, and the obsession with identity

In his theory of identity, Erikson favoured a relatively relaxed and flexible orientation towards psychological boundaries. He argued that the sense of 'wholeness' requires an open sensibility to new experience, to allow for the establishment of a harmonious relationship between the 'inner emotions and outer social circumstances', and that the establishment of an 'absolute boundary' between the inner and the outer world diminishes an individual's capacity to yield to new experience.[48] Despite his preference for a flexible approach towards psychological boundaries, Erikson understood that they provided a necessary infrastructure for the successful realisation of identity development.

Yet Erikson was a man of his times, and his writings in the late 1960s and 1970s appear to have absorbed the ascendant spirit of boundarylessness of the United States during that time. He became increasingly alienated from the cultural values that he initially saw as important for helping adolescents to overcome their identity crisis. In an interview with the psychiatrist Robert Coles, Erikson remarked that 'the concept of boundary might be the fitting symbol for the whole of my personal and social development', concluding that he had to adopt a form of thought that avoided being confined within the framework set by boundaries.[49]

Erikson's estrangement from boundaries was paralleled by his changing attitude towards identity in general and American identity in particular. In his 'Reflection on the American Identity', which was a chapter in the 1963 revision of his seminal work *Childhood and Society*, Erikson offered a sympathetic account of American character and a positive conclusion about its future development. He was optimistic about the ability of America to 'evolve a new world-image', one that 'encompasses all of mankind'.[50] Within a decade of making this statement, Erikson adopted a distinctly hostile approach toward national identity, which he condemned for its supposed exclusionary and dehumanising impulses.[51] Along with a significant section of adult society, he exchanged what he saw as the grim moral universe of the past for the promise of a much more permissive, boundaryless vision of the future. It was at this moment that the phenomenon of an identity crisis would be converted from a temporary psychological condition to a permanent feature of Western culture.

Where the loss of stable identity was previously perceived as a source of serious concern, in more recent times, the difficulty of adopting a stable identity is frequently portrayed as a potentially positive development. Postmodernist writers dismiss what they depict as traditional ideals of the self, asserting that 'the fixed subject of liberal humanistic thinking is an anachronism that should be replaced by a more flexible individual whose identity is fluid, contingent, and socially constructed'.[52] Within the academic world, where these sentiments exercise considerable influence, such writers make a virtue out of the destabilisation of identity.

Critics of this approach draw attention to the compulsive imperative of identity construction that leads individuals down a neurotic, consumerist path. The sociologist Charles Lemert has pointed to the pathologies of inventing yourself through body surgery, therapies, and sexual experimentation. He raises concerns about people on the Internet 'who essentially lose themselves in the self-transformation they undertake trying to catch up with the world', describing this development as a 'disturbing trend of early twenty-first century life'.[53] This sentiment is echoed by Anthony Elliott, who writes of a 'reinvention craze' driving people to undertake painful and expensive procedures to alter the way they look and 're-create their identities'. Examples of these 'reinvented identity practices' are cosmetic surgery, superfast weight loss diets, and body augmentation.[54]

Despite his eventual alienation from boundaries, Erikson intuited that the celebration of the fluidity of identity could have significant psychological and moral costs for the younger generations. In his Jefferson Lectures, delivered in 1973, he warned:

> I have said enough today about the nature of human conscience to indicate that where roles, in the name of multiple identity or of none, are played out licentiously, the old fashioned conscience is not liberated, but repressed. And the consequence is not greater freedom in informed permissiveness but an inability to personify and to convey to others any ethics except that of making a variety of role adjustments instead of a single one.[55]

Erikson was justified in his concern about the costs of attempting to detach identity from the boundaries set by 'old fashioned conscience'. But it is unlikely that he could have imagined the explosion of identity thinking and the transformation of identity into the destabilising and corrosive political phenomenon it has become today.

The unravelling of identities is often attributed to structural changes brought about by late capitalism. New communication technologies, the rapid flow of information and capital, and mass migration are some of the factors that are held responsible for the destabilisation of identity. While these changes have had an important impact on the way that people experience their place in the world, the problem of identity is mainly an outcome of the erosion of the web of meaning that served to provide guidance. A sense of belonging, which is a crucial component of identity, is historically rooted in a particular space that is defined by both the physical and the symbolic boundaries that surround it. Once individuals understand where lines are drawn, they can navigate their way in the world and develop their identity through reacting and learning from their experience.

By contrast, in the absence of authoritative cultural guidance and meaningful boundaries, people's sense of insecurity becomes intensified. Identities become decentred, free-floating, and the subject of perpetual preoccupation. Identity, and the crisis that often surrounds it, is thus inextricably linked to the confusion that often envelops conflicts of values and moral norms. Without the authoritative guidance provided through socialisation, the sensibility of boundarylessness, with its attendant crisis of identity, becomes the norm.

Notes

1 Martin and Barresi (2006) p. 275.
2 Agier (2017) p. 17.
3 Agier (2017) p. 15.
4 Agier (2017) p. 44.
5 Papastergiadis (2000) p. 212.
6 Gerth and Wright Mills (1954) p. 145.
7 Wolfenstein (1951) pp. 22 & 15.
8 Berger, Berger, and Kellner (1974) p. 73.
9 Erikson (1968) p. 26.
10 Erikson (1964) p. 95.
11 See Arnett (2000).
12 Hayward (2013) p. 525.
13 Erikson (1968) p. 16.
14 Erikson (1968) p. 17.
15 Erikson (1968).
16 Erikson (1964) p. 90.
17 Erikson (1964) pp. 90–91.
18 Erikson (1964) p. 93.
19 Erikson (1968) p. 30.
20 Erikson (1968) pp. 29–30.
21 Damian Carrington (2019) 'Greta Thunberg nominated for Nobel peace prize', *The Guardian*, 14 March, https://www.theguardian.com/world/2019/mar/14/greta-thunberg-nominated-nobel-peace-prize.
22 See https://friendsoftheearth.uk/climate-change/adults-are-failing-us-climate-thats-why-im-striking. (accessed 2 August 2019).
23 See Damian Carrington (2018) 'Our leaders are like children, school strike founder Greta Thunberg tells UN summit', *The Guardian*, 4 December, https://www.theguardian.com/environment/2018/dec/04/leaders-like-children-school-strike-founder-greta-thunberg-tells-un-climate-summit.
24 Porritt cited in Williams (2008) p. 82.
25 See www.thetimes.co.uk/edition/news/brexit-vote-a-vast-throng-too-posh-to-putsch-2876gg9n7.
26 See Bristow (2019).
27 For a discussion of arrested development, See Calcutt, A. (1998) *Arrested Development: Pop Culture and the Erosion of Adulthood*, Cassell: London.
28 A. O. Scott (2014) 'The Death Of Adulthood in American Culture', *New York Times*, 11 September, http://mobile.nytimes.com/2014/09/14/magazine/the-death-of-adulthood-in-american-culture.html?smid=tw-nytimes&_r=0&referrer=.
29 See Bristow (2019).
30 See Julie Beck (2016) 'When are you really an adult?', *The Atlantic*, 5 January, https://www.theatlantic.com/health/archive/2016/01/when-are-you-really-an-adult/422487/.
31 Erikson (1974) p. 123.

32 Erikson (1963) pp. 266–267.
33 Riesman (1964) p. 49.
34 Riesman (1969) p XIV.
35 Arendt (1956) p. 403.
36 Arendt (2006a) p. 54.
37 For an excellent discussion of the issues surrounding adulting, see Jennie Bristow's essay, www.spiked-online.com/2019/06/21/the-futility-of-generation-wars/.
38 See https://expressiontees.com/products/i-cant-adult-today-mens-t-shirt?variant=4297 4102854&currency=USD&utm_source=google&utm_medium=cpc&utm_campaign= google+shopping&gclid=CjwKCAjw1rnqBRAAEiwAr29II3eZnU50W_24ISXxvDT PylVJ0Q1r3cI8w9Q5I1unSJr66tRBpXP8fRoCovYQAvD_BwE (accessed 10 August 2019).
39 Krissy Pozatek, 'Why It's Important To Set Healthy Boundaries With Your Kids', https://www.mindbodygreen.com/0-17051/why-its-important-to-set-healthy-boundaries-with-your-kids.html.
40 See Furedi (2001) Chapter 8, 'The Problem of Holding The Line'.
41 Erikson (1968) pp. 16–17.
42 See Erikson (1970) pp. 11–22.
43 Erikson (1963) p. 138.
44 Twenge (2017) p. 41.
45 Smith (2011) pp. 23–24.
46 For a discussion of this development – see Furedi (2017).
47 Erikson (1963) p. 249.
48 Erikson (1964) p. 91.
49 Erikson is cited in Gutmann (1974) p. 60.
50 Cited in Friedman (1999) p. 252.
51 See Gutman (1974).
52 See the discussion in Lemert (2011) p. 18.
53 Lemert (2011) p. 18.
54 See Elliott (2013) pp. 11 & 94–95.
55 Erikson (1974) p. 108.

8

TARGETING BINARY THINKING

The attempt to dethrone conceptual boundaries

The previous chapters alluded to the trend towards what Jean Baudrillard characterised as the contamination and confusion of categories.[1] This chapter discusses a closely related phenomenon, which is the attempt to erode the fundamental conceptual and categorical distinctions used to interpret and give meaning to life. This has acquired its most striking form in its targeting of what is referred to as 'binary thinking'. Binary thinking and binary concepts – such as 'us and them', 'man and woman', 'normal and abnormal' – are portrayed not only as the product of rigid and inflexible thinking, but also as tools of discrimination used to maintain the domination of the weak by the powerful. Hence the practice of binary thinking is dismissed as morally wrong, and the deconstruction of conceptual boundaries advocated as the alternative.

Hostility towards binary thinking is motivated by a variety of concerns. These range from a sense of unease towards the boundaries set by conventional rules governing behaviour and speech, to a suspicion of moral boundaries, often derided as 'judgementalism'. Animosity towards the drawing of conceptual distinctions is frequently underpinned by a relativist ideological stance towards the categories used to give meaning to human experience. Anti-binary activism also seeks to undermine the biological distinctions between man and woman, advocating a gender-neutral approach towards the socialisation of children.

The crusade against the binary has been remarkably successful in influencing cultural attitudes and behaviour. In higher education, the mere mention of the word provokes knowing smiles of contempt towards those accused of simplistic binary thinking. In recent decades, binary attitudes towards sexuality court accusation of transphobia and heteronormativity. More widely, people accused of thinking in simplistic binary terms are indicted for polarising political life and held responsible for the rise of extremist political parties.

The aim of this chapter is to provide a critique of the critique of binary concepts and behaviour. It explains that hostility towards binary distinctions is ultimately motivated by the impulse of dethroning the conceptual distinctions that give meaning to human experience. Since, as Bourdieu and other social scientists explained, culture is itself built on boundaries, anti-binary trends implicitly negate the integrity of prevailing values. This chapter argues that the negative framing of the term 'binary' coexists with an escapist refusal to engage with the challenge of working with and developing moral and conceptual boundaries. In its more radical version, the anti-binary impulse directs its energy towards de-authorising the fundamental norms governing behaviour. It is devoted to the project of unbounding cultural norms.

Hostility towards binaries

In most spheres of everyday life, people continue to interpret and communicate their experiences through the aid of binary idioms and concepts. Most human beings spontaneously draw contrasts between short and tall, thin and fat, pleasant and unpleasant, near and far, or light and dark. In the course of attempting to understand an event and assess it, people constantly rely on distinctions such as normal and abnormal, good or bad, helpful or unhelpful, and harmful or harmless. People judge and value one another through such binary categories as trustworthy or unreliable, educated or uneducated, friend or enemy, clean or polluted, or true or false. Science and technology, too, have evolved through the use of binary categories; computer systems run on binary logic. More than any manifestation of boundarylessness, the revolt against the binary expresses its irrational and destructive impulses.

Human beings cannot do without thinking in terms of contrasting categories, which is why even devotees of the project of deconstructing traditional moral and conceptual boundaries implicitly rely on them. Deconstructionists are not averse to making distinctions between powerful and powerless, exploiter and exploited, oppressed and oppressor, or victim and victimiser. Yet in the face of both everyday reality and the experience of history, disdain towards binary thinking and the drawing of clear conceptual and moral distinctions has quietly emerged as the taken-for-granted 'sophisticated' outlook in education, culture, and the media. It is still begrudgingly accepted in science – but only just, as indicated by a commentary in *The Financial Times* titled 'Binary Thinking – right for computers, wrong for the real world'.[2] The author of this commentary claims that the use of binary thinking in the 'real world' simplifies matters and leads to poor decision-making.

At first sight, the singling out of binary thinking for criticism appears puzzling, since it is so integral to the pursuit of a meaningful life. If such criticism were simply directed at simplistic 'black and white' thinking, its motives would make perfect sense. However, the zeal with which the crusade against binary concepts is pursued suggests that it is not merely an expression of concern about the practice of inflexible and rigid thinking. In all but name, the anti-binary crusade has acquired the character of a rigid ideology. It can be most usefully interpreted as the intellectual expression of the borderless imagination. That is why those who denounce national border controls as inherently violent institutions also frequently adopt a hostile attitude towards the drawing of conceptual distinctions. Hostility towards binary categories should be understood as the intellectual and cultural manifestation of the revolt against boundaries. One critic of borders and sovereignty calls for perceiving group formations as 'overlapping, fluid, contingent, dynamic, and reversible boundaries and positions', rather than as 'zero-sum, discrete, binary groups which oppose each other from one side or the other of a boundary'.[3] Another opponent appears delighted that there 'has been a firm shift away from the binary and homogeneous logic that informed the creation of the borders of nation-states, and a firm shift toward something that is altogether less clear and/or more complex in terms of the relations between people, places, things and movement'.[4]

Over recent decades, commentators have drawn attention to the ascendancy of cultural relativism in higher education and the influence exercised by deconstructionist and postmodern ideas. Yet the widespread influence of the movement against binary thinking has been largely overlooked. In my review of popular and academic literature published in English, I have found very few attempts to defend binary concepts from their detractors: the critics of such concepts appear to dominate the intellectual and cultural landscape. In popular reviews and publications, a negative framing of conceptualising in binary terms tends to be the norm.

The hostility directed at binary thinking is fuelled, not simply by intellectual concerns, but also by ideological and political objections. The binary is sometimes portrayed as if it is a political foe that must be eliminated in order to make progress. For example, one academic, Nina Glick Schiller, argues that 'by rejecting binary thinking within various contemporary forms of social theory, scholars and activists can reconstitute identity studies in ways that highlight not only multiplicities and relationalities but their constant reconfigurations within structures of power'.[5] This call for the rejection of binary thinking is linked to a wider project of altering the way that identities are conceptualised. For Jacques Derrida, one of the leading deconstructionist thinkers of the 20th century, the main task at hand is to subvert the binary oppositions that underpin the outlook of Western societies and overturn the prevailing hierarchy of meanings.[6]

In recent times, binary thinking has often been held responsible for what are portrayed as destructive political outcomes. Xenophobia and racism are frequently associated with a simplistic binary mindset. Binary thinking is sometimes presented as a psychological deficit – a symptom of anxiety, and a marker for intolerance of ambiguity and complexity. One psychologist, Mark Baer, argues that 'healthy' groups need to 'transcend binary thinking in favour of more sophisticated forms of decision-making'.[7] Some commentators claim that political problems are reducible to the harm done by 'us and them' thinking and advise against thinking 'in binary terms'.[8] Critics of populism blame binary thinking for inciting citizens to vote against the policies proposed by their political elites. One academic commentator suggests that the use of the 'binary categories of the corrupt elites and the virtuous people' is culturally thin.[9] Writing in *The Economist*, Hans Kundnani blames populism for 'corrupting liberal thinking itself', fearing that liberals 'increasingly sees the world in simplistic, binary terms of "us" and "them" – doing exactly what it criticises in populism'.[10]

Attacks on binary categories have acquired a particularly aggressive tone in relation to issues associated with identity and gender. Devotees of identity politics claim that binary categories violate and harm the persona of people who do not identify in binary terms. One commentator vociferously attacks those who believe in a 'gender binary':

> You are imposing your concept of those things onto me, enforcing a binary that is paradoxical. Moreover, you are denying the gender fluidity of those who have a penis and identify as male, but prefer women's underwear or wear makeup or transgress norms in innumerable other ways.[11]

This gender fluid voice claims that 'by imposing the label "cisgendered" onto me, you do me psychological and intellectual violence'. For this individual, binary categorisation constitutes a form of violence against his gender-fluid identity.

The apparent valuation and appeal of gender fluidity, particularly in popular and youth culture, illustrates the influence of the anti-binary outlook. Celebrities are not only encouraged to defy gender stereotypes, but to flaunt their gender-fluid image. As Josie Appleton notes:

> The liberationary figure today is the non-binary, the trans; the position staked outside binaries, against them. In literature and cultural studies departments, binaries are deconstructed: made conscious, then reversed, then made to collapse under the weight of their internal contradictions.[12]

Calls for 'breaking binary boundaries' have migrated from the academy to the wider world. The enterprise of boundary-breaking is often oriented towards calling into question the very idea of normality and exposing the flaws of distinguishing between normal and abnormal. 'In modern society, there is a huge misconception as to what is normal and abnormal', wrote one blogger, before claiming that 'the fact that there are two such categories, normal and abnormal, is just a reaffirmation of this misconception'.[13] One psychotherapist questions the validity of using the terms to refer to the mental and emotional states of people. 'Indeed, it is a real question as to whether those words can be sensibly used at all, given their tremendous baggage and built-in biases and the general confusion they create', he writes.[14]

The impulse to erase the distinction between normal and abnormal is particularly strident in discussion around disorders of sexual development. Anti-binary advocates argue that the term 'disorders of sexual development' ought to be replaced with 'differences of sexual development' The attempt to blur the boundary between ordered and disordered development is motivated by the concern that the latter is stigmatising. However, the purpose for making a distinction between normal and abnormal in the medical sciences is not to stigmatise but to assist doctors in understanding the predicament faced by their patients. They are unlikely to be interested in treating conditions that they diagnose as normal and direct their energies at attempting to assist those they consider to be suffering from an abnormal condition. Without a concept of the normal, the very foundation of the medical sciences becomes eroded.[15]

It is no accident that boundary-breaking has its most well-known and publicised impact on gender. As Bourdieu explained in *The Logic of Practice*, gender is the fundamental binary division, which has historically influenced the structuring of distinctions in many spheres of life. Since the binary division between the sexes served as models for others, Bourdieu assumed that 'the limit *par excellence*, that between the sexes will not brook transgression'.[16] He believed in the durability of the distinctions drawn by analogy with gender because they were in some sense real. Now that his 'limit *par excellence*' is continually the target of contestation, it is evident that boundary-breaking has acquired an unexpected, unprecedented, and peculiarly unrestrained form.

Why we need binaries

Conceptual boundaries and binary categories have played a central role in the evolution of human thought. Since its inception, philosophy has relied on the use of dichotomies and dualist distinctions. For example, Plato's philosophy developed through distinguishing between the forms of appearance and their content. Other philosophers continued this tradition until Descartes elaborated the influential – but now contested – distinction between mind and body.

Both the Old and New Testaments rely on binary categories to make moral distinctions between good and evil. Jewish people's idea of a 'chosen people' offers an unambiguous contrast with those not chosen. Christianity makes a clear distinction between those who follow Christ and those who fail to believe. Binary concepts such as sacred and profane, heaven and hell, or saints and sinners serve as cultural tools for guiding people to make their way in everyday life. Other religions also rely on binary categories to give meaning to human experience. Zoroaster, the ancient Persian spiritual leader who founded Zoroastrianism, stressed the twofold nature of the world, which he believed could be understood as a struggle between light and wisdom versus darkness and evil.[17] The ying-yang distinction in Chinese philosophy offers a paradigmatic example of binary categorisation, symbolising the duality of all things in nature, such as male and female, light and dark, or motion and stillness. According to Confucian principles, the interaction to which ying and yang refer operates in every dimension of existence. This system of complementary binaries serves to explain the universe.

The use of the binary as a cultural tool is also widespread amongst small-scale societies and ethnic groups in Africa, Asia, and Latin America. Anthropologists influenced by Claude Levy Strauss's structuralist approach to the study of cultures stressed the central role played by 'binary opposites in culture'.[18] As Appleton explains:

> Faced with the mass of sensory experience, the waxing and waning of forms, the human mind fixes on the cardinal points: east/west, hot/cold. It fixes on the essential polarities, the extremes, the points of contrast, in relation to which the gradations of experience can be oriented. It is the *distinction*, the polarised difference, which strikes the human mind as meaningful.[19]

This point is stressed by Bourdieu, who concluded on the basis of his field work in Algeria and other ethnographies that fundamental contrasts, such as 'male and female, dry and wet, hot or cold' constitute the cultural tools for endowing community experience with meaning.[20]

Arguably, the most significant and influential study of the symbolic role of binary categories is Durkheim's pathbreaking study *The Elementary Forms of Religious Life* (1911). Durkheim, who is generally considered to be one of the founders of the discipline of sociology, argued that the distinction between religious and other forms of experience rests on the symbolic distinction between the domain of the sacred and that of the profane. From Durkheim's perspective, the binary concepts of sacred and profane possess a universal significance for understanding the workings of culture.

Durkheim argued that the distinction between what a community holds sacred and that which it situates in the realm of the profane governs the way that people conduct their lives. Moreover, the binary categories that emanate from this distinction play a key role in the maintenance of the moral order. As the French sociologist Marcel Fournier explains, 'dichotomies such as duty/passion and sacred and profane are, according to Durkheim, the basis of the moral order because the alternative is chaos'.[21] Durkheim's theory attaches great significance to the binary concept of the sacred and the profane because they provide the medium through which a community's internal bonds and shared meaning gain definition.

Durkheim's distinction between the sacred and the profane can also be understood as a reflection of the duality of individual and society. The sacred represents the collective outlook of society: its traditions, values, and shared emotions. The profane refers to the realm of individuals, where the plurality of minds interact with each other. In practice, this duality between individual and society is resolved through the socialisation of people into a collective outlook; as Fournier explains, 'the socialization of the individual involves an initiation into sacred things'.[22] The socialisation of the young helps them to understand what society holds sacred and provides them with the dichotomies and distinctions that they will need to make their way in the world. The domain of the sacred offers the members of a community the identifiable social norms that help them to understand who they are. These norms need not acquire an explicit religious form – for example, patriotism, loyalty, freedom, or democracy can serve as values that a community holds sacred.

Until recently, binary distinctions and systems of classification were perceived as integral to the maintenance of a moral order and culture by conservative, liberal, and radical thinkers alike. For example, Bourdieu wrote at length about what he saw as the discriminatory ideological power of distinction, arguing that distinctions such as that between 'high (sublime, elevated, pure) and low (vulgar, low, modest) spiritual and material, fine (refined, elegant) and coarse (heavy, fat, crude, brutal), light (subtle, lively, sharp, adroit) and heavy (slow, thick, blunt, laborious, clumsy)' constitute judgements that flatter the ruling elites and devalue the attributes associated with those who are ruled.[23] Nevertheless, he wrote that binary classifications provide the foundation for understanding the world and offer people shared meaning through which they could forge a sense of solidarity.

Bourdieu's sentiments were shared by one of the founders of cultural studies, the British Marxist Stuart Hall. Hall recognised that the 'marking of difference' was the prerequisite for the constitution of a symbolic order, 'which we call culture'. Though critical of the drawing of strong cultural boundaries, he noted that: Stable culture requires things to stay in their appointed place. Symbolic boundaries keep the categories 'pure', giving cultures their unique meaning and identity.[24] Hall himself preferred to unsettle culture by contesting its symbolic boundaries – but unlike contemporary opponents of binary thinking, he recognised that a culture could not survive without the assistance of symbolic boundaries.

What distinguishes contemporary opponents of binaries from the cultural radicals of previous generations is their aspiration to call into question prevailing boundaries for their own sake. They embrace the act of transgression not because they aspire to achieve a specific object but because they avow transgression as an act that is good in and of itself. Transgression without an object is the unconscious driver of this movement.

Thinking tools

Binary categories are not simply cultural tools. Thinking in terms of binary categories appears to be a fundamental feature of the practice of human conceptualisation. According to one account:

> Binary thinking seems to be the path of least resistance for the perceptual system, for thinking, and for linguistic structures. The easiest way to classify complex information is to clump it into two piles. Indeed the most instinctive and tempting clumps to use for complex data are the old favorites: like/don't like, ours/theirs, right/sinister, sheep/goats.[25]

The classification of complex information through a binary dichotomy helps provide people with a framework through which they can gain an understanding of their experience. This point is clarified by Appleton in the following terms:

> Thinking in binaries grasps an essential truth, which is that nature, and human life, proceed through the dynamic of *opposition*: there are conflicting forces, opposing elements, which play out beneath the surface of things. After all, nature itself contains poles: of positive and negative, attraction and repulsion.[26]

Binary categories are used to transform a confusing reality into a comprehensible one, providing the outline of a conceptual map that assists in the making of decisions and choices. When confronted with an unexpected challenge or problem, binary logic helps us to decide whether to tackle it or not; whether to fear it or embrace it. Binary concepts serve as interpretative themes not only for dealing with the problems of everyday life but for developing the aesthetic dimension of the arts. The literary critic George Steiner has outlined five binary oppositions, which he regards as universal interpretative themes in literature: age–youth; men–women; living–dead; the world of men–the realm of the gods; and public–private'.[27] As in literature, so in other spheres of life the human mind is drawn towards understanding its experiences through the making of contrasts.

In the social sciences, couplets such as traditional–modern, illiterate–literate, or inclusive–exclusive, and developed–underdeveloped provide conceptual contrasts through which a society, or different types of societies, can be understood. For example, Durkheim's model of development is based on the distinction between what he calls mechanical versus organic solidarity. The German social scientist Ferdinand Tönnies developed the binary categories of *Gemeinschaft* and *Gesellschaft*, which correspond to the distinction between a communal society and a more complex, modern community, where the ties between people are impersonal and instrumental. These binary categories need not be interpreted as rigid, mechanistic intellectual tools but can serve as the point of departure for their application, further development, and modification.

The boundaries that separate concepts are essential for ensuring that they are precise and rigorous constructs that can provide insights into understanding the problem under investigation. Politics professor George Schöpflin takes the view that 'what makes the social sciences scientific is the rigorous establishment of and adherence to conceptual boundaries, the application of logic, and the respect for consistency'.[28] Once thought is detached from conceptual distinctions, it acquires a free-floating and arbitrary character. Such an operation may momentarily assist the cultivation of an individual's imagination, but it will be at the cost of a loss of clarity about the workings of the world.

Over the centuries, binary categories and conceptual distinctions evolved to become associated with different academic disciplines. At first sight, the division of human knowledge into different subjects that are defined through their disciplinary boundaries may appear as an unnatural or inflexible way of developing knowledge. However, these boundaries have played an important role in assisting the development of ideas. As a theorist of education put it, 'boundaries are the condition of intelligibility of ourselves and of our world'.[29] An effective system of education requires the transmission of clearly bounded concepts through familiarising young people with different disciplines.

One of the challenges posed by the boundless spirit influencing cultural development lies in upholding the distinction between education and other forms of social activity. Opponents of binary thinking are often at the forefront of contesting disciplinary boundaries and the distinction between formal education and other forms of learning. Consequently, it has become fashionable to question the boundary between formal education and folk learning. Whatever the value of everyday knowledge, it does not provide young people with the theoretical knowledge and concepts that are essential to inspire them to go beyond their experience – whereas the rigorous adherence to conceptual distinctions offered by disciplinary knowledge provides students with the capacity to understand the world that lies beyond the boundaries of their own lives. The educationalist Leesa Wheelahan expresses her concerns with the tendency to erode the qualitative distinction between formal and informal learning in this way:

> [A]ttempts to collapse the boundary between abstract, theoretical knowledge that is primarily available in education and everyday knowledge available in the workplace in the interest of making it more "authentic" or "relevant" robs students of the capacity to recognise the boundaries between different kinds of knowledge and to successfully navigate them.[30]

The maintenance of boundaries is as important to upholding the integrity of the institution of education as it is to the development of thought through the use of conceptual distinctions.

Critics of binary thought often caricature it as a 'black and white' or 'either–or' form of thinking. Undoubtedly, binary concepts can be used in a simplistic and unreflective manner. However, binary contrasts also offer the potential for further conceptual elaboration and clarification by providing a framework through which thought can develop via an engagement with new experience. The binary categorisation of 'black and white' does not preclude the recognition of the phenomenon that is grey. The human imagination possesses the capacity to render concepts flexible; the dogmatic rejection of binaries overlooks the fact that through the use of judgement, we can modify, develop, and contextualise to ensure that categories are adequate for capturing the dynamic that they seek to address. Through yielding to new experience, concepts have evolved and transcended the boundaries within which they were formed. But this very transcendence requires the fixed points provided by conceptual boundaries.

Taking conceptual boundaries seriously does not mean seeing them as eternal and static. 'Disciplinary configurations are not fixed and will change, but the boundaries between different kinds of knowledge will remain important', argues Wheelahan.[31] Critics of disciplinary boundaries fail to realise that young people acquire a sense of intellectual independence through engaging with them. The framework provided by these boundaries provides them with the thinking tools they require to understand the distinction between different spheres of knowledge. As Wheelahan explains:

> engaging with disciplinary boundaries provides students with the basis for navigating those boundaries in multidisciplinary and interdisciplinary work. This is because, in understanding disciplinary boundaries, students are provided with criteria for legitimate and illegitimate uses of theory, for determining comensurability and incommesurability and for judging the validity of knowledge claims.[32]

Learning to navigate disciplinary boundaries is one the most important accomplishments of formal education. Working with concepts is essential for capturing the diverse features of reality and understanding their distinguishing features.

It is worth noting that the very formulation of the term 'binary thinking' is a politically motivated caricature. People rarely think only in binary terms. They may have strong views about what is right and wrong, but they are also open to making nuanced and subtle judgements that recognise that, in specific instances, an act may be both right and wrong.

Why have binaries become a target for scorn?

The hostility directed at what is now referred to as 'binary thinking' is a relatively recent development. My review of English-speaking publications suggests that hostility towards binary thinking first emerged in academic publications in the 1970s and gradually gained momentum in the following decades, to the point where it began to influence public discourse and gradually acquire influence within wider popular culture.

My study of the historical career of 'binary thinking' found very few references to it until the 1990s. According to a search of the Google Ngram database, the first reference to this term was in 1955, in a discussion of computers; while its first negative framing is to be found in a 1960 edition of *Art Journal*. An article in this journal discusses 'the perception of a crisis in category in late nineteenth-century French culture, an interruption of the kind of binary thinking that generates reassuring labels like "male and female", "orient and occident", "Christian and Jew"'.[33] The next reference I found in this database is to a journal article published in 1975, discussing the 'western sense of racial superiority as well as the power philosophy inherent in "binary thinking"'.[34]

A search of the *Nexis* database of English language newspapers and publications confirms this pattern. The first reference to binary thinking is in 1977, when *Newsweek* carried a book review that uses the term 'binary thinking' to refer to the simplistic outlook of 1960s political radicals.[35] There are few further references to the term until the turn of the 21st century. The numbers begin to rise in the decade between 2000 and 2010 (82 results) and gain momentum during the years that follow – 480 hits between the years 2010 and August 2019.

Hostility towards binary categories and conceptual distinctions is most consistently promoted by advocates of cultural and conceptual hybridity, who regard transdisciplinarity and the transgression of symbolic boundaries as the prerequisite for liberating themselves from the shackles imposed by the supposed inflexibility of traditional thought. This sentiment is widely held within institutions of education, where radical activists believe that the transgression of boundaries 'exposes the way in which boundaries are imposed by the powerful in their own interests and then universalized and naturalized as the ideal that pertains to the whole society'.[36]

The language used by educators contesting disciplinary boundaries is imbued with the borderless spirit discussed in previous chapters. As one advocate of transdisciplinarity explains, 'transdisciplinary boundaries vision which replaces reduction with a new principle of relativity is transcultural, transnational and encompasses ethics, spirituality and creativity'.[37] According to this outlook, disciplinary boundaries enforce the interests of the powerful and serve to justify their hegemony over society. It is important to realise that this sentiment is not confined to a handful of academics and teachers. As Muller explains, in education 'to live a life beyond bounds and without boundaries is the dominant ethical ideal'[38] – the 'central premise' of which is the belief 'that boundaries are always and by definition imprisoning, and should therefore be crossed, transgressed, combated and otherwise wished away wherever they appear to manifest themselves'.[39]

Astute analysts such as Tester characterise this 'intimation of boundlessness' as a reflection of postmodernity. However, the embrace of transgression as an inherently positive and ethically desirable project can best be understood as a rejection of both the integrity of knowledge and of cultural (symbolic) boundaries.

The contestation of conceptual boundaries is a recurrent theme in cultural studies. These debates often focus around the distinction between *insulation* versus *hybridity*. Insulation is associated with traditionalism and conservatism, and hybridity is promoted on the grounds that it challenges the domination of cultural imperialism and the influence of outdated traditions. Hybridity is embraced on the ground that its very existence negates conventional boundaries. As Muller outlines:

> Insulation stresses the interdictory and impermeable quality of cultural boundaries, of textual classification and of disciplinary autonomy. It

highlights the integral differences between systems of knowledge and the differences between the forms and standards of judgement proper to them. It stresses the virtues of purity and the dangers of transgression. Hybridity, by contrast, stresses the essential identity and continuity of forms and kinds of knowledge, the permeability of classificatory boundaries and the promiscuity of cultural meanings and domains.[40]

The most systematic theoretical expression of the borderless spirit is deconstructionism. It conveys the beliefs that binary distinctions are unfair and biased, and that portraying phenomena in terms of opposites is likely to be unjust. From this perspective, the very act of constructing dichotomies, such as master–servant, white–non-white, male–female, Christian–non-Christian, legitimates injustice and oppression. As Elbow writes, 'according to this critique, binary thinking almost always builds in dominance or privilege–sometimes overtly and sometimes covertly'.[41] From this standpoint, the binary distinction between the private and the public is an illustration of a dichotomy that mystifies relations of power. The political theorist James Panton remarks that critics of this distinction claim that its 'binary logic obscures the real complexity of social life' and 'disguises the underlying dynamics of social power and domination'.[42]

Deconstructionists argue not only that binary categories are arbitrary and inherently unstable, but also that they privilege one term and devalue the other. According to this view, the use of binaries helps establish a hierarchy of values that replicate prevailing biased views about superiority–inferiority. The belief that the drawing of distinctions is itself morally wrong has led some to conclude that the very act of drawing distinctions is discriminatory and racist. Undoubtedly, some conceptual contrasts convey judgement about what is considered desirable or undesirable or superior and inferior – as with the binary 'civilised–uncivilised'. However, in such cases, the problem is not so much the drawing of a line of contrasts, but the premise on which such distinctions are constructed. Hostility to the drawing of distinctions has led many deconstructionists to become suspicious of the very act of categorisation, based on the assertion that the act of categorisation assists cultural domination and the construction of unjust categories.

The tendency to attribute dark and prejudiced motives to the act of making distinctions is at first difficult to understand, and it is worth reflecting on the question of why deconstructionists choose to mediate their critique of power through a condemnation of binaries. My review of this trend suggests that the attack on the drawing of dichotomous distinctions represents a covert or unconscious attack on judgement. This point was already noted by Trilling in the late 1940s, when he noted that reluctance to make intellectual distinctions was allied to the belief that judgement would have 'undemocratic' consequences.[43] As noted previously, non-judgementalism exercises a powerful influence over Western culture. The appeal of anti-binary ideology, particularly in higher education, is not so much an accomplishment of the philosophical power of deconstruction but a consequence of the underlying *zeitgeist* of limitlessness.

Alienation from binary identity and binary gender roles

The crusade against binary thinking does not confine its activities to the deconstruction of moral and conceptual boundaries. It has effortlessly moved from challenging cultural contrasts to contesting biological distinctions such as those between humans and animals and between man and woman.

Until recent times, it was taken for granted that the concept of sex is, by definition, binary. As Deborah Soh explains, 'biological sex refers to whether we are female or male, based on our anatomy and reproductive functions'.[44] Opponents of sexual binary now argue that the distinction between male and female is similar to the unjust dichotomous categories such as 'literate–illiterate' or 'civilised–uncivilised'. They claim that the 'binary relationship between men and women obstructs the development of sexual equality', and that the binary category of man and woman violates the identity of transsexual or intersex people. Biologically given sex differences are portrayed as inflexible, oppressive, and socially constructed binaries.[45] Whereas in the past it was argued that sex is a biological reality and that gender is a social construct, trans activists claim the opposite, which is that gender identity is 'destiny, while biological sex is a social construct'.[46]

Hostility to the binary distinction between man and woman have led activists to challenge scientifically established facts about the nature of sexual differences. Their mission – particularly in higher education – is to challenge what they regard as simplistic 'common sense views' on the subject of sexual differences. One university teacher, who is devoted to guiding students 'through their initial attempts to deconstruct sex/gender binaries', notes that while undergraduates are willing to 'accept that *gender* is fluid, they balk at abandoning long established views on biological sex'. She acknowledges that, 'when it comes to "biological sex" . . . I am often met with a more committed resistance: students take for granted that *sex* is fixed, stable and binaristic, and are generally uncomfortable having those assumptions called into question'.[47] For many anti-binary activists, the task of de-authorising not just gender but also the difference of biological sex has acquired the character of a religious duty.

Anti-binary activists are committed to denaturalising what has hitherto been perceived as natural. Moreover, they are committed to gaining acceptance for the idea that gender fluidity, rather than sexual binary, is the natural state of affairs. To legitimate the normalisation of gender fluidity and binary-less differences of sex, they put forward a couple of tendentious arguments. The first is that the binary conception of sex is essentially a Western construction; the second is that binary thinking about sex is relatively recent, and that history provides numerous examples of gender fluid practices.

Through the plundering of history, anti-binary activists present instances of supposedly gender-fluid behaviour to reinforce their claims. Writing in *Psychology Today*, Karen Blair asserts:

> Yet, while the gender binary is certainly well anchored within society and our social mores, there is actually a long history of gender not being viewed in such a black and white manner. Indeed, many indigenous cultures around the globe held more fluid and dynamic understandings of gender before encountering Western theories of gender. Even within Western cultures, the characteristics associated with one gender or the other have changed stripes so many times through history that it is almost surprising how adamantly we now argue that heels, wigs, makeup, and the color pink are *only* for women and girls, when all of these things were previously reserved *only* for men and boys.[48]

That men wore wigs, makeup, and heels in the past is not in doubt. But historical differences in the way man and woman presented themselves does not in any way undermine biological binary between people with XX and those with XY chromosomes. All that it means is that the way that male and female identities are framed is historically specific.

The argument against the binary of sex is frequently justified on the ground that it is merely a Western construction, and not one that is biologically founded. Despite their anti-binary ideology, these claims-makers casually reintroduce a binary contrast (Western–non-Western), albeit in a reversed form. In some instances, fanciful claims are made about supposedly enlightened practices in non-Western societies. One essay, titled 'Hijras: the unique transgender culture of India', claims that the existence of this community shows that 'Indian society has been tolerant of diverse sexual identities and sexual behaviors'.[49] In reality, the role assigned to Hijras has little to do with tolerance for sexual diversity. The Hijras originally comprised people who were born as men and made to undergo an initiation ritual involving the removal of their penis, testicles and scrotum. Since antiquity, men have been castrated and assigned a specific social and ritual function. That a community of eunuchs is now portrayed as an illustration of a society 'tolerant of diverse sexual identities' demonstrates the absurd attempts made to normalise transgender culture.

In recent times, non-governmental organisations (NGOs) and transgender activists have sought to gain official recognition of the hijra as a 'third sex', neither man nor woman. While it may be the case that members of the hijra community do not perceive themselves as men or women, it is important to remember that the act of castration does not lead to the biological transformation of a male to a new sex. The adoption of a third sex identity does not alter biological facts or the binary of sex.

Academics devoted to the elimination of the conventional binary view of sex often look to the alleged cultural practices of various Native American people to endorse their views. They often refer to their 'Two Spirit' identity, which was allegedly possessed by Native Americans who performed an allegedly third gender ritual role in communal ceremonies and assert that the term Two Spirit refers to native Americans who were 'born with masculine and feminine spirits in one body'.[50] Activists offer the existence of the Two Spirit Identity as proof that 'traditionally, many Native cultures acknowledged and accepted greater variation in how individuals expressed gender identification, which is in contrast with the Western tradition of adhering to a strict binary (male/female) conceptualization of gender'.[51] Native American traditions are favourably contrasted to the narrow-minded approach of Western civilisation. 'The point is that Native Americans don't force each person into a neat box, but they allow for a diverse range of sexual and gender identities', argues one critic of supposedly unimaginative Western cultural practices.[52]

The idealisation of a gender fluid Two Spirit identity is closely connected to the practice of myth-making. People who identify as possessing both a female and male spirit are far more likely to be transgender activists than members of a Native American community. The Two Spirit identity is the product of an anachronistic reconfiguration through which the 21st century preoccupation with identity is reimagined as a feature of Native American tradition.

According to the story told by the inventors of this tradition, people who identified as Two Spirits flourished until they encountered narrow-minded Western settlers in the 19th century and were forced to accept sexual binaries. According to one account:

> This development was exacerbated by the fact that people in many Native communities began to adopt the negative attitude held by Europeans on homosexuality. Today, the overall impression is that while indigenous ways are generally cherished, preserved, and in many cases revived in Native American communities, the traditions of gender diversity are quite obviously something most people do not wish to see revitalized.[53]

In contrast to the attitudes expressed by actual Native Americans today, non-Native American activists are keen to reinvent the past and give life to the Two Spirit ideal. As one commentator explains, 'from the 1980s onward particularly the roles of women-men became elevated by some non-Native scholars to some universal supreme spiritual status held by people who were not heterosexual'.[54] That's another way of saying that the popularisation of Two Spirits has more to do with the narrative of non-heterosexual non-Native people than with the outlook of Native Americans.

The contemporary advocates of transgender ideals, seizing upon traditional rituals of transgression of sexual binaries, misunderstand the nature of these practices. There are numerous examples of ceremonies and rituals in a diverse range of communities that permit acts of transgression. Drawing on his field work,

Bourdieu suggests that the very purpose of rituals is to provide an opportunity for transgression in order to revitalise the distinction between the sacred and the profane.[55] These rituals are not directed at the elimination of binary distinctions or symbolic boundaries, but at the opposite: affirming them. Indeed, the very act of transgression presupposes a boundary to be transgressed. As Dennis Wrong explained in his exposition of Durkheim's view on this subject, 'an occasional crime or dramatic violation of a rule, serves to reaffirm the sanctity and authority of the rule for the community'.[56]

Paradoxically, the very attempt to embrace gender fluidity and escape beyond the boundaries set by biology forces those with a modicum of intellectual integrity to acknowledge the salience of the binary. The authors of the essay 'Beyond boundaries: Towards fluidity in theorizing and practice' note that even if they embrace the idea of 'multiple forms of masculinities or femininities', 'the binary divide' remains 'in place' and that the 'conceptualisation of fluidity relies on the existence of dualisms'.[57]

The great lengths to which opponents of binary sex categories go to provide an intellectual argument to sustain their case is motivated by the exigency of identity construction. Regardless of the poverty of the intellectual case for denaturalising the binary categorisation of male or female, the claim that the prevailing biological boundary between men and women ought to be overcome resonates with the prevailing boundless cultural spirit. The speed with which transgender culture and practices have gone mainstream in Western society is remarkable. While a tiny percentage of the population possesses the anatomical characteristics of both sexes, the overwhelming majority of people do not share these characteristics.[58] Nevertheless, non-binary, gender-fluid practices have become institutionalised and successfully permeate public life and popular cultures.

The dramatic reconceptualisation of the distinction between sex and gender is clearly outlined by the sociologist Rogers Brubaker:

> For much of the second half of the twentieth century, the distinction between them seemed relatively clear and stable. "Sex" denoted biological differences, "gender" the varied and complex systems of cultural meanings, norms, and expectations attached to sex differences. In recent decades, the distinction has been challenged by those who argue that sex is just as socially and culturally constructed as gender, and that it is therefore misleading to treat sex as biological and gender as cultural.[59]

In effect, the attempt to erode the distinction between sex and gender calls into question the boundary between nature (biology) and culture (human convention). It indicates that even this long-established boundary can lose its meaning for the borderless imagination. And that is precisely what has begun to happen. As Brubaker explained, 'the distinction between the terms has been eroded in everyday life, popular culture, and the media by the expansive use of "gender" to denote both biologically based differences and cultural codes and expectations'.

Not so long ago in the 1980s, social scientist believed that 'identities like transsexuals reinforces the normalcy of gender divisions'.[60] Many argued, that instead of challenging the biological binary of male and female, transsexuals related to them as normal and embraced 'natural attitudes towards gender'. These attitudes have given way to ones that are radically different. The ease and speed with which conventional distinctions between men and women have been eroded has surprised even trans-activists. As one American law professor sympathetic to this cause has noted:

> With stunning speed, nonbinary gender identities have gone from obscurity to prominence in American public life. The use of genderneutral pronouns such as "they, them, and theirs" to describe an individual person is growing in acceptance. "All gender" restrooms are appearing around the country and an increasing number of U.S. jurisdictions are recognizing a third-gender category. In June 2016, an Oregon court became the first U.S. court to officially recognize nonbinary gender identity. In October 2017, California passed its Gender Recognition Act, a law allowing any individual to change the sex[61]

The UK and parts of Northern Europe have been no less hospitable to a dramatic revision of the way that the relationship between men and women is conceptualised. Gender self-identification has trumped long-standing conventions. It is sufficient for a biological male to identify as a female in order to gain access to women's toilets, refuges, or prisons. Even hitherto girls-only institutions, such as the Girl Guides, and some single sex schools are now open to boys who identify as females. In the UK's National Health Service, transgender patients can choose to be treated in either male or female wards.[62] Consequently, the boundary between men and women is frequently depicted as artificial and even oppressive, and those who choose to transgress it are celebrated by the media as brave and inspirational role models.

The campaign to popularise gender-neutrality is not confined to winning hearts and minds. It is also fervently committed to forcing people to adopt new non-binary pronouns such as they, ze, or zee. In many parts of North America, the policing of gender-related language is backed up by formal and informal sanctions against individuals who refuse to alter their vocabulary. Directives issued in 2015 by New York City's Commission on Human Rights state that landlords and employers who intentionally use the wrong pronouns with their non-binary employees or tenants can face fines up to $250,000. In 2018, Jerry Brown, the Governor of California, endorsed a bill that threatened health professionals who 'wilfully and repeatedly' declined to use a patient's preferred pronouns.

In places of work and in institutions of higher education, people face strong pressure and informal sanctions should they refuse to embrace a gender-neutral vocabulary. It is increasingly common to provide people with a list of words that they can or cannot use at their workplace. One of the most disturbing targets of linguistic policing are day-care centres and primary schools, which are exhorted to socialise children into a gender-neutral culture by pre-empting them from adopting the language and values of the generations that preceded them. As far back as 1995, the day-care centre at La Trobe University in Australia banned the use of around 20 words, including the gender-related terms 'girl' and 'boy', to promote its mission of altering traditional sex roles. Those who violated the code were forced to pay a fine and treated as if they had used a dirty word.

The focus on altering children's vocabulary is not accidental. The project of purifying of language is motivated by the objective of altering people's behaviour. Language serves as a medium through which human relations are ordered and people's reality is shaped. Thus, socialising children into a gender-neutral culture and vocabulary aims to alter the meaning that youngsters attach to their identity and existence. For example, Virginia's Fairfax County public school system has replaced the term 'biological gender'; from its family life curriculum, with the phrase 'sex assigned at birth'.[63] The term 'sex assigned at birth' renders one's biological sex arbitrary and irrelevant. Biological sex, which is determined at the moment of conception, is rendered invisible and meaningless through the administrative fiat of rendering it transitory. The transformation of a birth certificate into a statement of identity preference implies that the description of a baby is a provisional one that is likely to alter as a child grows up. The premise of the phrase 'sex assigned at birth' is that it is the developing child and teenager who will eventually choose an identity – preferably a gender-neutral identity for themselves.

A significant cohort of 'up-to-date' parents have embraced the ideology of gender-neutrality and have adopted a style of childrearing that avoids assigning a biological gender to their child. Such parents assume that they are providing their offspring with the freedom to decide for themselves who they want to be. In reality, the embrace of gender-neutral parenting constitutes an act of adult irresponsibility. Instead of guiding their child to help understand their biological attributes and taking responsibility for the development of the child's identity, they place the burden of character formation on the child themselves. 'Leaving it up to the child' may sound very open-minded, but its effect is to allow the confusing influences and pressures of popular and peer culture to monopolise the identity formation of young people. Instead of providing direction and guidance, children are left to deal with a chaotic world dominated by the social media, consumer culture, and identity politics.

Conclusion

The reaction against conceptual distinctions and binaries has succeeded in undermining confidence in traditional symbolic boundaries. Millions of individuals who intuitively feel that there is something not right about the institutionalisation of trans culture nevertheless feel insecure about voicing their views. The mutation of the term 'binary' from an ostensibly neutral noun to a term of condemnation demonstrates the relative success of the anti-border project in the realm of intellectual life.

Yet despite its best efforts, the ideological fire directed at conceptual boundaries has not been able to rid the world of binary thinking. Opponents of binary thinking have themselves implicitly and sometimes explicitly adopted the use of binaries. They constantly voice their anti-border ideals through the drawing of binary contrasts that attempt to subvert the previous norms. Some of their binary preferences are outlined following:

- Inclusive not exclusive
- Fluid not stable
- Cosmopolitan not national
- Boundaryless not bounded
- Emotion not reason
- Feminine not masculine
- Binary neutral not binary specific
- Hybridity not insularity
- Heterogeneity not Homogeneity
- Openness not judgement
- Transparency not privacy
- Gender identity not biological sex

Despite their stated objective of 'going beyond binaries', they are actually in the business of displacing conventional binaries with ones that they prefer. The attempt to displace traditional forms of binary categorisation with new ones is paralleled by the project of delegitimating conventional borders and inventing new ones. The construction of new forms of bordering is the subject of the next chapter.

Notes

1 See Baudrillard (1993) pp. 8–9.
2 See Wolfram, C. (2015) 'Binary thinking-right for computers, wrong for the real world', *The Financial Times*, 30 October, www.ft.com/content/1327bc52-7eec-11e5-98fb-5a6d4728f74e.
3 Isin (2002) p. 30.
4 Green (2012) p. 585.
5 Glick Schiller (2012) p. 521.
6 See Derrida (1981) p. 41.
7 Baer (2017).
8 Chayenne Polimédio (2017) 'Fighting "Us vs Them" Populism', *Pacific Standard*, 25 May, https://psmag.com/news/fighting-us-vs-them-populism.
9 Bonikowski, Halikiopoulou, Kaufmann, and Rooduijn (2019) pp. 58–81.
10 Hans Kundani (2019) 'Liberalism's Betrayal of Itself – and the way back', *The Economist*, 14 February, https://www.economist.com/open-future/2019/02/14/liberalisms-betrayal-of-itself-and-the-way-back.

11 Aviance, J.N. (2016) 'I am not cisgendered', *Huffpost*, 2 February.
12 Appleton, J. (2008) 'In defence of binaries', *Notes on Freedom*, 25 April.
13 https://medium.com/@NicoleAshleyB/breaking-binary-boundaries-479ca95466b8.
14 See Eric Maiesel (2011) 'What Do We Mean by "Normal" ?', *Psychology Today*, 15 November, https://www.psychologytoday.com/us/blog/rethinking-mental-health/201111/what-do-we-mean-normal.
15 See Anderson (2028) pp. 91–92.
16 Bourdieu (1995) p. 211.
17 See Boyd and Donald (1979) pp. 557–588.
18 See Douglas (1999) p. xiv.
19 Appleton (2018) https://notesonfreedom.com/.
20 Bourdieu (1990) p. 223.
21 Fournier (2013) p. 282.
22 Fournier (2013) p. 319.
23 Bourdieu (1990) p. 470.
24 Hall (1997) p. 236.
25 Elbow (1993) p. 53.
26 Appleton (2018) https://notesonfreedom.com/.
27 Steiner's arguments in his essay on *Antigone* is discussed in Schöpflin (2012) p. 24.
28 Schöpflin (2012) p. 10.
29 Muller (2012) p. 71.
30 Wheelahan (2008) p. 207.
31 Wheelahan (2012) p. 151.
32 Wheelahan (2012) p. 151.
33 See https://books.google.co.uk/books?id=_D9UAAAAMAAJ&q=%22binary+thinking%22&dq=%22binary+thinking%22&hl=en&sa=X&ved=0ahUKEwim8ovEucbkAhWIShUIHXU8A_YQ6AEINTAC.
34 See https://books.google.co.uk/books?id=JqVRAQAAIAAJ&q=%22binary+thinking%22&dq=%22binary+thinking%22&hl=en&sa=X&ved=0ahUKEwjIwveAu8bkAhUgTxUIHYjUBK4Q6AEITjAG.
35 See 'A reader's christmas feat', *Newsweek*, 12 December 1977.
36 Wheelahan, L. (2012) p. 6.
37 Klein (2004) p. 516.
38 Muller (2012) p. 75.
39 Muller (2012) p. 77.
40 Muller (2012) p. 67.
41 Elbow (1993) p. 51.
42 Panton, J. (2010) *Public/Private Distinction: The Problematisation of Public/Private Relationship in Political Thought after World War II*, Ph.D. Thesis, New College, University of Oxford, Oxford, p. 11.
43 Trilling (1957) p. 234.
44 Deborah Soh (2018) 'Science Shows That Sex Is Binary, Not A Spectrum, *Real Clear Politics*, 31 October.
45 Linstead and Brewis (2004) p. 359.
46 Anderson (2018) p. 30.
47 Beyond the Binary: Thinking about Sex and Gender, https://www.hypatiareviews.org/content/beyond-binary-thinking-about-sex-and-gender.
48 Karen Blair (2008) 'Has Gender Always Been Binary?', *Psychology Today*, 16 September, https://www.psychologytoday.com/gb/blog/inclusive-insight/201809/has-gender-always-been-binary.
49 Kalra (2012) p. 121.
50 Sheppard and Mayo (2013) p. 262.
51 Sheppard and Mayo (2013) p. 262.
52 See https://medium.com/@ahanson8842/the-native-americans-two-spirit-people-67211116906c.

53 Lang (2016) p. 300.
54 Lang (2016) p. 318.
55 Bourdieu (1995) p. 211.
56 Wrong (1994) p. 79.
57 Linstead and Brewis (2004) pp. 356 & 359.
58 See Arboleda, Sandberg, and Vilain (2014).
59 Brubaker (2018) p. xii.
60 Weigert, Teitge, and Teitge (1986) p. 47.
61 Clarke (2019) p. 896.
62 Gabriella Swirling (2019) 'Transgender patients can choose to be treated on male or female wards, new NHS guidance says', *The Daily Telegraph*, 1 October, https://www.telegraph.co.uk/news/2019/10/01/transgender-patients-can-choose-treated-male-female-wards-new/.
63 Abigail Shrier (2018) 'Transgender Language War', *The Wall Street Journal*, 29 August, https://www.wsj.com/articles/the-transgender-language-war-1535582272.

9

INVENTING NEW BORDERS
FOR A BOUNDLESS WORLD

Since the beginning of time, people's existential need for security has expressed itself through attempts to draw lines and construct borders. Despite the influence of the borderless *zeitgeist*, human beings rely on boundaries no less than in the past: society cannot exist without the assistance they give to people attempting to interpret their experience and give meaning to their lives. This chapter is devoted to exploring how society's disengagement from conventional symbolic and moral boundaries has paradoxically created a demand for new ways of drawing lines in everyday life.

Western culture's alienation from judgement has played an important role in promoting a cultural climate hostile to borders and boundaries. Yet the ethos of non-judgementalism is fiercely committed to do what it can to protect itself from criticism, thereby building borders against judgement. Activists are fervently dedicated to the demarcation of criticism-free zones, in the form of 'safe spaces'. In this regard, the moral confusion that has encouraged a loss of boundedness has also created a demand for new boundaries. The policing of cultural and identity-related borders is pursued with a vigour that more than matches that of the most zealous defender of a national border.

A distinct feature of the new borders that have emerged in recent decades is their narrow personal and interpersonal character. The sense of security underwritten by the authority of conventional boundaries has given way to a climate of concern about individual safety and personal boundaries. It seems that a loss of solidarity, a growing sense of atomisation, and the presumption that you are on your own and therefore feel a sense of wariness and mistrust towards others, creates a demand for drawing up new lines. Through exploring the way that the contemporary demand for boundaries manifests itself, this chapter will attempt to shed further light on the phenomenon of the *paradox of borders*.

Even the spirit of limitlessness that informs the outlook of open border activists is forced to embrace some kind of limits. Human beings cannot detach themselves entirely from a physical or symbolic sense of space that they can call their own. In the absence of authoritative boundaries, an individual's sense of insecurity becomes intensified, leading to a quest for new boundaries. So when someone states 'I need some space', they are not simply referring to physically distancing themselves from another person. They are also looking to establish boundaries within which they can cultivate their identity and protect themselves from the pressures of everyday life.

In some instances, the paradox of borders is acknowledged by those who are dedicated to eradicating them. Judith Lorber, a former professor of Gender Studies, is committed to 'melding categories' and blurring boundaries; however, she recognises that there are 'dilemmas and paradoxes in crossing borders and erasing boundaries'. According to Lorber, the 'first paradox is that to erase boundaries one must fight to recognize them'.[1] In other words, the very attempt to erase boundaries presupposes their existence; those who wish to erase boundaries for their own sake soon discover that new lines have taken their place.

The quest for personal boundaries

Unlike national borders, the boundaries that promise to protect an individual's personal identity and shield them from criticism or the unwanted attention of others are highly valued by contemporary Western culture. The affirmation of transgression does not extend to the subversion of personal boundaries. On the contrary, as one commentary in *Psychology Today* explains, 'concerns about boundary crossing' into personal space 'have become greater than usual'.[2] Indeed, the issue of personal space has become a constant topic of concern in the workplace and institutions of education.

The paradox of borders is strikingly illustrated by the flourishing of a self-help industry, whose mission is to assist individuals to establish robust personal boundaries. The titles of self-help literature portray the 'setting' of a personal boundary as a duty to the self, as in Charles Whitfield's *Boundaries and Relationships: Knowing, Protecting and Enjoying the Self* (1993). Anne Katherine's *Where to Draw the Line: How to Set Healthy Boundaries Every Day* (2000) communicates the conviction that drawing lines is a daily ritual. Numerous books, such as Henry Cloud and John Townsend's *Boundaries in Marriage* (2002), offer advice about how to set boundaries between yourself and others, including (and often, especially) the people that you love. Jennifer Miller and Victoria Lambert's *How to Draw the Line in Your Head and Home* (2018) aims to provide assistance to readers who need to find ways of establishing personal boundaries in their domestic life. Adelyne Birch's, *Boundaries After a Pathological Relationship* suggests that it is never too late to establish personal boundaries.

Personal boundaries are sometimes referred to as *embodied boundaries*. This focus on the personal body is accompanied by a sense of anxiety about how to construct a boundary around the self. Numerous seminars and workshops are devoted to guiding individuals to come to terms with their embodied boundary.

An invitation to one such workshop asks 'where does self end and other begin?' It continues: How can 'we' be a safe experience? Learn about the natural development of 'boundary' from a somatic and developmental perspective. This workshop will help therapists work psychophysically with clients around self regulation and relational issues.[3] Professional advice is now available on 'the hard work of creating healthier boundaries in your day to day life'.[4]

Opponents of national borders often condemn them on the grounds that they exclude 'others' by artificially distancing groups of people from one another. There is no doubt about the fact that a national border reinforces the social and symbolic distance between those who live on its different sides. However, this act of distancing pales into insignificance compared to the act of distancing involved in the setting of boundaries between one's self and one's intimates. Here, individuals are called upon to distance themselves not just from one group, but from the entire world.

Advice on setting personal boundaries tends to encourage the establishment of hard, inflexible lines. Mark Manson's *Guide to Strong Relationship Boundaries* advises that, 'A person with **strong boundaries** understands that it's unreasonable to expect two people to accommodate each other 100 per cent and fulfil every need the other has'.[5] Manson's strong boundaries implicitly encourage the psychic and personal distancing of people involved in a relationship. He states that 'a person with **strong boundaries** understands that they may hurt someone's feelings sometimes, but ultimately they can't determine how other people feel'. Statements such as this seek to reconcile people to their estrangement from one another and to protect them from being disappointed with other people.

When it comes to drawing and maintaining lines between human beings, boundaries are anything but open. The literature that continually draws attention to the 'invention' of borders and their unnatural and artificial qualities has very little to say on the construction of personal boundaries. And yet, the call to construct personal boundaries is often self-consciously directed at encouraging the drawing of imaginary lines. One commentator poses the question of 'What Are Boundaries and Why Do I Need Them?' before answering in the following terms:

> All relationships need **boundaries.** A **boundary** is an imaginary line that separates me from you. They separate your physical space, your feelings, needs and responsibilities from others. . . . Without **boundaries**, people may take advantage of you because you haven't set limits about how you expect to be treated.[6]

In a different context, appeals to people's insecurity and anxiety about being taken advantage of would be labelled by critics of national borders as an example of the politics of fear.

In contrast to the unbounded spirit of limitlessness, personal boundary-setting is unambiguously about setting limits. A contributor to *Psychology Today* explains that, 'boundaries can be defined as the limits we set with other people, which indicate what we find acceptable and unacceptable in their behaviour towards us'.[7] Another counsellor states that 'it can be useful to think' about boundaries 'as our "limits"'.[8] The call to 'know your limits' is invariably linked with the project of defining 'your intellectual, emotional, physical, and spiritual boundaries' with 'strangers, work colleagues, friends, family, and intimate partners'.[9]

The exhortation to set your personal boundary is often conveyed through warnings about the psychological costs of failing to do so. The failure to set boundaries has become medicalised. The condition co-dependency is presented as a mental health problem suffered by individuals who fail to set limits about what an individual does for others or allows others to do for them. Borderline personality disorder is often used to refer to people who focus on the problems of others rather than tending to their own needs. The inability to set boundaries is often diagnosed as due to the loss of a sense of self where an individual does not see others as fully separate from themselves.

At first sight, the ritualistic emphasis on setting personal boundaries appears to contradict the ethos of cosmopolitan openness, which claims to overlook distinctions between people. In fact, it follows this logic. The alienation of individuals from their communities, and the abstract quality of their existence, reinforces the demand for personal space and boundary. The insecurity of a sense of self-identity, emanating from a loss of meaningful boundaries, intensifies the psychic distance between people and exacerbates confusion about one's place in the world. For many, finding refuge within imaginary personal boundaries appears to provide a provisional solution to this dilemma.

The endeavour of setting personal boundaries coexists with the problematisation of personal space. The exhortation 'give me some space!' signifies a demand for a zone that is protected from the physical and emotional intrusion of others.

Psychologists, in particular, are keen to offer advice on how to maintain and protect your personal space and avoid encroaching and invading other people's. Even neuroscience has been mobilised to support the legitimacy of this personal zone. Michael Graziano, author of *The Spaces Between Us*, argues that there 'really is such thing' as personal space[10] – it is a 'protected zone that provides an invisible spatial scaffold that shapes the way humans interact with one another'.[11] What psychologists also dub 'peripersonal space' is depicted as a buffer zone around the body, which protects the individual from invasive remarks, gestures, and physical touches.

The seriousness with which the inviolability of personal space is upheld more than matches calls to protect the integrity of national borders. After noting that 'don't invade my personal space' and 'respect my boundaries' are 'phrases we hear a lot today', a reviewer in *National Geographic* asks 'are we in danger of becoming too obsessed with the idea of personal space?' His answer is an unequivocal 'no' – in fact, 'we're in danger of the *opposite*!'.[12]

One reason why personal space has become an issue in recent times is because Western society has become confused about how to give meaning to the boundaries guiding human interaction. In such circumstances, many people tend to withdraw into themselves and become more conscious and territorial about the space immediately surrounding them.

One symptom of the insecurity regarding personal boundaries is the politicisation of touching. In 2019, during the course of his campaign for Democratic Party presidential candidate, former Vice President Joseph Biden was frequently accused of getting too physically close to people. Biden was forced on the defensive when two women alleged that he made them feel uncomfortable by coming too close to them and being too familiar. Biden responded by releasing a video in which he reflected on the importance of personal space, noting that 'social norms have begun to change' and affirming that the 'boundaries of protecting personal space have been reset – and I get it'.[13]

That Biden, along with many others, is not sure how close he can stand near other people illustrates the difficulty that many people have in knowing where and how to draw lines between themselves and others. As previous chapters discussed, the problem of drawing lines is closely linked to the weakening of the moral authority of conventional symbolic boundaries. The recent outburst of concern with personal boundaries and personal space is, to a significant extent, a reaction to this development. The insecure manner with which ideas about personal space are conveyed speaks to a loss of confidence about knowing where to draw the line.

As Biden discovered, interpersonal boundaries are increasingly subject to controversy. Some commentators associate the trend towards the policing of interpersonal boundaries with the rise of the *#MeToo* movement. However, the policing of personal boundaries predates *#MeToo*, at least in the workplace and in higher education. Articles with titles such as 'Physical contact at work – what are the boundaries', written in 2010, indicate that touching had already become an important boundary-setting issue.[14] Policing the boundaries of physical contact has been paralleled by a proliferation of advice about what is and what is not an acceptable form of touching.[15] That mature adults are now instructed by human resources managers about how to touch, or not touch, one another shows that the setting of personal boundaries is no longer allowed to be left to common sense. The intensely personalised form of boundary consciousness has acquired its disturbing and frenzied dimension in the policing of the boundary that separates children from adults. Previous chapters noted the difficulty that adults have in drawing lines between adulthood and childhood. Paradoxically, the absence of a clear line between what were previously seen as two distinct stages in the life cycle exist alongside the attempt to bar adults from entry into the world of childhood. Throughout the Anglo-American world, children are shielded from the attention of adults by boundaries that are both physical and symbolic. Numerous American towns and cities have adopted municipal ordinances that ban 'adults unaccompanied by a minor child from entering and/or remaining in a park playground'. Signs warning 'No adults unaccompanied by children' in New York City playgrounds serve as reminder of the existence of a hard boundary separating generations.[16] The creation of adult-free parks – ostensibly to protect youngsters from the attention of child predators – coincides with a more general trend towards protecting a child's boundaries from adult trespass.

The focus on protecting the boundary surrounding childhood has become particularly striking in relation to physical contact. Adult carers and teachers are constantly warned not to touch a child. In the UK, teachers, nursery workers, and play workers are warned about the danger of putting sun cream on youngsters. Numerous day-care and primary education institutions have what Professor Heather Piper has characterised as 'no-touch' rules. There is considerable evidence that in the Anglo-American world, a 'no-touch' culture exercises a decisive role in the management of adult–children encounters. Researchers report that some child carers are reluctant to put a plaster on a child's scraped knee. Youngsters have been asked to manage their injuries themselves, with a teacher instructing them how to take out a plaster from a First Aid box and stick it on their bodies. Teachers report that they feel awkward about giving a reassuring hug to a crying child.

The 'no-touch' ethos has gradually expanded beyond the boundary of the professional setting, with parents often being reluctant to hold or touch their children's friends. Some fathers even feel uncomfortable about touching their own children in public. Physical contact between an adult and a child can no longer be assumed as a spontaneous gesture of care and affection: it is an act that must be self-consciously justified as absolutely necessary and 'appropriate'.

Concern about adults not overstepping the boundary that divides them from children has become a constant theme in the regulation of the relationship between the generations. The policing of this boundary is widely practised, and grown-ups who cross the line face not only social stigma but also legal penalties. If present trends are indicative of future developments, the newly-established border demarcating childhood from the adult world is likely to become even more heavily guarded.

From personal space to safe space

Until recent times, the demand for a safe space was confined to a handful of individuals and small groups who wanted to create a secure, private environment in which they could discuss matters with those with whom they shared common problems and experience. But now, the demand for safe space has exploded into a veritable movement that demands protection from unwanted pressure, criticism, and – above all – judgement. For many young people, a safe space possesses an important symbolic significance, with many claiming that it offers protection for those individuals who require a 'supportive' and 'non-judgemental' environment in order to flourish

Just as many people believe that secure national borders are essential for the well-being of their community, so supporters of safe space rely on its boundaries to insulate them from unwanted pressure. Like a gated community set up to keep out undesirable outsiders, the purpose of a safe space is to protect its inhabitants from unwelcome criticism and thoughts. Many opponents of national borders, who regard the call for border security as unreasonable and oppressive, are often in the forefront of campaigns for clearly delineated and bounded safe spaces.

A safe space aims to regulate social distance and psychic boundaries between people, and the language used to articulate safe space policies frequently deploys the metaphors of space, distance, and boundaries. Contemporary protest movements often adopt conventions and guidelines that espouse respect for personal boundaries and provide its supporters with safe spaces. Though the Occupy Movement prided itself in blurring the boundary between private and public places, it adopted a hard-line commitment to respecting the boundaries of the personal. It also undertook the task of providing a safe space for its supporters, particularly 'those suffering from depression and alienation caused by a system that prioritises consumerism and mass media communication over genuine interpersonal communication and community'.[17]

The protest campaign Occupy Bristol demanded respect for 'people's physical and emotional boundaries', and exhorted its supporters, 'Be responsible for your own actions and safety and the safety of those around you'.[18] Occupy London's Safe Space policy also focused on the enforcement of maintaining a psychic space, advising: 'respect each other's physical and emotional boundaries' and 'Be aware of the space you take up and the positions and privileges you bring'.[19] This conception of a safe space was not simply directed at insulating people from external pressures but to keep them safe from those closest to them, in case they intruded on their personal space.

Social workers, school-teachers, psychologists, educators, doctors, sex workers, and probation officers are some of the interest groups who have raised support for safe spaces. Safe space is often portrayed as a human right for vulnerable groups such as refugees,[20] and it has also become integrated into the vocabulary of 21st-century political protest. As indicated previously, the international Occupy Movement, which emerged in September 2011, is committed to the provision of safe spaces, often on the grounds that these were vital for helping the movement's supporters gain confidence. During the conference of the British Labour Party in Brighton, a safe space was established for female delegates fed up with listening to heated debates.[21] Support for safe space is not confined to the left of the political divide: a leader of the University of California at Los Angeles' Bruin Republicans described her group as 'a space for conservative students to share opinion without facing criticism or attacks from faculty and students who disagree with them'.[22]

The adoption of safe space practices is often justified on the ground that these help protect an individual from exposure to unwanted comments and attention. At an academic conference on transgender issues held at Roehampton University in London in 2019, delegates were given traffic light 'safe space' badges. The wearing of a red badge signalled that the delegate did not wish to engage with other academics, and a yellow badge indicated that a person did not want to be approached and would only communicate with others if they made the first move. Academics who dared to wear a green badge were open to conversing with others. The use of safe space badges communicated the idea that some individuals needed to affirm their personal boundaries in order to protect themselves from unsafe conversation.[23]

Probably the first reference to the idea of a safe space in the sociological literature is found in the work of Karl Mannheim, one of the founders of the sociology of knowledge. Mannheim was interested in understanding the application of the concept of *social distance* to cultural life. Throughout history, groups have sought to maintain a distance between themselves and other groups. Those others were sometimes deemed polluting, as in the case of the caste system of India, or as a threat to safety to the people living behind the walled cities of feudal Europe. Mannheim would have been surprised to learn that in the 21st century, safe space has become personalised to the point of protecting one academic from the views of another.

Mannheim claimed that social distance could signify both 'an external or spatial distance' or an 'internal or mental distance'. He believed that the impulse towards distancing was bound up with the need to regulate and control anxiety. The current social distancing imperative driving the demand for safe space is the desire to protect the self from judgement. This point was clearly echoed by an editorial written by the staff of Harvard University's student newspaper, the *Crimson*, which stated that there 'can be no doubt that certain safe spaces on campus can serve a positive purpose, especially when acting as judgement-free zones or havens for marginalized students'. '[W]orthwhile safe spaces' were defined as those which 'give individuals the opportunity to voice their concerns without fear of judgement'.[24] In this regard, a safe space should be interpreted as a metaphor of validation: as the legal scholar and former head of the American Civil Liberties Union (ACLU) Nadine Strossen has stated, the meaning of this metaphor now implies protection from 'exposure to ideas that make one uncomfortable'.[25]

The impulses motivating the demand for safe spaces are not qualitatively different to those calling to 'keep America safe'. What distinguishes them are different perceptions of the nature of the threat from which an individual requires protection. The narrative of fear and insecurity that drives a call for strong borders can, in a different context, lead to the demand for safe spaces. The very idea of a safe space invokes a symbolic boundary between 'safe' and 'unsafe', which aims to segregate one group from another.

Space itself can become a focus of competition where groups may feel that their safety depends on excluding people who are not like them. The divisive potential of the safe space ideal was exposed in late 2015, when Afro–American university students on a number of US campuses raised demands for segregated safe spaces on campuses. Here, the issue of safe space acquired an explicitly racialised dimension. At Edinburgh University in Scotland, a conference organised by the Resisting Whiteness group included an 'anti-racism' event where white people would be banned from asking questions. The event advertised the availability of two safe spaces – one which barred white people from entering.[26] Studies indicate that identity politics frequently leads to the establishment and ossification of boundaries between different groups. Joshua Gamson's study of disputes between competing identity groups concluded that the achievement of 'collective identity is inevitably tied to some degree of boundary patrol'.[27] For example, trans activists are in the forefront of silencing their critics from speaking out by preventing them access to spaces.

Indeed, as discussed next, the policing of cultural boundaries has become a widely practised activity, which goes way beyond designated 'safe spaces'.

Policing cultural boundaries

Cosmopolitan commentators appear to possess a double standard when it comes to assessing national and cultural borders. While they are vehemently hostile to the border of a nation and call for opening it to the rest of the world, they adopt a benign attitude towards policing the borders that separate different identity groups and cultures. So, while the cosmopolitan imagination is vehemently antagonistic towards national consciousness and sensibility, it appears to be either indifferent or positively receptive to assertions of cultural identity and lacks awareness of the potential for divisive – even violent – conflict between different identity groups.

During the past decade, the policing of culture has become increasingly focused around the issue of cultural appropriation. With the rise of identity politics, culture has become a fiercely contested resource. People are now regularly condemned for their hairstyles, clothes, or the food they cook on the grounds that they have apparently appropriated someone else's culture. Our consumerist ethos treats culture as a group's private property to which others have no right of access. The appropriation of this resource by members of other groups, particularly those from a 'privileged' community, is now habitually condemned as akin to an act victimisation or oppression.

In all but name, the charge of cultural appropriation serves as the 21st century's moral equivalent of religious sacrilege.

The representation of culture as a resource that is owned by its representatives is the inescapable outcome of the fetishisation of cultural identity. Susan Scafidi gave voice to this sense of ownership in her 2005 study *Who Owns Culture? Appropriation and authenticity in American law*. Scafidi defines cultural appropriation as 'taking intellectual property, traditional knowledge, cultural expressions, or artifacts from someone else's culture without permission'.[28] The underlying assumption here is that members of a culture have a monopoly of ownership over its practices and products, and that everyone else must gain their permission before they can access it – otherwise, such access can be deemed an insulting act of dispossession. Policing the boundaries of culture follows logically the theory that it is something that is owned by a group.

Back in the 1970s, cultural appropriation was an obscure term of interest only to small groups of radical academic scholars. Yet, as a result of the ascendancy of identity politics, it began to acquire wider recognition in the 1990s. Identity politics regarded its cultural underpinning as vital for its legitimation, and therefore looked upon culture as a precious resource that it was reluctant to share with others. This disposition towards a zero-sum view of culture encouraged an insecure and anxious sensibility towards its ownership, and the right to represent a culture, or to access its accomplishment, became a jealously policed issue. Thus, cultural entrepreneurs claimed that only women had the right to write about female characters, or that the authorship of books on black history should be the prerogative of black people, or that only Native Americans could tell stories about the life and customs of their people. Such claims often stressed the unbridgeable difference in the way an identity was lived and experienced. Through their elevation of these differences, cultural entrepreneurs encouraged the widening of the chasm dividing cultures.

Since the turn of the 21st century, the cultural borders dividing different identity groups has hardened. Culture and identity are the main examples of a domain where the call for open borders is usually trumped by the demand to close them down. This is particularly striking in the spheres of art and popular culture, where the issue of who is entitled to create and what has become a constant topic of controversy. In 2017, calls to destroy a painting by a white artist, Dana Schutz, of a black victim of a lynch mob, which was on display in the Whitney Museum of American Art, indicates that for many, even artistic freedom has become a negotiable commodity in the crusade against cultural appropriation. Condemnation of a white painter crossing a racial boundary to depict an instance of black suffering was widely echoed in a supposedly open-minded cultural establishment. That the imposition of new limits on artistic creativity were increasingly acceptable was shown by the readiness with which the American museum industry accommodated to the imposition of cultural boundaries: as one commentator explained, after this experience 'museums will never be the same'.[29] It is frequently argued that only gay actors should be given LBTQ roles in films and plays.[30] There is even a discussion about whether or not non-Jewish actors should be able to play Jewish characters.[31]

Insecurity about who can create what, and which boundaries can be and cannot be crossed, is now frequently signalled by authors and artists. One author of historical fiction, Emma Darwin, asked 'are there multicultural boundaries we must not cross in historical fiction?' – adding, 'if so, what are they?'[32] Another commentator asked 'how do we objectively define the boundary between showing appreciation of a culture or blindly appropriating it?'[33]

The sponsorship of 'transgression' and of 'border crossing' is conspicuously absent in the controversy surrounding cultural appropriation. It appears that unlike other boundaries, the one separating culture cannot be challenged – and attempts to do so are condemned as exploitative and oppressive. 'When white people invoke the concept of culture-sharing as an excuse to overstep cultural boundaries, they mimic colonization', argues one angry opponent of cultural appropriation.[34]

In some instances, the Durkheimian distinction between the sacred and the profane is invoked to legitimate the policing of cultural boundaries. 'The main issue pertinent to the study of Hindu symbols concerns the boundaries between purity (sanctity) and impurity', writes cultural theorist Rina Arya, adding that the 'boundary remains permanent to protect the culture from desecration'.[35] To illustrate this point, she explained that is why 'the presence of a bindi [on a Western] festival goer, or an image of the goddess Laxmi on a swimsuit, is regarded as blasphemous'.

Conflict between identity groups is increasingly conducted through the prism of culture, where the policing of cultural boundaries is communicated through a self-righteous, sometimes hysterical, tone. Metaphorical 'Keep Out' signs are proliferating throughout the landscape dominated by the outlook of identity activists. Indeed, the principal achievement of the crusade against appropriation is to turn every form of cultural interaction into a potential site for conflict. This idea of appropriation has as its foundation the conviction that culture is the sacred property of its moral guardians. It is based on the premise that unless cultural artefacts, practices, rituals, and even food are used in a reverent and respectful manner, something akin to religious sacrilege has been committed. Such pious attitude towards culture does not merely apply to religious rituals and symbols, but to the most banal features of everyday existence, such as the label on your shirt or the snack you are munching.

In a further paradox, the constant demand for culturally-correct behaviour actually serves to desensitise people from knowing how to distinguish between rituals and practices that are genuinely worthy of respect, and those that have little moral significance. If the demand for respect for everything becomes automatic, making distinctions between truly important practices such as a religious ritual, and trivial matters such as your hairstyle, becomes complicated – if not impossible. But then, as we noted previously, the capacity to make distinctions has become one of the casualties in the culture war against borders.

The fashionable boundaries that coexist with the borderless imagination are intensely personalised and can best be understood as cultural tools used to manage identity crisis-related issues. Calling on people to protect themselves with healthy boundaries, one psychologist explains:

> By definition, a boundary is anything that marks a limit. Psychological limits define personal dignity. When we say, "You just crossed a line," we are speaking about a psychological limit that marks the distinction between behavior that does not cause emotional harm and behavior that causes emotional harm.[36]

The insistence with which these psychic boundaries are upheld constitutes an indirect recognition of humankind's need for borders. It is as if the historic sense of an inviable territory now acquires meaning mainly through the idealisation of personal space. 'Personal space is a private, intimate, and exclusive territory which nobody can invade or claim', declares a commentary on this subject.[37] Unfortunately, in this personalised form, boundaries are too individualised and fragmented to provide the guidance and meaning demanded by today's insecure world.

The turn towards process

Throughout the modern era, relations between people have tended to be guided by informal rules of conduct that were guided by a community's taken-for-granted assumptions. These informal rules worked in part because people could rely on the fixed points provided by society's symbolic boundaries to navigate their personal encounters. In this environment, personal judgement played an important role in the management of everyday life. Even the professions, which were to some extent formally regulated, possessed considerable scope for the exercise of informality. Professional judgement was respected and provided teachers, academics, doctors, and others with considerable latitude to make context-specific decisions.

In recent decades, society's estrangement from judgement has had a significant impact on the conduct of informal life. Once people are discouraged from acting in accordance with their personal judgements, a demand is created for more formal guidance. The aim of these new rules and codes – often referred to by institutions as *process* – is to draw new lines and formalise everyday behaviour. The formalisation of hitherto informal rules of behaviour leads to the drawing of new lines that criss-cross different dimensions of people's interactions. So paradoxically, the cultural devaluation of judgement leads to the proliferation of (new) boundaries in everyday life.

Unlike the symbolic boundaries of the past, which evolved organically from the ethical habits and reciprocal moral obligations of a community's experience, formal process is administratively constructed. The codes of conduct manufactured by the human resources industry are literally invented by professionals who have no moral or organic connection with the people who will be subjected to the new rules. The boundaries they attempt to draw are inherently fragile and transient. That is why administratively created process inevitably leads to yet more process. Its main outcome is to continually contract the space available for the exercise of professional discretion and judgement. Consequently, professionals devote far more time to ticking boxes rather than to exercising judgement.

The purpose of the new rules governing people's relationships and of the implementation of processes in public institutions is to regulate and ultimately control people's behaviour. This exposes the limits to the idealisation of the value of openness. Administratively constructed boundaries are designed to contain the free and spontaneous interaction that is associated with genuine openness to experience. That is why the opening up of the private sphere and the erosion of the line that protects it from public gaze coincides with the construction of new rules governing the conduct of intimacy.

Rule-making through process strives to restrain informality through establishing new and unprecedented limits on the exercise of judgement. For example in the UK, many universities insist that newly arriving students attend consent classes.[38] The aim of these classes is to lay down the law about how to gain and give consent in sexual relationship. Evidently the powers that govern higher education do not trust university students to possess a capacity for judgement on even the most personal and intimate matters.

Until recently, the idea of consent was associated with an act that is freely given and is not the product of coercion or compulsion. The classical definition of consent emphasises this act as a voluntary one. According to the *OED*, consent is a 'voluntary agreement to or acquiescence in what another proposes or desires' – so it is ironic that, in many universities, advocates of consent workshops wish to make them compulsory for all students. The coupling of compulsion with consent suggests that these workshops have little to do with attributes associated with 'voluntary agreement' or freely expressed desire. Rather, an examination of the workings of these workshops indicates that they are devoted more to policing intimacy than to providing an opportunity for deliberating on the meaning of consent.

The institutionalisation of consent workshops indicates that, when it comes to everyday human interaction, the culture of boundarylessness suddenly mutates into its opposite. Newly constructed hard borders that regulate the conduct of personal affairs expose the ethos of double standards that pervades the boundaryless outlook.

Notes

1 Lorber (1999) p. 363.
2 F. Diane Barth (2015) '5 ways to protect your personal space', *Psychology Today*, 6 September, https://www.wsj.com/articles/the-transgender-language-war-1535582272.
3 www.eventbrite.com/e/embodied-boundaries-establishing-safety-differentiating-self-from-other-registration-52868112949.
4 www.facebook.com/events/18-hook-ave-toronto-on-m6p-1t4-canada/embodied-boundaries-workshop-in-toronto/237487486797353/.
5 Mark Manson, 'The Guide to Strong Relationship Boundaries', https://markmanson.net/boundaries.
6 Sharron Martin, 'What are boundaries and why do I need them?, https://livewellwith sharonmartin.com/what-are-boundaries/.
7 See Bockarova, B., Ph.D. (2016) '4 ways to set and keep your personal boundaries', *Psychology Today*, 1 August, www.psychologytoday.com/gb/blog/romantically-attached/201608/4-ways-set-and-keep-your-personal-boundaries.
8 Jo Baker (2018) 'Knowing your limits. What are boundaries and why are they important?', *Counselling Directory*, 6 November, https://www.counselling-directory.org.uk/counsellor-articles/knowing-your-limits-what-are-boundaries-and-why-are-they-important.
9 See Bockarova, M., Ph.D. (2016) '4 ways to set and keep your personal boundaries', *Psychology Today*, 1 August, www.psychologytoday.com/gb/blog/romantically-attached/201608/4-ways-set-and-keep-your-personal-boundaries.
10 Graziano is cited in www.nationalgeographic.com/news/2018/01/personal-space-between-us-graziano-peripersonal-dyspraxia/.
11 See Graziano (2018).
12 Worrall, S. (2018) 'You need your personal space-here's the science why', *National Geographic*, 20 January, www.nationalgeographic.com/news/2018/01/personal-space-between-us-graziano-peripersonal-dyspraxia/.
13 Cited in Carey, B. (2019) 'Beyond biden: How close is too close', *New York Times*, 4 April.
14 http://edition.cnn.com/2010/LIVING/worklife/02/08/cb.getting.physical.at.work/index.html.

15 See for example Kate Neilson (2019) 'Touching at work: how far is too far?', *HRM*, 26 April, https://www.hrmonline.com.au/sexual-harassment/touching-at-work-how-far-too-far/.

16 James Kozlowski (2015) 'Park playground ban on adults unaccompanied by children', *Parks & Recreation*, 28 February, https://www.nrpa.org/parks-recreation-magazine/2015/march/park-playground-ban-on-adults-unaccompanied-by-children/.

17 Roth, Saunders, and Olcese (2014) p. 3.

18 See www.occupybristoluk.org/about/safe-space-policy/. (accessed 2 February 2016).

19 http://occupylondon.org.uk/about/statements/safer-space-policy/. (accessed 4 March 2016).

20 www.newtactics.org/conversation/creating-safe-spaces-tactics-communities-risk.

21 Tim Sculthorpe (2017) 'No politics here please! Labour sets up a "safe space" for delegates worn out by tribal battles at party conference', *The Daily Mail*, 24 September, http://www.dailymail.co.uk/news/article-4915050/Labour-sets-safe-space-delegates.html.

22 Emily Guo (2016) 'Bruin Republican members encourage students to accept election results', *The Daily Bruin*, 17 November, https://dailybruin.com/2016/11/17/bruin-republicans-members-encourage-students-to-accept-election-results/.

23 Phoebe Southworth (2019) 'Academics criticise traffic light "safe space" badges at transgender conference', *The Daily Telegraph*, 22 September, https://www.telegraph.co.uk/news/2019/09/22/academics-criticise-traffic-light-safe-space-badges-transgender/.

24 See www.thecrimson.com/article/2015/3/26/staff-better-safe-spaces/.

25 Strossen is cited in www.telegraph.co.uk/news/worldnews/northamerica/usa/12022041/How-political-correctness-rules-in-Americas-student-safe-spaces.html. (accessed 14 January 2016).

26 Auslan Cramb (2019) 'Anti-racim event hosted by Edinburgh University bans white people from asking questions', *The Daily Telegraph*, 27 September, https://www.telegraph.co.uk/news/2019/09/27/anti-racism-event-hosted-edinburgh-university-bans-white-people/.

27 Gamson (1997) p. 181.

28 Scafidi (2005).

29 Halperin, J. (2018) 'How the Dana Schutz controversy—and a year of reckoning—have changed museums forever', 6 March, https://news.artnet.com/art-world/dana-schutz-controversy-recent-protests-changed-museums-forever-1236020.

30 Dino-Ray Ramos (2018) 'Daren Chriss says he will no longer play LGBTQ characters', *Deadline*, 24 December, https://deadline.com/2018/12/darren-criss-lgbtq-gay-glee-the-assassination-of-gianni-versace-1202525793/.

31 See for example https://forward.com/schmooze/416384/is-it-kosher-for-non-jewish-actors-to-play-jewish-characters/.

32 Emma Darwin (2018) 'Are there multicultural boundaries we must not cross in historical fiction?', *Historia*, 14 March, http://www.historiamag.com/dr-darwin-cultural-appropriation/.

33 Jessica Michault (2016) 'Cultural Appropriation or Appreciation: Where to Draw the Line', *Antidote Magazine*, Summer, https://magazineantidote.com/english/cultural-appropriation-or-appreciation-where-to-draw-the-line/.

34 Nami Thompson (2018) 'I'm Done Answering Questions About Cultural Appropriation', *WYV*, 29 May, https://wearyourvoicemag.com/race/im-done-answering-questions-cultural-appropriation.

35 Arya, R. (2017) 'Cultural appropriation: Analysing the use of Hindu symbols within consumerism', *LSE Blog*, 8 September, https://blogs.lse.ac.uk/religionglobalsociety/2017/09/cultural-appropriation-analysing-the-use-of-hindu-symbols-within-consumerism/.

36 www.guidetopsychology.com/boundaries.htm.

37 See https://exploringyourmind.com/stress-and-personal-space-when-people-invade-your-privacy/.

38 Nicola Woolcock (2019) 'Universities teach consent classes to cut sexual assault', *The Times*, 9 October, https://www.thetimes.co.uk/article/universities-teach-consent-classes-to-cut-sexual-assault-kg62ld5nw.

10
CONCLUSION

Hostility towards conventional boundaries and borders coexists with the demand for new borders. Our exploration of the spirit of limitlessness and boundaryless-ness needs to be qualified by the recognition that these trends work alongside ones that are apparently contradictory. The rejection of limits and boundaries discussed in previous chapters refers principally to those that have their roots in the conventions and values of the past and have now come to be regarded as unacceptable barriers and archaic restrictions on people's capacity to be who they want to be. They may now seem to some as unacceptable, but they pro-vided people with a measure of meaning and security. In their absence, a sense of defensiveness prevails, leading many to invest their energy in securing their personal boundary.

The previous chapters have drawn attention to the casual manner with which long established boundaries are disregarded and cast aside. According to some commentators, even the boundary separating humans and animals is now open to question: one study writes of the 'permeability of the human–animal bound-ary, transcended by thinking animals, bestial ancestors, and trans-species empa-thy'.[1] The moral dimension of being human, which has been so important to enlightened thought, is now dismissed by some as an anthropocentric conceit.

Age-old boundaries, such as those between adults and children or between men and women, are regarded by some as either unnecessary or as illegitimate obstacles that stand in the way of the realisation of personal identity.

The story of Dr David Mackereth illustrates the spirit of the times: Dr David Mackereth, a disability assessor at the British government's Department for Work and Pensions, shows how the unbounding of cultural norms impacts on everyday life. Mackereth lost his job because he refused to use recently invented transgen-der pronouns on the ground it went against his Christian faith. In October 2019, the Employment Tribunal assessing his case ruled that 'a lack of belief in trans-genderism and conscientious objection to transgenderism in our judgement are incompatible with human dignity and conflict with the fundamental rights of others'.[2] Without any hesitation, the centuries-old distinction between male and female was casually dismissed in favour of the establishment of a new boundary between what is, and is not, 'incompatible with human dignity'. This judgement underlines the proclivity for new boundary-setting, and the extent to which, despite the non-judgemental cultural turn, there is still plenty of scope for judgement: 'lack of belief in transgenderism' is judged to contradict the values upheld by the Tribunal.

Outwardly, the questioning of limits and boundaries can appear as a genuinely bold and radical act. Yet the radical anti-border rhetoric that aggressively questions national, sexual, generational, and other boundaries runs in parallel with a trend that I characterise as the *culture of fear*.[3] This trend is particularly powerful in the Anglo-American world, where an obsession with safety has acquired unprecedented proportion. Concern with safety and security directly contradicts the spirit of risk-taking and adventure. That is why these societies are anything but open to exploration and experimentation: they are busy micromanaging every dimension of human experience. Little is left to chance in private and public institutions, where, as we have noted, process governs just about every contingency. The ethos of openness disrupts everything that it scrutinises, creating a demand for the monitoring and auditing of everyday life. Once openness is instrumentalised, it turns into a medium for regulating behaviour It encourages the construction of a network of micro-boundaries, hoops to be jumped through, and boxes to be ticked.

Spontaneous and informal behaviour, which was once associated with the character trait of openness to new possibilities, is now explicitly discouraged. Rules of conduct, speech codes, and micromanaged procedures establish a complex range of administratively constructed boundaries for the management of people's behaviour. The rhetoric of openness sits uneasily alongside the reality of an intensely scrutinised and regulated institutional setting. Even people's language is regularly patrolled to ensure that it does not threaten the emotional safety of people who might find it offensive. The outward display of limitlessness is paralleled by demands for the imposition of new forms of security.

Why?

The coexistence of the cultural authority of openness with an apparent political, social, and psychological demand for new borders is a paradox that requires explanation. Writing about this phenomenon, the historian Daniel Jütte observes: 'I have long been intrigued by the question of why, exactly, in our time it is common to think of openness as something that must be intrinsically (and morally) superior to all other forms of knowledge circulation'. This question puzzles Jütte, because 'there certainly seems to be a gulf between the invocation of openness as an ideal, on the one hand, and the undeniable persistence – sometimes even proliferation – of boundaries, on the other'.[4]

To make sense of this paradox, it is important to reflect on the question of 'why?' Why is such an influential section of the cultural elite drawn towards the denigration of boundaries? What motivates individuals to communicate their protest against boundaries with placards declaring 'No Borders, No Nations!'. Is this merely an example of rhetorical hyperbole? Do they really desire and envisage a world of unbounded and deterritorialised people? Or are they merely mouthing a fashionable narrative in order to secure a reputation for being of the moment?

Some suggest that the call for 'No Borders' should be interpreted as a rhetorical gesture, since in their heart of hearts even the most zealous border critics realise that borders are not going to go away. Žižek dismissed open border advocates as the 'greatest hypocrites', contending that 'they play the Beautiful Soul, which feels superior to the corrupted world while secretly participating in it' and that 'they need this corrupted world as the only terrain where they can exert their moral superiority'.[5] From this perspective, today's defenders of mass migration are the contemporary equivalent of the child-saving movement of the 19th century. Many of those child savers assumed that they possessed the right to save children from their parents. They regarded most parents as their moral inferiors who inhabited a different moral universe to them. The movement against borders is also strongly motivated by the similar desire of distancing themselves from their moral inferiors.

The non-judgemental, relativist temper that infuses the anti-border imagination attempts to project its values forwards to the future. The possibility of socially engineering new values was raised by Ruth Benedict, one of the leaders of the cultural relativist movement in 1934, when she wrote that, 'no society has yet attempted a self-conscious direction of the process by which its new normalities are created in the next generation'.[6] Benedict claimed that 'cultural relativity' challenges 'customary opinions and causes those who have been bred to them acute discomfort'. She believed that breaking with the customs of the past was a price well worth paying for an enlightened alternative and promised that as 'soon as the new opinion is embraced as customary belief, it will be another trusted bulwark of the good life'.[7]

The invention of 'new normalities' speculatively discussed by Benedict was mainly driven by the desire to displace the old with the new. What the art critic Harold Rosenberg described as the 'tradition of the new' strives to break down boundaries, because it believes that superior values will be found on the other side.[8] However, experience has shown that the quest for new normalities is more effective at breaking with the normalities of the past than it is in constructing a bridge towards the future. It does not lead to major discoveries but to valuing the new for its own sake. Unfortunately, when the customs of the past are broken as a matter of course and old boundaries are undermined, 'new opinion' does not necessarily offer a meaningful guide to life. Cultural relativity deprives society of the capacity for judgement, which in turn diminishes its ability to draw meaningful lines. The accommodation to the erosion of lines by advocates of open borders constitutes one response to this development. The patrolling of personal space represents another.

In this regard, openness, transparency, and transgression are not about the project of opening doors that humanity has not yet opened but about refusing to engage with the legacy of the past. They exercise a corrosive influence on the conventions that still influence people's lives. Openness does not leave what has been opened intact. The private sphere does not remain the same after it has become the target of transparency. The celebration of transgression represents the revolt of the individual against symbolic boundaries that it does not really care about. This is a case of a revolt for its own sake; transgression without an object. This pattern is strikingly apparent in relation to the campaign against binaries: a campaign fuelled by an *objectless* desire to start anew but without a clearly formulated *objective*.

There is something truly performative about the self-conscious manner with which some people boast about their commitment to transgression. One illustration is the enthusiasm with which numerous French social theorists and philosophers discuss the legacy of the Marquis de Sade and interpret his acclamation of sexual cruelty and perversion as an overdue blow against a prudish society and against the artificial restraint of social conventions. As an essay on 'The Pleasure of Transgression' outlines:

> Postmodern philosophy abounds with the ideas of flouting, breaking and overcoming of various socio-cultural boundaries, the ideas that are generalized by the concept of transgression. Any reflection on a boundary presupposes a possibility of crossing it, for the act of mentally grasping a boundary amounts to already transgressing it, which will sooner or later manifest itself in creative or practical action.[9]

There is something insincere and affected about the self-satisfied manner with which commentators offer hints about their transgressive inclinations. Typically, they fail to acknowledge that in a world where the spirit of boundarylessness exercises significant power, the 'flouting, breaking and overcoming of various socio-cultural boundaries' rarely incurs serious costs.

With all the flattery directed at the transgressor, it is easy to overlook the real meaning of the act. Unlike its contemporary connotation, transgression was classically perceived as a serious matter, for it touched on the violation of a moral norm. The *OED* refers to it as the 'action of transgressing or passing beyond the bounds of legality or right; a violation of law, duty, or command; disobedience, trespass, sin'.[10] Historically, philosophers and writers such as Baudelaire and Nietzsche self-consciously challenged moral standards in an attempt to go beyond prevailing conventions and boundaries.[11] By contrast, today's transgressors transgress as a matter of routine. Their behaviour meets with little resistance, since crossing a line is considered quite normal. The way has been cleared for them by a culture that willingly opens all the doors. Walking through an open door does not require a determination to go beyond long-established boundaries, nor the desire for transcendence. Supported by the hegemonic status enjoyed by the values of openness and transparency, the act of transgression has never been so easy.

The numerous academic conferences devoted to transgression show an obsessive and sometimes pornographic interests in the subject. No surprise that the focus of the 'Transgressive Cultures Conference' organised by the University of Chicago in Paris in December 2019 is the Marquis de Sade. The call for papers for this event seeks proposals on topics such as 'new approaches to transgressive philosophy, explorations of pornography and erotica, aberrant behaviour and outsiders'.[12] Other academics conferences have as their themes, 'Taboo – Transgression – Transcendence', 'Boundaries and Transgression', 'Gender Transgressions – Historical perspectives', 'Transgressive Romanticism' or 'Gender and Transgression in the Medieval World'. It appears that a section of academia is drawn towards the performance of transgression and gets a buzz out of being part of a transgressive intellectual community.

Playing at transgressing has also become a constant theme in consumer culture. Advertisers promote their products by appealing to potential customers to 'dare to be different'. A Europe-wide sales campaign for Honda Civic cars 'outlines a path that pushes the boundaries' of a 'Honda Civic driver'. A voiceover instructs would-be drivers to go 'where different takes you'. Its message of 'dare to be different' has become a theme that is constantly promoted by the advertising industry.[13] Breaking boundaries is also a theme of Land Rover advertisements.[14] The NatWest bank's 'No Boundaries' campaign boasts that 'we created 'Cricket has no boundaries', a fully integrated campaign to showcase and celebrate NatWest's commitment to diversity and inclusion through the lens of modern cricket'.[15] Even the manufacturer of Barbie Dolls plays the transgression card. Its sales pitch for its range of Shero Dolls leads with the statement that, 'since 2015, we've honoured women who continue to break boundaries'.[16]

As far as the advertising industry is concerned, 'breaking taboos' and 'breaking boundaries' are the markers of creativity. In June 2018, a 'boundary breaking ad' by the sanitary product brand Libresse won the Glass Lion for Change Prix at Cannes. The advertisement shows us:

> scenes of young women clutching themselves in pain from cramps, others having sex on their cycle and, perhaps most notably, plenty of blood – blood running down a leg in the shower and even realistic red liquid on a pad. The ad, we hope, has served to change the conversation around the category even more than ever before, in a year when women's voices have come powerfully to the fore.[17]

The breaking of the boundary of the intimate is thus celebrated in an advertisement that 'dares' to display red liquid on a sanitary pad, rather than the customary blue one.

The analysis presented in this book suggests that transgression alters its meaning when, as now, it has gone mainstream. This point is overlooked by present-day commentaries, which fail to distinguish between the classical notion of transgression and its contemporary caricature. A study titled *Transgression* has as its premise the assertion that a feature of modernity is 'the desire to transcend limits – limits that are physical, racial, aesthetic, sexual, national, legal and moral'.[18] No doubt there is a powerful trend towards the dissolution of these boundaries – but it is not fuelled by the desire to 'transcend limits'. The sense of limitlessness discussed in previous chapters is characteristically indifferent to conventional forms of restraint. It is worth noting that the word 'transcend' conveys the connotation of 'to exceed' and 'to go beyond', even 'to rise above, surpass, excel'.[19] Such accomplishments are markedly distinct from the studied indifference to, or ignorance of, prevailing limits that we see today.

In a context where limits lack clear markers, transgressive behaviour does not involve the violation of powerful socially sanctioned moral and social boundaries. In the domain of sexual identity in the Western world, with the possible exception of paedophilia, transgression has become emptied of meaning. Individuals can brag about their transgressive sexual identities without incurring stigma. That is why a report directed at the advertising industry urges its members to 'push the boundaries of gender stereotyping' and 'help' consumers 'break free from the shackles of identity norms'.[20]

The celebration of breaking taboos, and the call to help people 'break free from the shackles of identity norms', implicitly communicates the conviction that the regime of border controls to which people are subjected in their everyday life constitutes a serious barrier to the development of their potential. Precisely at a time when conventional limits are barely perceptible, they are portrayed as a major obstacle that must be overcome. The more symbolic boundaries lose their moral force, the more they are regarded as unacceptable impositions on the conduct of life. Breaking free from the 'shackles of identity norms' constitutes an invitation to adopt a consumerist orientation towards identity.

Human beings have always sought to overcome the limits confronting them. However, the aim was to overcome a specific limitation, rather than to abolish limits as such. Today, when there is widespread disagreement about values and norms, there is also a lack of consensus, not only about *where* meaningful limits could be set, but about *whether* they should be set at all. In this regard, the feeling of limitlessness emerges as a sublimated manifestation of society's alienation from meaningful limits.

It is important not to confuse the *zeitgeist* of limitlessness with that of the historical meaning of transgression. There is a qualitative difference between acts of transgression and the testing of boundaries, which are normal – if rare – features of human life, and the pursuit and acclamation of these activities as an end in itself. Though the imagination can fly beyond existing limits in order to undertake a journey into the unknown, it is evident that human beings and their communities can only flourish within established limits. This point is recognised by the unprecedented concern that people today, adrift in a sea of limitlessness, express towards securing their personal space.

One striking feature of the paradox of borders is that scepticism about the practice of border security runs alongside an increasingly aggressive demand to respect personal boundaries. It is as if the space around an individual's body is the one frontier that really counts, and one which requires constant protection. That personal boundaries have a very real meaning in a way that all the other ones discussed previously do not can be dismissed as yet another example of the hyper-individuated world that we inhabit. Such an interpretation would merely confuse the symptom of the problem with its cause – for the real problem pertains to matters that have wreaked havoc and confusion in the domain of meaning. As the previous chapters have indicated, the loss of confidence in borders and symbolic boundaries is intimately connected to the loss of judgement. Without the social connection realised through judgement, human estrangement acquires a powerful influence over the conduct of human affairs.

At first sight, the controversy over upholding dichotomous concepts seems a million miles from taking seriously the security of a border. However, both of these endeavours are founded on the mutually complementary acts of making distinctions and setting and enforcing limits. Through an act of judgement, these acts acquire moral connotations so that boundaries, such as those between nations, between children and adults, or between the private and the public, are not seen as arbitrary or morally irrelevant, but as points of reference essential for navigating our existence.

One of the aims of this book has been to discuss Western society's loss of self-belief, which is most strikingly expressed through its reluctance to make judgements of value, draw symbolic boundaries, and take existing borders seriously. Although arguments against borders are often framed through the language of humanitarian internationalism, my argument is that they have little to do with the Enlightenment tradition that inspired the ideals of universalism. The humanist tradition portrayed its ideal of the human as not only free but also as responsible. As Hannah Arendt explained, the exercise of freedom and responsibility is territorially bounded and gains clarity through interacting with citizens within a limited space.

This book argued that there is a close link between the different manifestations of the boundaryless spirt. The heated controversy surrounding national borders and arguments about what attitude to adopt towards mass migration understandably dominate the media landscape. But the prevailing defensive attitude that large sections of Western society have adopted towards upholding the integrity of their national borders is refracted through its loss of confidence in the numerous boundaries that regulate life. Ultimately, the boundaryless *zeitgeist* calls into question all taken-for-granted distinctions, even the legitimacy of conceptual boundaries.

Of course, not everyone who condemns national borders feels the need to question the boundary between childhood and adulthood, or between the private and public spheres. Nor does every critic of binary categories wish to eliminate the boundary between health and illness. Critics may even be surprised to learn that their animosity towards one particular boundary is fuelled by attitudes towards culture and morality that motivate others to contest other forms of borders and boundaries. What the previous chapters have shown is that the different tensions and conflicts over borders and boundaries should be interpreted as different symptoms of common cultural trends.

At the same time, a loss of solidarity, a growing sense of atomisation, and a resulting sense of wariness and mistrust towards others creates a demand for drawing up new lines. The prevailing *zeitgeist* of boundarylessness does not abolish people's need for the security provided by boundaries. But too often, the demand for boundaries assumes a personal and individualised form which is incapable of connecting with a community's need for meaning and solidarity. Self-help books that purport to answer questions such as, 'can I set limits and still be a loving person? What are legitimate boundaries?' are not the solutions to but the symptoms of the problem.[21] How to draw 'legitimate boundaries' requires the help of wider cultural norms, not the top tips provided by self-help manuals – and in its atomised personal form, this question is likely to remain unanswered.

Answering the existential questions of our era requires that society adopts a positive orientation towards judgement and the making of moral distinctions. At present, acts of judgement are often made and communicated in a semi-clandestine and surreptitious form. The hesitant and defensive manner with which judgement is expressed deprives society of the moral clarity it needs to deal with uncertainty. Western society needs to relearn how to draw lines in order to provide communities with the guidance they need to face the future. It needs to learn to draw lines that can guide young people to make their way to the adult world and assist them to overcome their crisis of identity.

Borders matter because they provide communities with the security they require in a world of uncertainties. Borders also matter because they provide the cultural infrastructure necessary for the constitution of self-identity. Commentators have drawn attention to the difficulty of establishing a common sense of identity without some form of symbolic or physical demarcation from others. Some argue that people 'must feel as individuals that their own personal identities are in part defined by their identification with their territorially delimited country'.[22] A sense of belonging, which is a crucial component of identity, is historically rooted in a particular space that is defined by both the physical and the symbolic boundaries that surround it. Once individuals understand where lines are drawn, they can navigate their way in the world and develop their identity through the making of choices.

Arguably the most disturbing driver of the problems under discussion in this book is the trend towards the devaluation of moral judgement. In turn, this trend contributes to the detachment of identity from moral norms, lending identity an unstable, arbitrary, and fluid form. Most accounts claim that the fluidity of identity is a consequence of the postmodern condition and the rapid acceleration of change. While these conditions influence the forms that identity assumes, I contend that the decisive influence on the problematisation of identity is a lack of clarity about the moral values that underpin the self. As the philosopher Christine Korsgaard pointed out, 'you can't maintain the integrity you need in order to be an agent with your own identity on any terms short of morality itself'.[23]

A living morality is not reducible to a system of norms written down on a piece of paper. Morality is mediated through the symbolic boundaries and rituals that help individuals endow their experience with meaning, and refreshed and made relevant through acts of judgement and the drawing of lines.

Notes

1 Russell (2010) p. 3.
2 David Mackereth (2019) Christian doctor loses trans beliefs case', *BBC News*, 2 October.
3 See Furedi (2018b).
4 Akbari, Herzog, Jütte, Nightingale, Rankin, and Weitzberg (2017) p. 1540.
5 Žižek (2017) p. 8.
6 Benedict (1989) p. 271.
7 Benedict (1989) p. 277.
8 See Rosenberg (1962).
9 Rubavičius (2008) p. 68.
10 'transgression, n.', OED Online, September 2019. Oxford University Press, www.oed. com.chain.kent.ac.uk/view/Entry/204777?redirectedFrom=Transgression& (accessed 1 October 2019).
11 Jenks (2003) pp. 84–85.
12 See call for paper – www.facebook.com/events/the-university-of-chicago-center-in-paris/transgressive-cultures-conference/2358221884496519/.
13 www.campaignlive.co.uk/article/honda-civics-typographic-film-champions-breaking-norm/1494998.
14 Ionut Ungureanu (2014) 'World-renown adventurers talk about breaking boundaries in Land Rover ads', *Autoevolution*, 19 August, https://www.autoevolution.com/news/world-renown-adventurers-talk-about-breaking-boundaries-in-land-rover-ads-video-85874.html.
15 https://sportandentertainment.mcsaatchi.com/project/natwest-no-boundaries/.
16 https://barbie.mattel.com/en-us/about/role-models.html.
17 Alexandra Jardine (2018) 'Boundary-breaking by Libresse wins the Glass Lion for Change Grand Prix at Cannes', *AdAde*, 22 June, https://adage.com/creativity/work/blood-normal/53003.
18 Jenks (2003) p. 8.
19 "transcend, v.", OED Online, September 2019. Oxford University Press, www.oed. com.chain.kent.ac.uk/view/Entry/204606?redirectedFrom=transcend (accessed 18 October 2019).
20 Nicola Kemp (2017) 'Consumers urge brands to push the boundaries of gender stereotyping', *Campaign*, 25 July, https://www.campaignlive.co.uk/article/consumers-urge-brands-push-boundaries-gender-stereotyping/1440353.
21 These questions are posed in ad for Henry Cloud's *Boundaries: When to Say Yes, When to Say No, To Take Control of Your Life: When to Say Yes, How to Say No, to Take Control of Your Life*. See www.amazon.co.uk/Boundaries-When-Take-Control-Your/dp/0310247454.
22 Lucian Pye in cited in Mackenzie (1978) p. 63.
23 Korsgaard (2009) p. xii.

BIBLIOGRAPHY

Agamben, G. (1995) 'We refugees', *Symposium: A Quarterly Journal in Modern Literatures*, vol. 49, no. 2.

Agamben, G. (1998) *Homo Sacer: Sovereign Power and Bare Life*, Stanford University Press: Stanford.

Agier, M. (2017) *Borderlands, towards an Anthropology of the Cosmopolitan Condition*, Polity Press: Cambridge.

Akbari, S.C., Herzog, T., Jütte, D., Nightingale, C., Rankin, W. and Weitzberg, K. (2017) 'AHR conversation: Walls, borders, and boundaries in world history', *The American Historical Review*, vol. 122, no. 5.

Altheide, D. (2002) *Creating Fear: News and the Construction of Crisis*, Aldine Transaction: New Brunswick, NJ.

Anderson, R.T. (2018) *When Harry Became Sally: Responding to the Transgender Moment*, Encounter Books: New York.

Anderson-Gold, S. (2010) 'Privacy, respect and the virtues of reticence in Kant', *Kantian Review*, vol. 15, no. 2.

Appleton, J. (2008) 'In Defence of Binaries', *Notes On Freedom*, 25 April.

Arboleda, V.A., Sandberg, D.E. and Vilain, E. (2014) 'DSDs: Genetics, underlying pathologies and psychosexual differentiation', *Nature Reviews Endocrinology*, vol. 10, no. 10.

Arendt, H. (1956) 'Authority in the twentieth century', *The Review of Politics*, vol. 18, no. 4.

Arendt, H. (1959) 'Reflections on little rock', *Dissent*, vol. 6, no. 1.

Arendt, H. (1970) *Men un Dark Times*, Jonathan Cape: London.

Arendt, H. (1998) *The Human Condition*, 2nd ed., The University of Chicago Press: Chicago.

Arendt, H. (2006) 'The crisis in culture', in Arendt, H. (ed.), *Between Past and Future*, Penguin: London.

Arendt, H. (2006a) "What is authority?", in Arendt, H. (ed.), *Between Past and Future*, 91–141. Penguin: London.

Arnason, A. (2000) 'Biography, bereavement story', *Mortality*, vol. 5, no. 2.

Arnett, J.J. (2000) 'Emerging adulthood: A theory of development from the late teens through the twenties', *American Psychologist*, vol. 55, no. 5.

Bacevich, A.J. (2009) *American Empire*, Harvard University Press: Cambridge, MA.

Baer, M. (2017) 'When binary thinking is involved, polarization follows', *Psychology Today*, vol. 27, January.

Balibar, E. (2004) *Alexander von Humboldt Lecture in Human Geography*, Radboud University: Nijmegen.

Balos, B. (2004) 'A man's home is his castle: How the law shelters domestic violence and sexual harassment', *Saint Louis University Public Law Review*, vol. 23.

Barth, F. (1969) 'Introduction', in Barth, F. (ed.), *Ethnic Groups and Boundaries: The Social Organization of Culture Difference*, Allen & Unwin: London.

Baudrillard, J. (1993) *The Transparency of Evil: Essays on Extreme Phenomena*, Verso: London.

Baugh, B. (2016) 'The open society and the democracy to come: Bergson, Deleuze and Guattari', *Deleuze Studies*, vol. 10, no. 3.

Bauman, Z. (1996) 'From pilgrim to tourist: Or a short history of identity', in Hall, S. and Du Gay, P. (eds.), *Questions of Cultural Identity*, Sage: London.

Bauman, Z. (2013) *Liquid Modernity*, John Wiley & Sons: London.

Beck, U. (2002) 'The cosmopolitan society and its enemies', *Theory, Culture & Society*, vol. 19. nos. 1–2.

Beck, U. (2003) 'Understanding the real Europe', *Dissent*, vol. 50, no. 3.

Beck, U. (2005) *Power in the Global Age: A New Global Political Economy*, Polity Press: Cambridge.

Beck, U. (2006) *The Cosmopolitan Vision*, Polity Press: Cambridge.

Benedict, R. (1989) *Patterns of Culture*, Houghton Mifflin Harcourt: Boston.

Benhabib, S. (2016) 'The new sovereigntism and transnational law: Legal utopianism, democratic scepticism and statist realism', *Global Constitutionalism*, vol. 5, no. 1.

Berger, P., Berger, B. and Kellner, H. (1974) *The Homeless Mind*, Penguin: Harmondsworth.

Bergson, H. (1956) *The Two Sources of Morality and Religion*, Doubleday: Garden City, New York.

Bertram, C. (2018) *Do States Have the Right to Exclude Immigrants*, Polity Press: Cambridge.

Birchall, C. (2019) Draft manuscript, 'Opaque openness: The problem with/of transparency'.

Blom-Cooper, L. (1967) 'Forward' to Wesin, A.F. (ed.), *Privacy and Freedom*, The Bodley Head: London.

Bloom, A. (1987) *The Closing of the American Mind: How Higher Education Has Failed Democracy and Impoverished the Souls of Today's Students*, Penguin Books: London.

Bodhi, B. (1991) 'A Note Openness', *Buddhist Publication Society*, no. 17, https://www.bps.lk/olib/nl/nl017.pdf.

Bonikowski, B., Halikiopoulou, D., Kaufmann, E. and Rooduijn, M. (2019) 'Populism and nationalism in a comparative perspective: A scholarly exchange', *Nations and Nationalism*, vol. 25, no. 1.

Bosniak, L. (1999) 'Citizenship denationalized', *Indiana Journal of Global Legal Studies*, vol. 7, no. 2.

Bourdieu, P. (1984) *Distinctions: A Social Critique of the Judgement of Taste*, Routledge: London.

Bourdieu, P. (1995) *The Logic of Practice*, Polity Press: Cambridge.

Boyd, J.W. and Donald, A. (1979) 'Is zoroastrianism dualistic or monotheistic?', *Journal of the American Academy of Religion*, vol. 47, no. 4.

Bristow, J. (2019) *Stop Mugging Grandma: The 'Generation Wars' and Why Boomer Blaming Won't Solve Anything*, Yale University Press: New Haven.

Brown, W. (2017) *Walled States, Waning Sovereignty*, Zone Books: New York.

Brubaker, R. (1992) *Citizenship and Nationhood in France and Germany*, Harvard: Cambridge, MA.

Brubaker, R. (2018) *Gender and Race in an Age of Unsettled Identities*, Princeton University Press, Princeton, NJ.

Burrill, D.R. (1966) 'The changing status of moral authority', *Harvard Theological Review*, vol. 59, no. 3.

Calcutt, A. (1998) *Arrested Development: Pop Culture and the Erosion of Adulthood*, Cassell: London.

Canovan, M. (1996) *Nationhood and Political Theory*, Edward Elgar: Cheltenham.

Canovan, M. (1999) 'Is there an Arendtian case for the nation-state?', *Contemporary Politics*, vol. 5, no. 2.

Carens, J. (1987) 'Aliens and citizens: The case for open borders', *The Review of Politics*, vol. 49, no. 2.

Chemaly, S. (2018) *Rage Becomes Her: The Power of Women's Anger*, Simon and Schuster: New York.

Clarke, J.A. (2019) 'They, them, and theirs', *Harvard Law Review*, no. 894.

Cohen, J. (2013) *The Private Life*, Granta: London.

Cooper, B. (2018) *Eloquent Rage: A Black Feminist Discovers Her Superpower*, St. Martin's Press: New York.

Debray, R. (2010) *Éloge Des Frontières*, Gallimard: Paris.

Delanty, G. (2006) 'Borders in a changing Europe: Dynamics of openness and closure', *Comparative European Politics*, vol. 4, nos. 2–3.

Delsol, C. (2003a) *Icarus Fallen: The Search for Meaning in an Uncertain World*, ISI Books: Wilmington, DE.

Delsol, C. (2003b) *The Search for Meaning in an Uncertain World*, ISI Books: Wilmington, DE.

Delsol, C. (2015) *Unjust Justice: Against the Tyranny of International Law*, ISI Books: Wilmington, DE.

Derrida, J. (1981) *Positions*, The Athlone Press: London.

Derrida, J. and Ferraris, M. (2000) *A Taste for the Secret*, trans. Giacomo Donis, Polity Press: Cambridge.

Diener, A.C. and Hagen, J. (2012) *Borders: A Very Short Introduction*, Oxford University Press: Oxford.

Dineen, T. (1999) *Manufacturing Victims: What the Psychology Industry Is Doing to People*, Robert Davies Publishers: Toronto.

Douglas, M. (1999) *Implicit Meanings Selected Essays in Anthropology*, Routledge: London.

Dunn, R.G. (1998) *Identity Crisis: A Social Critique of Postmodernity*, University of Minnesota Press: Minneapolis.

Elbow, P. (1993) 'The uses of binary thinking', *Journal of Advanced Composition*, vol. 13, no. 1.

Elias, N. (2000) *The Civilizing Process*, Wiley-Blackwell: Oxford.

Elliott, A. (2013) *Reinvention*, Routledge: London.

Elshtain, J.B. (1993) *Public Man, Private Woman: Women in Social and Political Thought*, Princeton University Press: Princeton.

Erikson, E.H. (1963) *Childhood and Society*, W.W. Norton & Company: New York.

Erikson, E.H. (1964) 'Identity and uprootedness in our time', in Erikson, E.H. (ed.), *Insight and Responsibility*, Faber & Faber: London.

Erikson, E.H. (1968) *Identity: Youth and Crisis*, W.W. Norton & Company: New York.

Erikson, E.H. (1970) 'Reflections on the dissent of contemporary youth', *International Journal of Psychoanalysis*, vol. 51, nos. 11–22.

Erikson, E.H. (1974) *Dimensions of a New Identity: The 1973 Jefferson Lectures in the Humanities*, W.W. Norton & Company: New York.

Falk, R. (2002) 'Revisioning cosmopolitanism', in Nussbaum, M. (ed.), *For Love of Country*, Beacon Press: Boston.

Flege, M. (2016) *Conceptualizing Cruelty to Children in Nineteenth-Century England: Literature, Representation, and the NSPCC*, Routledge: London.

Fournier, M. (2013) *Émile Durkheim: A Biography*, Polity Press: Cambridge.

Fox, C.R. (1977) 'The medicalization and demedicalization of American society', *Daedalus*, vol. 106, no. 1.

Franklin, B. (1995) 'The case for children's rights: A progress report', in Franklin, B. (ed.), *The Case for Children's Rights: A Progress Report: The Handbook of Children's Rights: Comparative Policy and Practice*, Routledge: London.

Friedman, L.J. (1999) *Identity's Architect: A Biography of Erik H. Erikson*, Free Association Books: London.

Frye, D. (2018) *Walls: A History of Civilization in Blood and Brick*, Faber & Faber: London.

Furedi, F. (2001) *Paranoid Parenting: Why Ignoring the Experts May Be Best for Your Child*, Alan Lane: London.

Furedi, F. (2002) *Therapy Culture: Cultivating Vulnerability in an Anxious Age*, Routledge: London.

Furedi, F. (2011) *On Tolerance: A Defence of Moral Independence*, Bloomsbury Press: London.

Furedi, F. (2013) *Authority: A Sociological History*, Cambridge University Press: Cambridge.

Furedi, F. (2017) *What Happened to the University? A Sociological Exploration of Its Infantilisation*, Routledge: London.

Furedi, F. (2018a) *Populism and the European Culture Wars: The Conflict of Values between Hungary and the EU*, Routledge: London.

Furedi, F. (2018b) *How Fear Works the Culture of Fear in the 21st Century*, Bloomsbury: London.

Gamson, J. (1997) 'Messages of exclusion: Gender, movements, and symbolic boundaries', *Gender and Society*, vol. 11, no. 2.

Gerson, G. (2019) 'Nationality in the open society: Popper versus Hayes and Kohn', *Nations and Nationalism*, vol. 25, no. 1.

Gerth, H. and Wright Mills, C. (1954) *Character and Social Structure: The Psychology of Social Institutions*, Routledge & Kegan Paul: London.

Glick Schiller, N. (2012) 'Situating identities: Towards an identities studies without binaries of difference', *Identities*, vol. 19, no. 4.

Goffman, E. (1959) *The Presentation of Self in Everyday Life*, Doubleday: New York.

Gormley, K. (2011) *The Death of American Virtue: Clinton vs. Starr*, Broadway Books: New York.

Götz, N. (2014) 'The Concept of Openess: Promise and Paradox', in Götz, N. and Marklund, C. (2014) (eds.). The paradox of openness: transparency and participation in Nordic cultures of consensus. Brill: Leiden.

Götz, N. and Marklund, C. (2014) *The Paradox of Openness: Transparency and Participation in Nordic Cultures of Consensus*, Brill: Leiden.

Graziano, M. (2018) *The Space between Us: A Story of Neuroscience, Evolution, and Human Nature*, Oxford University Press: New York.

Green, S. (2012) 'A sense of border', in Wilson, M. and Donnan, T.M. (eds.), *A Companion to Border Studies*, Wiley Blackwell: Chichester.

Grieder, A. (2009) 'What are boundary situations? A jaspersian notion reconsidered', *Journal of the British Society for Phenomenology*, vol. 40, no. 3.

Gurstein, R. (1996) *The Repeal of Reticence*, Hill and Wang: New York.

Gutmann, D. (1974) 'Erik Erikson's America', *Commentary*, vol. 58, no. 3.

Habermas, J. (1991) *Moral Consciousness and Communicative Action*, MIT Press: Cambridge, MA.

Habermas, J. (1996) *Between Facts and Norms: Contributions to a Discourse Theory of Law and Democracy*, MIT Press: Cambridge, MA.

Habermas, J. (2016) *The Crisis of the European Union: A Response*, Polity Press: Cambridge.

Hall, S. (1997) *Cultural Representations and Signifying Practices*, Sage: London.

Hardt, M. and Negri, A. (2000) *Empire*, Harvard University Press: Cambridge, MA.

Hayward, K. (2013) 'Life stage dissolution in Anglo-American advertising and popular culture: Kidults, Lil'Britneys and middle youths', *The Sociological Review*, vol. 61, no. 3, p. 525.

Heidegger, M. (1997) 'Building, dwelling, thinking', in Leach, N. (ed.), *Rethinking Architecture: A Reader in Cultural Theory*, Routledge: London.

Herskovits, M.J. (1951) 'Tender-and tough-minded anthropology and the study of values in culture', *Southwestern Journal of Anthropology*, vol. 7, no. 1.

Herskovits, M.J. (1958) 'Some further comments on cultural relativism', *American Anthropologist*, vol. 60, no. 2.

Himmelfarb, G. (2002) 'The illusions of cosmopolitanism', in Nussbaum, M. (ed.), *For Love of Country*, Beacon Press: Boston.

Hardt, M. and Negri, A. (2004) *Multitude: War and Democracy in the Age of Empire*, Penguin: London.

Held, D. (2003) 'Violence, law and justice in a global age', in Archibugi (ed.), *Debating Cosmopolitics*, Verso: London.

Hobbsbawm, E. (2004) *The Age of Extremes: The Short History of the Twentieth Century, 1914–1991*, Abacaus: London.

Holmes, M. (2000) 'When is the personal political? The president's penis and other stories', *Sociology*, vol. 34, no. 2.

Holmes, S. (1993) *The Anatomy of Antiliberalism*, Harvard University Press: Cambridge, MA.

Ingold, T. (2016) *Lines: A Brief History*, Routledge: London.

Isin, E. (2002) *Being Political: Genealogies of Citizenship*, University of Minnesota Press: Minneapolis.

Jacobson, D. (1997) *Rights across Borders Immigration and the Decline of Citizenship*, The John Hopkins University Press: Baltimore.

Jarvie, I.C. (2003) 'Popper's ideal types: Open and closed, abstract and concrete', in Jarvie, I.C. and Pralong, S. (eds.), *Popper's Open Society after Fifty Years: The Continuing Relevance of Karl Popper*, Psychology Press: London.

Jarvie, I.C., Milford, K. and Miller, D.W. (eds.) (2006) *Karl Popper: A Centenary Assessment Volume I*, Ashgate Publishing, Ltd.: London.

Jaspers, K. (1964) *Way to Wisdom: An Introduction to Philosophy*, Yale University Press: New Haven.

Jenks, C. (2003) *Transgression*, Routledge: London.

Kalra, G. (2012) 'Hijras: The unique transgender culture of India', *International Journal of Culture and Mental Health*, vol. 5, no. 2.

Kant, I. (1991) 'Perpetual peace: A philosophical sketch', in Kant, I. (ed.), *Political Writings*, 2nd ed., Cambridge University Press: New York.

Keaten, J.A. and Kelly, L. (2000) 'Reticence: An affirmation and revision', *Communication Education*, vol. 49, no. 2.

Klein, J.T. (2004) 'Prospects for transdisciplinarity', *Futures*, vol. 36, no. 4.

Kluckhohn, C. (1950) 'Anthropology Comes of Age'. *American Scholar*, vol. 19.

Korsgaard, C.M. (2009) *Self-Constitution: Agency and Integrity*, Oxford University Press: Oxford.

LaFontaine, J. and Sapford, R. (1993) 'Endnote: Public and private', in Muncie, J. (ed.), *Wetherell, Understanding the Family*, Sage: London.

Lamont, M. and Molnár, V. (2002) 'The study of boundaries in the social sciences', *Annual Review of Sociology*, vol. 28, no. 1.

Lang, S. (2016) 'Native American men-women, lesbians, two-spirits: Contemporary and historical perspectives', *Journal of Lesbian Studies*, vol. 20, nos. 3–4.

Lasch, C. (1979) *The Culture of Narcissism: American Life in an Age of Diminishing Expectations*, Warner Books: New York.

Lasch, C. (1985) *The Minimal Self: Psychic Survival in Troubled Times*, WW Norton & Company: New York.

Lemert, C. (2011) 'A history of identity: The riddle at the heart of the mystery of life', in Elliott, A. (ed.), *Routledge Handbook of Identity Studies*, Routledge: London.

Lindahl, H. (2003) 'Give and take: Arendt and the nomos of political community', *Philosophy and Social Criticism*, vol. 32, no. 7.

Linklater, A. (2007) *Critical Theory and World Politics: Citizenship, Sovereignty and Humanity*, Routledge: New York.

Linstead, A. and Brewis, J. (2004) 'Beyond boundaries: Towards fluidity in theorizing and practice', *Gender, Work and Organization*, vol. 11, no. 4.

Lorber, J. (1999) 'Crossing borders and erasing boundaries: Paradoxes of identity politics', *Sociological Focus*, vol. 32, no. 4.

Lowney, K. (1999) *Baring Our Souls;TV Talk Shows and the Religion of Recovery*, Aldine de Gruyter: New York.

MacIntyre, A. (1997) *After Virtue: A Study in Moral Theory*, Gerald Duckworth & Co.: London.

Mackenzie, W.J.M. (1978) *Political Identity*, Penguin: Harmondsworth.

MacKinnon, C. (1987) *Feminism Unmodified: Discourses on Life and Law*, Harvard University Press: Cambridge.

Maier, C.S. (2016) *Once within Borders: Territories of Power, Wealth, and Belonging since 1500*, Harvard University Press: Cambridge, MA.

Manning, H.E. and Waugh, B. (1866) *The Child of the English Savage*, Kessinger Reprints: Whitefish, MT.

Martin, R. and Barresi, J. (2006) *The Rise and Fall of Soul and Self*, Columbia University Press: New York.

McMahon, C. (1990) 'Openness', *Canadian Journal of Philosophy*, vol. 20, no. 1.

Melucci, A. (1989) *Nomads of the Present: Social Movements and Individual Needs in Contemporary Society*, Hutchinson Radius: London.

Merlau-Ponty, M. (1974) *Adventures of the Dialectic*, Heinemann: London.

Mhurchú, A.N. (2014) *Ambiguous Citizenship in an Age of Global Migration*, Edinburgh University Press: Edinburgh.

Midgley, M. (2017) *Can't We Make Moral Judgements*, Bloomsbury Academic: London.

Miller, D. (2016) *Strangers in Our Midst: The Philosophy of Immigration*, Harvard University Press: Cambridge, MA.

Miller, D. (2017) 'Migration and justice: A reply to my critics', *Critical Review of International Social and Political Philosophy*, vol. 20, no. 6.

Moran, M. (2015) *Identity and Capitalism*, Sage: London.

Moran, M. (2018) 'Identity and identity politics: A cultural materialist history', *Historical Materialism*, vol. 25, no. 2.

Muller, J. (2012) *Reclaiming Knowledge: Social Theory, Curriculum and Education Policy*, Routledge: London.

Müller, J.-W. (2006) 'On the origins of constitutional patriotism', *Contemporary Political Theory*, vol. 5, no. 3.

Nagel, T. (1998) 'Concealment and exposure', *Philosophy & Public Affairs*, vol. 27, no. 1.

Ngnoumen, C.T. and Langer, E.J. (eds.) (2014) *The Wiley Blackwell Handbook of Mindfulness*, Wiley Blackwell: London.

Nicholson, L. (2008) *Identity before Identity Politics*, Cambridge University Press: Cambridge.

Nussbaum, M. (ed.) (2002) 'Patriotism and cosmopolitanism', in Nussbaum, M. (ed.), *For Love of Country*, Beacon Press: Boston.

Ober, J. (2017) *Demopolis: Democracy before Liberalism in Theory and Practice*, Cambridge University Press: Cambridge.

Ochoa Espejo, P. (2018) 'Why borders do matter morally: The role of place in immigrants' rights', *Constellations*, vol. 25, no. 1.

O'Dowd, L. (2010) 'From a "borderless world" to a "world of borders": Bringing history back in', *Environment and Planning D: Society and Space*, vol. 28, no. 6.

Panton, J. (2010) *Public/Private Distinction: The Problematisation of Public/Private Relationship in Political Thought after World War II*, Ph.D. Thesis, New College, University of Oxford, Oxford.

Papastergiadis, N. (2000) *The Turbulence of Migration, Globalization, Deterritorialization and Hybridity*, Polity Press: Cambridge.

Parekh, B. (2006) *Rethinking Multiculturalism: Cultural Diversity and Political Theory*, Palgrave Macmillan: London.

Parker, N. (ed.) (2008) *The Geopolitics of Europe's Identity: Centres, Boundaries and Margins*, Palgrave Macmillan: London.

Parsons, T. (1965) *Social Structure and Personality*, Free Press: New York.

Parsons, T. (1978) *Action Theory and the Human Condition*, Free Press: New York.

Popper, K. (2003) *The Open Society and Its Enemies; Volume One: The Spell of Plato*, Routledge: London.

Popper, K. (2012) *In Search of a Better World: Lectures and Essays from Thirty Years*, Routledge: London.

Prozorov, S. (2008) 'De-limitation: The denigration of boundaries in the political thought of late modernity', in Parker, N. (ed.), *The Geopolitics of Europe's Identity: Centres, Boundaries and Margins*, Palgrave Macmillan: London.

Purdy, J. (1999) *For Common Things: Irony, Trust, and Commitment in America Today*, Alfred A. Knopf: New York.

Rauch, J. (1993) *The Kindly Inquisitors: The New Attacks on Free Thought*, The University of Chicago Press: Chicago.

Riesman, D. (1964) *The Lonely Crowd: A Study of the Changing American Character*, Yale University Press: New Haven.

Riesman, D. (1969) *The Lonely Crowd: A Study of the Changing American Character*, Yale University Press: New Haven.

Rippe, J.M. (2017) *Nutrition in Lifestyle Medicine*, Springer International: Cham, Switzerland.

Rodriguez, D. and Boahene, A. (2012) 'The politics of rage: Empowering women of color in the academy', *Cultural Studies? Critical Methodologies*, vol. 12, no. 5.

Rosen, J. (2000) *The Unwanted Gaze: The Destruction of Privacy in America*, Random House: New York.

Rosenberg, H. (1962) *The Tradition of the New*, Horizon Press: New York.

Roth, S., Saunders, C. and Olcese, C. (2014) 'Occupy as a free space-mobilization processes and outcomes', *Sociological Research Online*, vol. 19, no. 1.

Roy, O. (2004) *Globalized Islam: The Search for a Ummah*, Columbia University Press: New York.

Rubavičius, V. (2008) 'The pleasure of transgression: Consumption of identities', *Athena: filosofijos studijos*, vol. 3.

Rumford, C. (2006) 'Theorizing borders', *European Journal of Social Theory*, vol. 9, no. 2.

Rumford, C. (2012) 'Bordering and connectivity', in Delanty, G. (ed.), *Routledge Handbook of Cosmopolitanism Studies*, Routledge: London.

Russell, N. (2010) 'Navigating the human-animal boundary', *Reviews in Anthropology*, vol. 39, no. 1.

Sassen, S. (1996) *Losing Control? Sovereignty in an Age of Globalization*, Columbia University Press: New York.

Saxonhouse, A. (2015) 'Public man/private woman in context', *Politics & Gender*, vol. 11, no. 3.

Scafidi, S. (2005) *Who Owns Culture?: Appropriation and Authenticity in American Law*, Rutgers University Press: New Brunswick, NJ.

Schöpflin, G. (2012) *Politics, Illusions, Fallacies*, TLU Press: Tallinn.

Sennett, R. (2003) *Respect: The Formation of Character in Age of Inequality*, W.W. Norton: New York.

Sennett, R. (2017) *The Fall of Public Man*, WW Norton: New York.

Sheppard, M. and Mayo, J.B., Jr. (2013) 'The social construction of gender and sexuality: Learning from two spirit traditions', *The Social Studies*, vol. 104, no. 6.

Showalter, E. (1997) *Hystories: Hysterical Epidemic and Modern Culture*, Picador: London.

Simmel, G. (1918) 'The transcendent character of life', in Simmel, G. (ed.) (1971), *On Individuality and Social Forms*, The University of Chicago Press: Chicago.

Simmel, G. (1994) 'Bridge and door', *Theory, Culture & Society*, vol. 11.

Smith, C., Christoffersen, K., Christoffersen, K.M., Davidson, H. and Herzog, P.S. (2011) *Lost in Transition: The Dark Side of Emerging Adulthood*, Oxford University Press: New York.

Soderberg, S., Lundman, B. and Norberg, A. (1999) 'Struggling for dignity: The meaning of women's experiences of living with fibromyalgia', *Qualitative Health Research*, vol. 9, no. 5.

Song, S. (2012) 'The boundary problem in democratic theory: Why the demos should be bounded by the state', *International Theory*, vol. 4, no. 1.

Steinworth, U. (2006) 'On popper's concept of an open society', in Jarvie, I.C., Milford, K. and Miller, D.W. (eds.), *Karl Popper: A Centenary Assessment Volume I*, vol. 1, Ashgate Publishing, Ltd.: London.

Stephens, A.C. (2010) 'Citizenship without community: Time, design and the city', *Citizenship Studies*, vol. 14, no. 1.

Strauss, M.A., Gelles, R.J. and Steinmetz, S.K. (1980) *Behind Closed Doors: Violence in Families*, Anchor Books: New York.

Sue, D.W., Bucceri, J., Lin, A.I., Nadal, K.L. and Torino, G.C. (2007) 'Racial microaggressions and the Asian American experience', *Cultural Diversity and Ethnic Minority Psychology*, vol. 13, no. 1.

Szary, A.L.A. (2015) 'Boundaries and borders', in *The Wiley Blackwell Companion to Political Geography*, Wiley Blackwell: Oxford.

Tester, K. (1993) *The Life and Times of Post-Modernity*, Routledge: London.

Theodorakis, K. (2014) 'Refugees, citizens and the nation–state: Unrecognised anomalies and the need for new political imaginaries', *The ANU Undergraduate Research Journal*, vol. 6.

Thompson, D. (2017) 'An exoneration of black rage', *South Atlantic Quarterly*, vol. 116, no. 3.

Traister, R. (2018) *Good and Mad: The Revolutionary Power of Women's Anger*, Simon and Schuster: New York.

Trilling, L. (1957) *The Liberal Imagination: Essays on Literature and Society*, Doubleday Anchor Book: New York.

Turner, B.S. (ed.) (1993) *Citizenship and Social Theory*, Sage: London.

Twenge, J. (2017) *iGen: Why Today's Super-Connected Kids Are Growing Up Less Rebellious, More Tolerant, Less Happy and Completely Unprepared for Adulthood*, Atria: New York.

Wacks, R. (2014) *Philosophy of Law: A Very Short Introduction*, Oxford University Press: Oxford.

Weigert, A.J., Teitge, J.S. and Teitge, D.W. (1986) *Society and Identity: Towards a Sociological Psychology*, Cambridge University Press: Cambridge.

Weintraub, J.A. and Kumar, K. (eds.) (1997) *Public and Private in Thought and Practice: Perspectives on a Grand Dichotomy*, University of Chicago Press: Chicago.

Waiton, S. (2016) 'Third way parenting and the creation of the "named person" in Scotland: The end of family privacy and autonomy?', *Sage Open*, vol. 6, no. 1.

Wellman, C.H. (2008) 'Immigration and freedom of association', *Ethics*, vol. 119, no. 1.

Westin, A.F. (1967) *Privacy and Freedom*, The Bodley Head: London.

Wheelahan, L. (2008) 'A social realist alternative for curriculum', *Critical Studies in Education*, vol. 49, no. 2.

Wheelahan, L. (2012) *Why Knowledge Matters in Curriculum: A Social Realist Argument*, Routledge: London.

Williams, A. (2008) *Enemies of Progress*, Societas: London.

Witmer, H. (1934) *The Field of Parent Education: A Survey from The Point of View of Research*, National Council of Parent Education: New York.

Wolfe, A. (1997) 'Public and private in theory and practice', in Weintraub, J.A. and Kumar, K. (eds.), *Public and Private in Thought and Practice: Perspectives on a Grand Dichotomy*, University of Chicago Press: Chicago.

Wolfe, A. (1998) *One Nation, after All: What Middle-Class Americans Really Think about*, Viking: New York.

Wolfenstein, M. (1951) 'The emergence of fun morality', *Journal of Social*, vol. 7, no. 4.

Wrong, D. (1994) *Problem of Order*, Simon and Schuster: New York.

Wuthnow, R. (1989) *Meaning and Moral Order: Explorations in Cultural Analysis*, University of California Press: Berkeley.

Yack, B. (2012) *Nation and Individual: Nationalism and the Moral Psychology of Community in Modern Political Life*, University of Chicago Press: Chicago.

Yuval-Davis, Y., Wemyss, G. and Cassidy, K. (2019) *Bordering*, Polity Press: Cambridge.

Zebrack, B. (2000) 'Cancer survivor identity and quality of life', *Cancer Practice*, vol. 8, no. 5.

Žižek, S. (2017) *Against the Double Blackmail*, Penguin: London.

INDEX

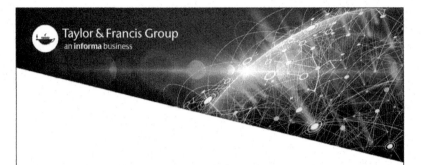